We Should
Not Be Friends

All friendships of any length are based on a continued, mutual forgiveness. Without tolerance and mercy all friendships die. —DAVID WHYTE

After all, what can a first impression tell us about someone we've just met for a minute in the lobby of a hotel? For that matter, what can a first impression tell us about anyone? Why, no more than a chord can tell us about Beethoven, or a brushstroke about Botticelli. By their very nature, human beings are so capricious, so complex, so delightfully contradictory that they deserve not only our consideration, but our *reconsideration*—and our unwavering determination to withhold our opinion until we have engaged with them in every possible setting at every possible hour. —AMOR TOWLES, *A Gentleman in Moscow*

The only way to have a friend is to be one. —RALPH WALDO EMERSON

Contents

Note to the Reader

THIS IS A story about the forty-year friendship Chris Maxey and I have shared. While the writing is mine, the remembering has been a joint effort. The dialogue is in most cases what we recall having said or heard. When memory failed us both, we did our best to conjure up what we believe we would have said. For the details throughout, we relied on contemporaneous notes we kept and interviews with others who were with us on parts of our journey. The emails we exchanged are quoted verbatim, but our letters have proved unfindable so we re-created them as best we could.

In a few instances, we've changed names and identifying details to preserve the privacy of people with whom we've lost contact.

We've checked our memories against the facts whenever possible. But friendships like ours proceed largely unchronicled, which is one of the reasons I wanted to write this book and Maxey wanted to be my partner in it. We may have misremembered some of the dialogue and descriptions, but we've tried to get the spirit right.

We Should Not Be Friends

Bright College Years

NERDS AND JOCKS

By the time I was a junior at college, I'd already met everyone I cared to know. I was friends with most of the other gays
and lesbians; this wasn't difficult because, in the early 1980s,
not many of us were out of the closet. I was also cordial with
most of the lesbians and gays who were still in the closet; it
was pretty obvious who they were. I knew the theater people,
a group that overlapped almost completely with the gays and
lesbians, uncloseted and closeted. I knew many of the people
who styled themselves writers. I knew absolutely everyone in
my major—there were only a few of us who had chosen to get
degrees in Latin and Greek, so it would have been Herculean
not to. And I knew a splattering of visual artists, a handful of
comparative lit majors, the odd philosopher, and three mathematicians, along with an assortment of other obsessive, quirky
characters with whom I'd fallen into conversation in a dining
hall line or bonded over the cinnamon toast at Naples Pizza
when we should have been studying.

I also knew those I didn't want to know. The jocks. And they didn't seem to want to know me. In the dining halls, they filled boisterous tables. They wolfed down epic platters of scrambled eggs. They wore baseball caps backwards and moved in packs. The jocks and I were like planets in different orbits, circling one another but not colliding. I felt that if we did, I would be obliterated.

During the spring of my junior year, I'd taken to wearing a turquoise acid-washed blue jean jacket, and I wore a studded leather wristband that served as a wallet—a souvenir from Los Angeles, where I'd spent the previous term away from school, working in the realer world. I had my hair permed down the center but cut shorter on the sides, in a recent fit of enthusiasm for the artist who was still then known as Prince and also for the look of a singer named Adam Ant. Despite my stylist's valiant efforts, my hair looked nothing like theirs. But I did look like someone trying very hard not to look like everyone else; I was elaborately disguised as someone who didn't care what other people thought of me.

I now can't be sure the jocks gave me much thought at all, but I assumed they didn't like me or considered me ridiculous, as was suggested by the occasional sneer directed my way. Certainly, many of my women friends, especially the very out lesbians, as well as my more feminine gay friends had contended with derision, menace, and worse from the college jocks. There was good reason to leave space between myself and anyone wearing a letter jacket.

All that dramatically changed at the end of my junior year, when I collided with one jock in particular: Chris Maxey, known to just about everyone as Maxey. From the start it was clear that Maxey and I should not be friends. What was less obvious was that I was much more prejudiced against him than he was against me. Yet we became friends and have remained so for the next forty years—right up to the present day.

Perhaps I didn't care to know Maxey, but fortunately the matter was taken out of my hands. Because if I hadn't met him, my life would have been less rich and less fun. Had it not been for Maxey, the me that is here today wouldn't be me. Also, I never would have learned how to breathe. He tells me I had a similar effect on his life. Except he figured out how to breathe all by himself.

INITIATION

Just beyond Yale's campus, a three-story building composed of limestone blocks presents a sheer, windowless front. An iron fence separates the sidewalk from a moat of carefully tended grass. Two handsome shrubs stand sentry at either side of a short flight of rough-hewn granite steps. The decorative stonework at knee level and around the building's door makes a nod to Ancient Greece, but there's no hint as to what lies inside. A gray slate path leads to the unwelcoming black door, the intricate details on its exterior visible only when the sun hits it just right. There was no sun the first time I entered; it was the middle of the night.

EVERYTHING BEGAN WITH a visit from my friend Tim. We'd been at high school together; he was a year older. Tim was one of those kids who is equally popular with adults and other teens. He had the floppy hair sported by the stoners in our class, but his wry smile and willingness to chat with anyone set him apart from the floppy-haired kids who wouldn't meet an adult's eye.

Once I arrived at Yale, Tim and I kept in touch the way students did in the early 1980s before there were mobile phones and personal computers. We had phones in our rooms (where we rarely were) but no answering machines—so calling one another almost always resulted in endless ringing. Instead, we would drop by unannounced and leave notes on someone's door if a knock went unanswered. The visit from Tim that would change my life came in early 1983, in the spring of my junior year, when he stopped by my room to ask if I could join him for lunch the following day.

Tim refrained from commenting on the number of Matt Dillon posters I had on my walls. At the time, I lived for Matt Dillon but had to make do with pictures of him in his first five movies: *Over the Edge* Matt, *Little Darlings* Matt, *My Bodyguard* Matt, *Tex* Matt, and *Liar's Moon* Matt. In my small dorm room, that left only enough wall space for a modest corkboard.

The next day, as arranged, we met up at the dining hall, dutifully stood in line with our trays, helped ourselves to sandwiches and coffee—I drank about a dozen cups of coffee a day throughout college—and found an empty table. I assumed that it would just be the two of us, but as soon as we sat down, we were swarmed from all sides by friends of Tim who had been loitering in the vicinity. None of them seemed to have anything in common—a girl I knew only by face; a jock I'd never seen before, but not the threatening kind; a few other kids I couldn't immediately classify. Sure, they could join us. High school gossip could wait.

Tim asked me a series of questions about myself—which was odd because they were mostly ones to which I was certain he already knew the answers. *Where had I grown up?* Cambridge, Massachusetts. *Activities during high school?* A lot of theater and also debating, but I'd stopped debating after a beloved classics teacher told me that it was sophistry and that I would condemn my soul to eternal damnation if I continued to do it. *Sports?* Not if I could help it. *Music I liked?* In high school, I'd listened to punk rock, country ballads, bluegrass, Bruce Springsteen, and show tunes; now, I preferred new wave and disco, with Blondie and Hazell Dean in constant rotation. And Prince, of course. Nothing compared 2 him.

Before long, despite the oddity of the situation, I'd segued into a monologue that required no prompts. I told Tim's friends how I'd just come back from a term away from college in Los Angeles, but explained that I could graduate with my class because I had some extra credits towards my major; I talked about being part of the university's gay student group and how far we'd come from meeting furtively on the edge of campus when I joined as a freshman to now co-hosting Gay and Lesbian Awareness Days; I described how I'd become involved with Gay Men's Health Crisis, a group in New York City that had recently been formed to help people with a new disease called AIDS.

I loved the lunch, of course—what was not to like? What a remarkable friend I had in Tim, I later said to myself, and what a wonderful group of friends he has! It didn't occur to me that the lunch had accomplished anything other than spotlighting how effortlessly I had managed to captivate such a random and diverse group of seniors. Of course, I had asked Tim's friends some questions about themselves, as well. Or had I?

Some weeks later, by which time I had acquired another Matt Dillon poster (*The Outsiders* Matt, now covering my corkboard and whatever reminders had been pinned to it), Tim stopped by my room again.

"You might have guessed that our lunch was an audition of sorts," he said.

"Yes," I lied. "I figured as much." In fact, I had no idea what he was talking about.

That's when Tim told me that he was in a secret society and that the other seniors who had joined us were some of his fellow members. Had I ever noticed a granite building on the edge of campus? That was the hall where they'd been gathering twice a week all year. Now, they were in the process of choosing fifteen juniors to replace themselves. Those juniors would inherit the hall, would meet there throughout the coming year, and then choose their own successors in turn. If the current members chose me, would I want to join?

I was confused. The only secret society at Yale I'd ever heard of was Skull and Bones, famously all male and symbolizing much that was wrong not just with Yale but with the country as a whole. Tim was expecting this.

"Before you say no, I need to tell you a few things," he continued. "We are one of the oldest secret societies and have a decent amount of money. That means it doesn't cost you anything to join or belong. That also means the new students each year come from all different kinds of economic backgrounds. We also admitted women the same day Yale did. *And* we try to bring together the fifteen most different kids we can find so you'll meet people who are nothing like you."

"What about the gay thing?"

Tim laughed. "Not a problem. In fact, it's a plus."

I still wasn't sold. "What do you have to do to belong?"

"Just show up," Tim said. "But you have to show up. It's two dinners a week for your entire year. You aren't supposed to miss a single one unless you really have to. Oh, and then there are the audits. But I'll tell you about those later."

"And how secret is this place?"

"Not very," Tim explained. "I mean, you can tell people about it, just don't be a jerk—the idea is not to make a big deal out of it. Oh, and you can also take your friends there anytime except for the two nights when you have the dinners—but only other seniors."

I couldn't think of a good reason to do it. I mean, I already knew everyone I needed to know—and two dinners a week was a big commitment. Still, I trusted Tim, and he'd obviously said yes when he was asked.

"How's the food?" I asked.

"Excellent and free," Tim replied.

"Oh, and one more question: Are there free drinks?"

"Unlimited account at the liquor store and a keg in the basement."

That changed the calculus: unlimited alcohol seemed well worth two nights a week. "There's also a pool table," Tim added. This wasn't of interest; I didn't play pool. Then Tim delivered the coup de grâce. "And there's a television with cable."

Cable meant MTV, the music channel that had launched two years before. And MTV meant Prince videos.

"Okay then. Tell them that if they ask, I'll say yes."

Tim smiled but couldn't let it go at that. "This is going to change your life," he told me. Then he added, "It's going to open you up." I found this curious. I thought I was already as open as I could be.

ACROSS CAMPUS, FOURTEEN similar conversations to the one I had with Tim were taking place. In one of them a brawny senior from Colorado named Colin was trying to convince a junior from Berwyn, Pennsylvania, to join if asked. Both were wrestlers, brothers of sorts, though Colin consistently beat the junior to a pulp when they wrestled against each other in practice. The junior had never wrestled a grizzly bear, but he imagined he knew what it must be like whenever he wrestled Colin.

"This will be the best chapter in your soft, preppy, silver-spoon, privileged life," Colin told the junior. "It's a chance to meet different kinds of people. People very different from you. People who aren't even on your planet, Maxey."

Maxey laughed, thinking this couldn't possibly be the case. The team had wrestlers from all different backgrounds and parts of the country—even from abroad. In fact, he was the only prep school kid who wrestled. He spent every day with other jocks who weren't like him at all. It also sounded like a huge time commitment on top of practice and meets, and for what? But Colin wasn't asking Maxey to join if asked: he was telling him. Besides, there was free beer—and a pool table.

THE NIGHT OF "tap," when the secret societies offer membership to juniors and induct them, I had been told to wait in my room—but I had also been warned that I might wait up all night for nothing: only on tap night would the seniors make their final choices. I would later find out that wasn't true—if they asked you if you wanted to join and you said yes, you were in. But I remember waiting anxiously in my room, excited but nervous, and still unsure what my answer would be if I were asked.

I'd recently lost a friend to an illness that was almost certainly AIDS; he was someone I'd met in Los Angeles and with whom, on five or six occasions, I had done just about everything sexual that gay men did with each other. It had only been six months since the CDC had named this new syndrome, and no one knew how it was transmitted. But men who slept with men were dying in ever-increasing numbers. Most of the time I was able to convince myself that even if this terrifying new thing had killed my friend, the odds were in my favor. Maybe it wasn't spread through intimate contact at all; there were dozens of theories, all possible. After all, there were four hundred gay men horrifyingly dead but millions of us still healthy. Other times, especially during sleepless nights, all I could think of was the other men I'd slept with whose fates were entirely unknown to me, and the disease's near one hundred percent mortality.

So, it wasn't just the free liquor and MTV that made me want to join this society: it was the need for distraction. But if anything about the initiation alienated me, I would simply bail. After all, I didn't need to join this thing. It definitely wasn't going to change my life.

The longer I waited in my room, the more I convinced myself that this wasn't for me. Two nights a week? With fourteen kids I might not know—or might not like once I got to know them? Even worse, what if I liked them and they didn't like me? Maybe because I was gay? Or maybe because I was me? The whole idea of an initiation was preposterous, if not offensive. The whole idea of a secret society was as well. We were twenty years old! I became certain I would say no.

I had homework for a course on Greek lyric poetry, but rather than study the poem that had been assigned, I turned to a fragment I revisited often, which was attributed to Sappho: "The moon has set along with the Pleiades / It's the middle of the night and time goes by / and I am in bed alone." When I was feeling low, I often took comfort in indulging my melodramatically melancholy side. Even if I *didn't* want to join this thing, I wanted them to want me to.

Suddenly, there was a knock on the door. Outside stood Tim and several of the people from our lunch, looking extremely serious. One of them had a blindfold in her hand. Right before she asked me to put it over my eyes, Tim stage-whispered something in my ear—that is, he said it so loudly that everyone could hear him. Clearly this was said to every potential initiate.

"Will, this is supposed to be fun. If you aren't having fun, you need to let us know right away. You don't have to do anything. You're already in, and we're happy to have you. Seriously. We mean it."

I felt a wave of relief. So maybe the initiation would be okay, after all. Then I remembered the other kids but decided that I could just avoid the ones I didn't care for. And as for their not liking me, that was easy: I wouldn't let them get to know me. Why should I?

*　　*　　*

WE LEFT MY dorm and walked for about a mile, my companions making sure to guide me gently so that I wouldn't trip. Then I was led up a few steps and into some kind of a building, seated in a chair, and told to take off my blindfold. I found myself in a magnificent hall lit by candlelight. The style was Addams Family baronial: a wood-paneled anteroom furnished with chesterfield sofas and leather library chairs led to a two-story dining room hung with flags. In the center of the dining room was a massive oak table that could seat sixteen. Soon, scattered around the building, there were also fourteen rising juniors I'd never met. One of them was Maxey, the wrestler from Berwyn, Pennsylvania.

I didn't know he was a wrestler right away, but he was clearly some kind of athlete. His biceps were so large that he'd cut Vs into his T-shirt so his arms could fit through the sleeves. He had a big grin on his face and was looking around at everyone, taking everything in. The rest of us were pretty quiet, but not Maxey. He shouted hellos to all of us before bounding up to people and introducing himself.

Two members of our group he recognized. The first, a guy named Tom, was obviously a football player: tall, thick-necked, ruddy-faced. I'm five-eight on a good day and have always been nervous around big people. Tom was big, but careful not to loom over me when we shook hands. Happily, the other guy Maxey knew was my size, if more compact: David Singer, a soccer player from D.C. He and I soon discovered we had lots of friends in common—then I remembered having heard about him: he had a reputation for being maddeningly smart and endlessly argumentative.

After a while I'd met almost everyone except for Maxey; I

studied him from across the room. Maxey had neatly combed strawberry-blond hair and a classically square jaw, but the thing that was most striking was the blue of his eyes—not the blue of an ocean, or of a precious stone, but more like oxford-cloth blue. He was undeniably handsome, but also had a mischievous nervous energy that played against his looks. His pointy ears made him resemble Disney's Peter Pan and gave you a sense that he was just about to pull a prank—or that you were just about to discover the one he'd already set in motion.

When Maxey walked up to me and stuck out his hand, I shook it quickly. He said he'd seen me before; he remembered my crazy hair. He said it with a smile, but it sounded almost menacing. We stood awkwardly for a few minutes. Someone was trying to get my attention. Maxey smiled again and politely backed off.

What followed was a lot of stupid initiation stuff. I remember being taken to a bar near the hall, where I was instructed to talk to my imaginary pet rabbit, Harvey. This was a challenge designed for a movie lover like me. Maxey was once again blindfolded and instructed to drink from a leathery cup that was alleged to be a sheep's scrotum.

After about five minutes of talking to Harvey at the bar, I called it quits and we retreated to the hall. Soon we were all gathered together again.

I talked with just about everyone in my group that night. I was drawn to an exuberant dancer named Renata, who was matching those of us who were drinking shot-for-shot without seeming the slightest bit drunk. It was soon clear that she had such an ebullient personality that the liquor only mellowed it. I talked with David Singer's sophomore roommate—David

Kelly, an economics and political science major with a boyish face and warm laugh. I chatted with Molly, a pixieish presence with a wide grin, just back from a term abroad studying in Leningrad, and with a track star named Julia, who volunteered as a Big Sister and taught swimming at the YMCA. I met an art historian with a sly smile who introduced herself to everyone as Alice, and then, when she got more comfortable, said we could also call her Huei-Zu (pronounced "Way-Roo") or Zoo, her nickname. We were soon joined by yet another David, a tall kid from Texas, and then by Brooke, who had long hair and seemed to have her act together far more than any of the rest of us.

I had a lively conversation with a trim, curly-haired runner named Morris, who launched into a discussion about journalism and politics. He told me that for his initiation task he'd been instructed to deliver a soliloquy to a vending machine in the Cross Campus Library. I was delighted to meet Jane, also a writer but an outdoorsperson and athlete as well. And there was Clark, a guy from Newark, who was the best dressed of the lot of us. He and David Kelly knew each other from the Black Church at Yale, but not well. It was soon clear that each of us knew no more than one or two of the others; we were, for the most part, strangers to one another.

Maxey was the loudest among us. He took up space and knocked things over, and he was drinking vast quantities of beer. He was also trying way too hard, and I found it a bit much—the high fives and the instant nicknames and the questions to everyone about everything. Whenever he went to one part of the hall, I went to another. My efforts to avoid him were thwarted by Singer, the argumentative soccer player, who told me to wait a second and then walked over to Maxey, grabbed him by the neck, and led him back to me.

"I want you guys to meet," he said.

Maxey said we already had, although he seemed happy to meet again.

"Schwalbe is a theater jock and Maxey's an actual jock, a star wrestler," Singer said. An awkward silence followed.

"What do you think about this place?" I asked Maxey.

"Feels like a great opportunity to meet new people," Maxey said.

"You are such a dork," Singer said, punching Maxey in the arm.

"I almost said no when they asked me to join because I wasn't really sure that I *wanted* to meet more people," I said. I was trying to be honest, but it sounded hostile. I grinned to compensate.

By this time people were dancing, and Maxey dragged Singer and others out onto the impromptu dance floor. After more drinking and talking, I even found myself dancing briefly when Michael Jackson announced over a hypnotic beat that Billie Jean was not, in fact, his lover. I didn't dance with any-one in particular; I danced with everyone, just as I had in Los Angeles when I would go to Studio One every Saturday night and lose myself in a crush of gay men for hours at a time, bliss-ful to have found my tribe.

The next morning, I had a pounding hangover. I winced as I remembered talking too much about myself with everyone I met: about LA, about Studio One, about Prince, about my love for Matt Dillon. Some parts of the night were blurrier than oth-ers, but one thing was clear: I had let down my guard. I'd been loud and theatrical. I didn't know whether my jerry-rigged persona was still in shape or in tatters. I knew I would never see most of the seniors again, but what about my classmates? Whatever impression I'd made was the one they would carry with them all summer until we met again. It had been a long time since I'd felt so vulnerable and exposed.

I took some comfort in knowing that there was one kid who'd behaved more outrageously than I had: Maxey. I kept seeing him out of the corner of my eye as he jumped around the room, shout-singing along with the music, mangling names, wrestling Singer.

I vowed that when I came back, I wouldn't do anything to attract notice. I would not get drunk. I would not talk too much. I certainly wouldn't open up anymore. And I would give Chris Maxey a wide berth.

ANGEL

The summer between junior and senior year in college would be my last school summer ever. I didn't know what I wanted to do, but I was certain that I didn't want to be a doctor, lawyer, architect, teacher, or anything else that required further study: I was keen to get on with life. Meanwhile, the news of AIDS kept getting worse. The straight media was still largely ignoring it, but a few doctors, journalists, and activists in the gay media were warning that it was the tip of an unfathomably large and lethal iceberg. I found myself constantly remembering my friend in LA, who had died after suffering from the symptoms that were the hallmarks of this new disease: fevers, wasting, swollen glands, pneumonia, night sweats. I couldn't forget him and all we'd done together.

I was determined to make everything I could out of the summer between junior and senior year because it seemed to me possible that I might not live to see thirty or even twenty-five. In June, I worked as a temporary secretary in New York during the days and on an AIDS hotline in the evenings, and occasionally as a "buddy" to people with AIDS, to help with chores and visit people who were alone. At night I went to gay bars and dance clubs. I sometimes stayed out until dawn and once went right from a disco to the office, where I barfed on my boss's desk. (I told her I had a stomach bug; she pretended to believe me.) On the nights I didn't go out, I stayed in my room and wrote endless versions of a play called *Traitors,* about a young man right out of college who lets down his guard among his roommates and is destroyed for doing so.

I'd won a traveling research fellowship that started in July and wound up sharing an apartment in London with the play-wright Larry Kramer, a friend of my mother from the 1950s when they'd both worked in theater in adjacent offices, secretar-ies to two different producers. Larry had become a mentor and second father to me when I was in high school. We'd written a television show together when I was a college sophomore (sold, not made). It was because of Larry that I first became involved with Gay Men's Health Crisis; he had been a cofounder. That July, while I was busy doing research in the Victoria and Albert Museum, Larry was back at the apartment writing *The Normal Heart,* a play about gay men fighting for our lives.

Larry returned to New York at the end of July; I stayed on. One night that summer, after Larry left, I found myself in a strange bar near Earl's Court. I'd had a few drinks, but not too many. That's when I spotted, across the bar, the most ethereal person I had ever seen: he had blond curls, like a Botticelli angel. He smiled at me, shyly. I grinned back. After a while I had the courage to approach him. He was ghostly pale. I found myself transfixed by the blue veins on his neck, running like rivers under his translucent skin. It was a hot night, and yet he was wearing a long-sleeved shirt, buttoned to the wrists.

We shared a drink, as we both were low on cash, and then I wound up walking for miles with him through the city at night until we got to his studio apartment. We undressed, and that's when I noticed the scars all down his arms.

"A car accident," he explained, blushing. He showed me how he had put his hands up to protect his face when he went through the windshield. To me, they looked more like track marks from shooting drugs. I traced them with my fingers.

Once in bed, it was as though our bodies fit in a way I had never felt before. He kept the television on, but it was just the test pattern, dimly lighting the room with its unnatural colors. After we were done, I let my hand hang down from the bed—it was a twin and there was no room to stretch out—and my fingers grazed something cold and metallic. When the angel wasn't looking, I peered over the edge: there on the floor beside me lay an arm-sized knife, serrated and rusty, glowing blue and orange in the light of the television.

I was in bed with an angel whose name I didn't know and he didn't know mine. I wasn't sure where I was. He had been endlessly sweet. I so wanted to doze off in his arms and wake up to do again in the morning everything we had done the night before. But the knife. And the track marks. And the knife.

Here's the thing about being twenty: it all seemed worth the risk. Growing up gay had always involved risk, not just of rejection but of physical violence; maybe it wasn't a bad idea to keep a knife under your bed if you were inviting people you met in bars into your home. Or perhaps I had thought that he might indeed kill me, and if so, so be it. Whatever I was or wasn't thinking, I let myself fall asleep and woke up the next morning, next to my angel. He managed to make us some tea using an induction coil and offered me biscuits. We watched something on the news about the royals. We kissed and I left.

The next night I returned to the bar to try to find him, but he wasn't there. I described him to the bartenders. No one knew him or had ever seen him before. I left the bar and went hunting for his apartment, trying to retrace steps I couldn't remember. I had neglected to note both the street and the house number; all I could recall was walking by train tracks. We had also passed a large cast-iron structure—or had I dreamed that? I couldn't find anything familiar in any direction. Eventually, I was back on the twisting streets that led to my borrowed apartment. For several days in a row, I repeated this sequence: a trip to the bar followed by wandering with only longing, lust, and drunken fragments of memory as my compass.

Finally, I gave up.

I never saw him again, but I began to be plagued by a nightmare from which I would awaken in terror, gasping for breath. As I slept peacefully, I would become aware of my phantom angel standing over me, about to plunge his rusty knife into my heart.

*　　*　　*

IN MID-AUGUST, I got sick and couldn't get out of bed for two weeks. I was alone in London and pretty sure I knew what was wrong.

During those nights and days I read feverishly: *All Creatures Great and Small* by James Herriot; *Grand Hotel* by Vicki Baum; *The Good Companions* by J. B. Priestley. Only later did I realize that everything I read was set in Europe during the twenty peaceful years between the two great wars.

My glands didn't swell and I didn't lose weight. When I returned to New York my doctor told me that I'd had hepatitis B. But he couldn't test for AIDS; there was no test for that. My nightmare about the angel of death would haunt me for years to come.

MAXEY'S SUMMER

When we came back to college in September 1983 for our final year, the hall was ours. The seniors who had chosen us were now out in the world and we had to figure out everything by ourselves. Luckily, we'd been given some directions. We would first elect leaders. This we did in short order. In just the small time we'd spent together, it was clear that Brooke, with the long hair, had a practical bent and spoke her mind. Both seemed like good things in a president, so we made her ours. Although frequently Maxey's partner in crime, she also had the rare ability to inject a note of sanity when any of us got too wild. After we elected her, the other officers fell into place. I didn't put myself forward and no one suggested I do so. This was just as I wanted it. Maxey was literally climbing all over the place when it came time for the election, effectively taking himself out of the running.

Maxey could never hand anything to anyone; everything got thrown. "Think fast!" seemed to be his motto; the moment you heard it, something—a beer, an apple, a bag of chips—was sure to come whistling past your head on its way to someone's hand. I thought to myself, *This guy can't keep still.*

The first dinner together, people talked about their summers. Internships weren't as common as they would later become, and the job market was healthier. Many of us had worked in offices or in retail, restaurants or clothing stores, most staying close to home. A few had been able to travel a bit at the beginning or the end. Someone asked Maxey what he had done.

Maxey told us that he had answered an ad in the *Yale Daily News* that simply said: AEROBICS INSTRUCTORS WANTED. CANCÚN, MEXICO. He and a dormmate named Scott were interviewed by a woman who could tell right away that they didn't have a clue about aerobics. They'd never even participated in an aerobics class and didn't know that it was, essentially, a trendy dance routine and not just vigorous exercise. They both turned on the charm and promised that they would start to learn aerobics the minute the interview was over.

Within days, Maxey and Scott—along with two women also from Yale and also ignorant of all things aerobic—heard back from their prospective employer. It really wasn't about aerobics after all, the woman explained: she and her husband had developed a series of exercises for the mini-trampoline and were trying to get guests in the high-end hotels on Mexico's east coast to take this new kind of fitness class; it would be yet another amenity that hotels offered. The four Yalies would get transportation to Cancún, and their room and board would be covered for the summer. No pay, but they only needed to work four days a week trying to talk tourists into exercising while they were on holiday. The other days they could bartend or do whatever they liked to make money. Whether they actually taught aerobics or not didn't matter, as long as they sold trampolines.

They all jumped at it, Maxey said, smiling.

The women chose to go by air, but Maxey and Scott were pressed into service driving down to Cancún in their employers' Lincoln Continental and hauling a camper attached to it full of the trampoline entrepreneurs' belongings.

"Scott and I picked up the car at the end of the term and started driving," Maxey told us. "The camper kept getting flat tires. We got one on the New Jersey Turnpike and then we got another in Virginia and I asked this guy in Virginia at a gas station why we kept getting these flat tires. And he said, 'What the hell do you have in this camper?' And I said, 'I don't know. I'm just driving this shit down to Mexico for a lady.' So we open up the back of the camper and there's a BMW motorcycle. This huge BMW 750.

"So I called the woman, and she said it was her husband's and then put him on the phone. I told him we weren't going to make it down there with this motorcycle in the back and he asked me, 'Do you know how to ride a motorcycle?' I said, 'Well, I think I can figure it out!' So, starting in Virginia, I'm on the motorcycle and Scott is driving the Lincoln. It was awesome."

Did Maxey really teach himself to ride a motorcycle on the

spot? No one else seemed to doubt it, so I kept that question to myself.

"After a whole day on the road," Maxey continued, "we hit New Orleans. First thing we do is unhook the camper in a little camping place. Then we drive that Lincoln across the causeway into the city and the minute we get there we go to this Cajun place and we're eating crawfish—it's unreal—and then we find this great jazz place that looks like a warehouse. And we don't leave there until about two in the morning.

"We drive out of the parking lot and Scott turns left when he should have turned right and, you ready for this . . . ?" Maxey paused dramatically. ". . . The next thing is that we realize the car is on some railroad tracks. That's not all. It's *stuck* on the tracks. We can't go forward. We can't go backward. The body of the Lincoln is resting high and dry on the tracks with the wheels spinning. What's *more,* now a train is coming. Scott's standing next to the car, by the door, with his hand inside, flashing the lights, getting ready to bail. And it doesn't seem like the train is slowing down.

"Yo, can someone get me a beer?" That wasn't part of the story. Maxey needed a beer before continuing. Someone got him a beer. He took a swig and then started up again. "So, the car is stuck, we are standing next to it, the train is barreling toward us—and then this cop car pulls up on the tarmac that goes across the tracks, and the cop driving puts his car's lights and siren on, and the train sees that, and it stops about three hundred feet from our car.

"Then the cop—a big, burly New Orleans cop—comes up to us and drawls, 'You boys been drinking?' It was pretty obvious. But we'd sobered up pretty quickly. Long story short, he helped us out—found a trucker to get the car off the train track, and didn't even give us a ticket. He just said, 'Make sure you guys sit and drink some coffee.'"

Maxey confessed that he couldn't really sell any trampolines in Cancún—none of them could—so he wound up teaching tourists how to scuba dive, even though he'd just learned himself the summer before. He said he'd been about to hook up with one of the Yale girls but then found out she was a virgin, so he didn't. And he got wasted a lot.

He'd also managed to save some money and used it to buy a motorcycle. It was now parked outside the hall. A used Yamaha 850. "It's a big hog, like a Harley, but has a Japanese shaft drive," Maxey explained. "It's a good simple bike. Not a lot of maintenance. I call it the Bitch."

How was my summer? someone asked. I wanted to tell them about my weeks sick in bed in London and my search for the angel with the rusty knife. "Pretty boring," I replied.

FALL RETREAT

I started as a classics major at Yale. But I dreaded one of the requirements of the major: translating a John F. Kennedy speech into ancient Greek. First, it struck me as a breathtakingly pointless exercise. More important, I didn't think I could do it. I'd been studying Greek for seven years, but to this day I'm not sure whether I ever actually learned to read Greek. I suspect I memorized vast quantities of English translation that I'd painstakingly puzzled out, and was adept at matching the English to the correct passage in Greek as soon as I had sufficient clues.

The autumn of my senior year, right at the start, I switched to the much easier classical civilization major, which had a language requirement that I'd already fulfilled. That meant I would have more time to put on plays, more time for trips to New York, more time to spend on the New Haven AIDS hotline, and more time to read.

I doubted, however, that I would spend more time than I had to at the hall.

I liked the other kids a lot, but Maxey made me nervous. I couldn't think of anything to say to him, and the feeling seemed mutual. It was clear that the less time we spent together the better. We were similar in so many ways—we'd both grown up in prosperous, preppy worlds and, of course, had Yale in common. But this only served to highlight our differences, which seemed especially hard to bridge given that they stemmed almost entirely from our personalities and from the choices we'd made from earliest childhood about the kinds of people we wanted to have around us—and those we didn't.

IN ORDER FOR all of us to get to know one another quickly, we were supposed to go away together for an entire weekend early in the fall. It was a tradition. I was dreading it.

Seventy hours with a bunch of kids I didn't know seemed too much. I was particularly anxious about sleeping arrangements. I guessed that it wasn't possible we would have our own rooms and was worried about sharing.

There's a dance that goes on in the heads of many gay men around straight men, and it filled mine at that point. I had no idea how gay friendly or gay tolerant any of the guys were and whether sharing a room with a homosexual might cause them to panic. Yet I didn't want to be the one who didn't want to share a room with any of the other guys—it would make it seem like I couldn't trust myself around them, that I had designs on them. I was particularly worried about Maxey. I didn't know how he felt about gay people but was quite certain he didn't like us. And while we hadn't talked about the fact that I was gay, I knew he knew it.

Right up until the last minute I debated whether I should go. I could call in sick. Still, I prided myself on attendance. Someone had once told me that showing up is ninety percent of life. I scored it more at ninety-eight percent.

So, on the appointed day, we gathered for our big expedition. We were six women and eight men: one of the women had decided to take an extended break from college a few weeks in, so we were one shy of our original fifteen and would remain that way. Our destination was the country home of a family with strong ties to the society. This was a distinguished New England clan with achievements that went back generations. Another secret society was rumored to own an island. Ours didn't own this house, but the family loaned it to the group for this weekend every fall. I remember being impressed: it seemed to me that you had to be either pretty crazy or very loyal to let a bunch of college students stay unsupervised in your country house for a weekend.

Maxey was the only one of us who had wheels; in his case, two: his Yamaha 850, the Bitch. The rest of us had to rent or borrow enough cars to get us there, and I remember being squished into a back seat and distinctly uncomfortable. It wasn't simply because of the lack of room: I really don't like to touch other people unless I am sleeping with them. I never have. Some people are huggers; I'm the opposite. I also would have been anxious about a sufficient quantity of rest stops, due to my coffee intake. To refrain from drinking coffee would never have occurred to me.

When we got to the house, Maxey was waiting outside. We had driven fast; clearly, he had ridden much faster. He'd also almost wiped out in a huge way and had a tale to tell: something about changing lanes, an oil patch, a big truck. He had thought he was going to die, and it was clear that he wasn't exaggerating. Maxey seemed shaken, almost pensive.

The sun was setting, there was a chill in the air, and there wasn't a thing to eat in the house. I volunteered to go along on the grocery run. Others would fire up the grill. And still others would go stock up on beer, wine, and liquor.

I had recently reread William Golding's *Lord of the Flies,* and I felt apprehensive when we came back to the house: I knew how quickly things could devolve. Happily, the scene when we returned was a placid one: the home team, Maxey among them, were busy setting up the grill and prepping the coals. There was the requisite debate about how much lighter fluid to pour over the charcoal, but in the end, consensus was reached.

The shocking thing that happened next was that nothing shocking happened next. We ate. We talked. We drank. We cleaned up. When it came time to pick bedrooms, we filled empty beds in the order in which we retired, without giving much thought to whomever had filled the other bed in the room. One of the women and I shared. The next day was a repeat of the day before.

At the same time, I remained guarded, and I wasn't the only

one. Even while drunk, no one revealed much. No one did or said anything outrageous. Maxey and I gave each other a wide berth. There were fourteen of us, so it wasn't difficult.

Our last night we all stayed up far too late, and most of us drank way too much. When morning came, shockingly soon after our last drink, it was time to leave. I had a thick tongue, spikes in my temples, and weights pressing on my eyeballs. I couldn't imagine how I was going to make it back to campus squished again into the back seat of a car. It was a crisp fall morning, so I feared the windows would be rolled up tight.

I was hanging around the kitchen waiting for enough coffee to drip through the Mr. Coffee filter into the carafe to allow me to shortstop it before putting the carafe back in place. Maxey was in the kitchen with a few others, looking similarly worse for wear.

As we discussed our hangovers, I aired my concerns about being in the back of a car for the ride home. I think I was hoping that my confession might earn me the coveted shotgun seat, where I could crack the window and have my own space. Instead, next thing I knew, Maxey was insisting that I ride home on the back of the Bitch. The air would be good for me. He had an extra helmet.

I said I thought this was a terrible idea—that I didn't like motorcycles, that someone else might want to go—but Maxey wouldn't take no for an answer. When we got outside, he threw the helmet at me.

"Dude," he said, "you just got to promise me one thing."

I asked him what.

"If you feel like you are frickin' going to puke, you got to turn your head around and try not to get me or the Bitch."

He got on the bike. I got in back of him.

What came next was all my fears about choosing a bedroom made manifest.

Maxey is a handsome guy, but he wasn't my type. I've always liked wan aesthetes, goths, punks, spiky-haired dancers, dandies, and moody rebels. Maxey was classic all-American preppy. But he didn't *know* that he wasn't my type.

So I was on the back of his bike, worrying about the fact that I might need to wrap my arms around Maxey to keep from falling off, but also worrying that he might think I was coming on to him, and then worrying that I had no idea how he would react to that. However, if I *didn't* wrap my arms tightly around him when it was obviously a good idea, then he might assume that it was because I was afraid he might think I was coming on to him if I did. Which would have been accurate and awkward. Then there was my aversion to hugging people generally. This was why I didn't want to ride back with Maxey in the first place. This was why I wasn't even sure I should have come to the retreat. This was why I wasn't even sure I should have joined the secret society. It was all just too complicated. It was so much easier to be around other gay people and theater people and people just like me whom I never needed to touch.

Then Maxey started up the motorcycle, and we roared out of the driveway. As the bike screamed down the highway back to New Haven, I simply wrapped my arms around Maxey and held on for dear life. We couldn't talk or listen to music, but the soundtrack in my head was pure Bruce Springsteen with his "highways jammed with broken heroes on a last-chance power drive." Maybe I was born to run after all?

I suppose if I had thought more about the lyrics to that

particular anthem it would have been embarrassing in just the ways I had feared the whole ride might be—I wasn't looking for Maxey to guard my dreams and visions, and I doubt that he was asking me to help him find out if love was real. He was just giving me a ride home on his motorcycle. But the ride itself was so terrifying and exhilarating that for once I wasn't overthinking everything. Who I was, I was. Who I would be, I didn't know. At that moment I was just a guy on the back of a motorcycle piloted by a daredevil jock who wanted to push his machine to the maximum but didn't seem like he wanted to die.

MY AUDIT

I felt buoyant the following week. Maybe I wouldn't have to watch myself so carefully after all. Maybe I could be myself. Most of the others in the group had also begun to let down their guards a bit. This was particularly true of Huei-Zu, the art historian. She had barely said anything on the drive up. But over the course of the weekend, she'd started to talk about her true passion: contemporary art. She had a full-throated laugh that also appeared as the weekend progressed. Now that we were back, she and I found ourselves spending more time together, especially because we realized we had a friend in common who had a Datsun 280-Z and could be prevailed upon to drive us to New York on the flimsiest of pretexts.

As we felt less anxious with one another, our conversations turned more frequently to politics. At the start of the school year, a Korean airliner full of passengers had been shot out of the sky by Russia, killing all 269 people aboard; we debated what the global response to that should be. A few of us were following events in the Philippines after the assassination of Benigno Aquino Jr. And everyone had an opinion on our president, Ronald Reagan, who had few fans in the hall.

We talked about our courses. I had put together an eclectic mix: Film Studies, Black Women and Their Fiction, Minoan Archaeology, The Fundamentals of Financial Accounting, and ever more Greek. My assigned reading ranged from François Truffaut and Paule Marshall to the annual reports of United Technologies and Dow Chemical. With some Plato.

I was highly distractible in my room or in the library, so in the weeks after the retreat I often found myself wandering over to the hall with a book. I could stretch out on the ante-room sofa and read without anyone bothering me. Once or twice Maxey came in with friends, but they went right down to the pool table. One afternoon, though, when I walked into the hall I found Maxey alone there, quietly reading. I was on my way to the basement to watch some television, hoping to catch Dexys Midnight Runners' "Come On Eileen" video. It didn't occur to me to ask Maxey to join me. Or to ask him what he was reading.

YALE COLLEGE IS divided into residential dorms that are themselves called colleges. Confusing, but they are basically just dorms. When you arrive, you're assigned to one of these for your full four years. Unless you live off campus or are a freshman (they live and eat all together), it's where you sleep and have most of your breakfasts, lunches, and dinners. As you gain a nodding acquaintance with the others in your college, you also get a sense of who would welcome your company over a meal and whom you should avoid.

Still, you don't have to eat in *your* college; you can eat in any of them. When you arrange to share a meal with friends from another one, you might just as easily find yourself joining them in their college as your own. Which is why, a few weeks after the retreat, I found myself, tray in hand, waiting in line for dinner at a residential college where I knew few people except the student I was visiting that day.

This guy was one of the other gay kids at Yale who was totally out of the closet. He dressed in an even more extreme fashion than I did. For want of a better phrase, I would describe his style as Gay Spartan. He liked leather sandals with straps that crisscrossed up his thighs, mesh shirts that were made from sparkly metallics, and bracelets so thick that they covered his entire forearm. Classics major that I was, I referred to them by their proper name, vambraces.

Naturally, he attracted quite a lot of ridicule. Most of the time, he didn't seem to care.

There were a bunch of jocks ahead of us in the hot-food line, jostling one another, and one of them was Maxey. But before I could catch his eye, which seemed like the polite thing to do, there was a commotion of some kind. One of them had either dropped his tray or had it slapped out of his hand. Spaghetti with meat sauce was now splattered all over the floor. Lots of laughter among the jocks.

"I hate those guys," my friend said to me. "I really hate them. They just don't give a shit about anyone, and they make life really unpleasant. I mean, someone has to clean up that mess."

"Let's just go to the salad bar," I said. "I don't want to wait in line anymore."

My friend was up for that; he was underweight bordering on malnourished, but he had fat cheeks and so was always on a diet.

I don't know if Maxey saw me. I don't think he did. We went to opposite sides of the dining hall to eat and soon he was gone. This came as a relief. Our friendship seemed to me so tenuous that I wasn't sure it was up to a test: I didn't want to see how he would treat me when he was amongst his tribe—nor was I keen to have my lunchmate snub Maxey.

IN THE WEEKS following the retreat we were supposed to start our audits. An audit was a verbal presentation you shared with the group. You were meant to tell the others everything you had ever done and thought from your first memory to the present. Whatever was shared was to be treated with complete confidentiality: nothing was ever to leave the hall without the explicit permission of the person who had shared it. The audits, we were told, were the heart of the experience we would have that year. You were encouraged to do it—but it was up to you how deeply into your life you dove. Most of the time, people talked for two or three hours without stopping. Sometimes they went to four or five. Only one audit would be scheduled per week, and it was totally up to us what order we followed: who would give the first and who the last.

Having been a debater and actor in high school, I wasn't nervous about the idea of giving my audit. But many of the others were anxious bordering on hysterical.

Before the first audit, we were given a training by an alumnus of the society to set our minds at ease, and it did. I try to keep the lessons he taught us in mind to this day, whenever anyone is telling me anything sensitive or personal.

We were told that the most important thing was to listen, really listen, and to keep an open mind and heart. We weren't to ask any questions until and unless we were invited to do so. We were told to be thoughtful about our questions—that they had to be genuine. It was fine to ask for more information or clarification if we were curious or didn't understand what we'd heard. But questions were never to be used as challenges or veiled criticisms. We were warned particularly about "Why" questions. It's hard to ask about motivation without implying that you would have handled the same situation differently. Far better to ask "How" and "What" questions (as long as the "What" was never a sarcastic "What were you thinking?").

Also, we weren't to follow a person's audit with statements of our own values, share our own stories in the guise of questions, or use queries to show how smart we were. Finally, no matter how gentle or well-meaning we thought our questions to be, the person who had presented was under no obligation to answer, or to give a reason why she or he didn't want to elaborate or explain.

This wasn't an investigation or interrogation, the trainer said. It wasn't a commission or a hearing. It was a chance to share our lives and thoughts with one another.

One of us asked whether *audit* was really the right word, then, to describe what we would be doing, given that an audit is "an official inspection."

"Probably not," we were told. "And yet that's exactly the kind of question you shouldn't ask right after an audit."

*　　*　　*

I CAN'T REMEMBER whose audit was first, but I was soon after. I spent several days preparing, writing notes of every single thing I could remember about my life. As I was figuring out what to include, I started to become nervous. I put everything down on paper but would decide what to share in the moment.

The evening started with us gathering around the sofas for drinks. We were supposed to be prompt, and we were. Then we all sat down for dinner. Tim wasn't kidding about the food; the hall's caretakers were a couple who made delicious, hearty meals served family-style.

At the audit dinners everyone stayed quite sober. Since I was giving the one this night, I drank nothing. After pie for dessert, it was back to the sofas.

I pulled out my notes and began.

First, the facts. Both parents grew up in New York, and both went to PS 6—though they didn't know each other then, as my father was born in 1927 and mother in 1935. Father enlisted in the navy right after boarding school in time for the last year of World War II. Served on a destroyer out of Norfolk, Virginia. Mother had wanted to be an actress but then became assistant to a producer.

I was born in New York in 1962. Brother eighteen months older. Sister four years younger. Moved to Cambridge, Massachusetts, when I was four. Mother went into admissions first at Radcliffe and then at the combined office of Harvard and Radcliffe. Father managed Harvard's theater.

Then I tried to describe my personality and early life as an indoor child, reading and painting. I also talked about how

I loved to act. I mentioned a production of *Life With Father,* where I'd played one of the kids and had to dye my hair bright red the summer before I went to boarding school, and how, when I got there, everyone called me Red until it grew out.

I went into much more detail than that. I was probably well into an hour by the time I was fourteen. And that's when I started to talk about being gay.

I backtracked to my early crushes on boys when I was as young as six or seven, and talked about a recurring dream that began when I was in middle school, which so terrified me that I would wake up not just sobbing but grieving: in the nightmare, a boy in my class named Ben was killed by a mob while coming over to my house. The other emotion I felt in addition to grief, I explained, was guilt. In the dream-turned-nightmare he was on his way to see me; that's why he was killed.

I talked about wearing a shirt with pink stripes in ninth grade and my panic when a jock sidled up to me and said, "Nice shirt, wrong color." And about staring at my feet whenever I was in the locker room, lest anyone think I was looking at them, but really wanting to look at the same time. I talked about being an apprentice at a summer stock theater when I was fifteen where I lived with four other kids, including an older gay roommate named Hooch, who boycotted orange juice to protest the homophobia of Florida Citrus spokeswoman Anita Bryant. He became a friend that summer, but I still hid my feelings about men from him and everyone else.

Then I explained how a librarian at school introduced me to the works of James Baldwin and how I started to admit to myself that I was gay, confiding in a minister at school whom I strongly suspected of being a lesbian. "Don't tell anyone until graduation," she advised; I had been elected school president, but we were both sure I would have had to leave had anyone found out. There had never been an out gay student or teacher at my school.

I talked about other authors and books I'd discovered that helped me learn that I wasn't alone: *The City and the Pillar* by Gore Vidal; *The Lord Won't Mind,* a steamy gay romance by Gordon Merrick; and *City of Night,* the 1963 novel by John Rechy featuring a Los Angeles hustler, a celebration of gay men as outlaws that is as erotic as it is dark.

At this point in the audit, I paused to take a breath and see how people were reacting. Everyone was smiling encouragingly. So I decided to go further than I had before and tell this group things I had told only my closest friends: I talked about going to a bar when I was sixteen and getting plastered and going home with an older man and then throwing up in his bed. And how he had said, "You have to stop hating yourself." I talked about how much weed and cocaine I had done in high school, and about taking mescaline. And about the first time I had full-on sex, which I described in infinite detail. I talked about summer weeks working as a temporary secretary to fund weekends spent at the infamous St. Mark's Baths, formerly the home of James Fenimore Cooper, where I would prowl the halls hour after hour, rejecting and being rejected until I found a match. I talked about life in Los Angeles in the term I'd taken off, and how my friends and I would flirt for drinks in a bar called the Mother Lode and try to go home with someone from a different state every night. I talked about how proud I was to have had a story published in a gay literary magazine called *Christopher Street,* and how I loved that they had illustrated it with a drawing of an enormous male organ scrawled on a bathroom wall.

Throughout, I continued to keep an eye on the faces of the others in the group. The dancer, Renata, was no stranger to gay men and nodded in support throughout. I kept glancing at her and every time I did, she smiled. Every now and then I looked over at the football player, Tom, and at Maxey, who were sitting together. Where I had expected to see some kind of disapproval, there was none. Maxey was particularly focused, leaning forward and smiling.

I talked next about AIDS and working on the hotline and speaking with a man in his twenties who was clearly dying, and how there was almost nothing I could do for him; how everything I said felt wrong and how my apologies made it worse. I talked about that friend in LA whom I'd slept with many times, the one who had died, and about how I tried for months not to think about his death but couldn't stop, and how I was becoming increasingly convinced that I would be dead by twenty-five. I talked about a benefit I had just put on to raise money for Gay Men's Health Crisis and AIDS Project New Haven: it was a performance of a play I'd written about conjoined twins, one straight and one gay.

I told them about going home with the boy I met in the bar over that last summer, the angel of death with the rusty knife under the bed; how I still didn't leave after I discovered the knife, and the way he haunted my sleep.

I talked about the threat of violence I felt almost everywhere, whether cruising in New York's Greenwich Village—where a group of kids in a Jersey car had once thrown a beer bottle at my head that missed by inches—or even sometimes on Yale's campus. I talked about the homophobic gunman who had opened fire at a New York City bar I went to called the Ramrod; he had killed two men and injured six more. "I want to kill them all," he had said, referring to gay men: "They're no good. They ruin everything." I talked about the loathing and disgust I would so often hear when anything gay was mentioned. And the way politicians and the media constantly demonized or trivialized what they called our "lifestyle" and we called our lives. I explained how it was totally legal to fire someone for being gay in every state in America, except for Wisconsin.

Then I talked about the worst day of my life, after I had taken a Valium that a friend had given me to help me sleep. All my friends knew I could never get to sleep. I described how I had slept a blissful night with no dreams but woken up to a nightmare, in which I felt that my whole life was a farce, that I was a dreadful person, that I had no reason to go on living. I remember distinctly knowing that I was no less happy or blessed than I had been the day before —I was sure the Valium was the culprit— but I also remember the terror that maybe I would never be happy again, that I would eventually need to end my life to make the agony stop.

It was the first time—in that hall, surrounded by thirteen kids I barely knew—that I had told anyone I had ever thought of taking my own life. I shared with them my feeling that even talking about it filled me with shame; that it seemed obscene to me that I had thought, even for a day, of killing myself when so many gay people were dying too young. I also told them how relieved I was to be able to share both the story and the sense of shame.

And then, always the entertainer, and feeling a bit like I

had brought the room down, I talked about my crushes (Mark Lindsay of Paul Revere and the Raiders, Bobby Sherman, and always, always, Matt Dillon). And, of course, I was rhapsodic about Prince. I talked and talked and talked, for at least four hours, if not five.

And then I was done.

People did have questions. One listener wanted to know when I had come out, which was just about the only story I'd forgotten to tell. I explained that it was at a senior party on the last day of high school. I'd confided in a handsome friend from San Francisco (I hoped that maybe he was gay, given his native city, but he was not) and asked him not to tell anyone; he told everyone. Right there. At the party. And far from being mad at him, I'd been grateful. Another member of the secret society asked me to recommend the best Matt Dillon film, and someone else asked me about my favorite author, which gave me a chance to talk about Christopher Isherwood.

Maxey hadn't asked anything, but he also hadn't looked the slightest bit shocked at anything I said. Eventually, there were just a few of us left drinking beer in the hall, and I realized that he had something to say to me before we called it a night.

"You know, Schwalbs," he said, giving me a new nickname on the spot. "I've never really met a gay person before." Then he amended that: "I mean, I'm sure I've met a gay person, but I've never been friends with one. I got to tell you: I still don't really get it. But when you talked about being in the gym surrounded by hot guys and having to look at your feet, I really understood. I was trying to think what I would do in a locker room full of naked girls. And your other stories: you're as boy crazy as I am girl crazy. So maybe I do get it. But I have to tell you one other thing: when you talked about that beer bottle being thrown at your head, that really pissed me off. I just wanted you to know, if anyone ever gives you a hard time, tries to hurt you, or even looks at you funny, you just let me know—and I'll kick the shit out of them."

I should have disapproved, firmly believing that violent retribution is never the right answer to violence. Yet I couldn't help smiling.

MAXEY'S AUDIT

Several audits followed mine and each drew the group closer. One of us spoke about growing up the only child of parents who had lost the rest of their family in the Holocaust. Another about the Svengali-like role that coaches and teachers had played in her life. Another about the death of a beloved father when she was in high school. It wasn't the stories that bound us; it was the way we framed them for one another and the fact that we shared them in the first place. We had come from all over: suburbs and small towns; an industrial city whose factories had closed a generation ago; a university campus; our nation's capital and NYC. Yet we had all wound up in the same place—if with different theories about how we got here and what that meant.

Most of us admitted to suffering from imposter syndrome; there was relief in that admission. Inadequacy loves company. We also discovered over the course of the fall that we had an eclectic array of fears, ranging from common childhood terrors (Spiders! Mimes!) to more esoteric phobias (Swiss cheese!

Guinea pigs!) to thoroughly adult concerns. Several in our group had grown up in alcoholic homes and were terrified of their fathers.

We discovered at least one shared fear. We were children of the Atomic Age: our communities had well-marked fall-out shelters, and we had been taught how to huddle under our school desks in case of nuclear attack. Other fears common to our generation included overpopulation, pollution, and hijack-ing. Then there were fears about our own futures and whether we would be happy. There was an Auden line I thought of often: "Every young man fears that he is not worth loving." Of course, every young woman, as well. I believe we shared this, too, though not all of us admitted it.

The audits provided, for many of us, our first chance to share our fears without adding one more to the list: the fear that those fears would be weaponized against us. Week after week, over beers and candles, we handed one another the nuclear mat-ter of our lives, yet there was no thought of mutually assured destruction, no anxiety that we would use our secrets against one another, no need for any treaties.

As the audits multiplied, we learned that there was another fear we all shared in addition to thermonuclear destruction of our planet and being unworthy of love: we worried that we might squander the almost obscene opportunity we had been given. We knew that *because* we were there—not just in the hall but at the college—others hadn't been given this chance. Each week that went by brought us closer to graduation and the obligation to do something with our lives. We all had hopes and thoughts—but even by late autumn few of us had anything that resembled a plan.

While we were meeting, talking, drinking, competing, acting, sleeping, and worrying, the world was far from quiet. In October, two suicide bombers had struck US and French barracks in Beirut, killing 241 American Marines, 58 French servicemen, and six Lebanese citizens. Days later, the United States had invaded the tiny Caribbean nation of Grenada. At Yale, the clerical and technical workers were negotiating a new contract; relations between their union and the university were growing increasingly strained. As for AIDS, I had yet to convince most of my friends that this would affect more than a few thousand gay men, Haitians, and hemophiliacs.

Outside the hall, students were constantly arguing about issues from around the world and problems at the college itself, and inside we began arguing, too. The two most frequent combatants were David Singer and David Kelly, continuing the sparring that had begun when they were roommates. It was a sure thing that if one of them made a statement, the other would challenge it. I usually kept quiet, as did most of the others, but Maxey liked to fan the flames, which I sometimes found entertaining but often made me cringe. On the evenings when there were audits, everyone behaved; the other dinners, however, could be a free-for-all.

If we had been friends of friends at an ad hoc dinner party, we probably would have vowed never to see one another again. This person was condescending; that one shouted everyone else down; a third refused to concede even the smallest point. But we *had* to see one another again. Twice a week. Thankfully, no matter how acrimonious things got, the audits always brought us back together. Sharing our stories forced us to reexamine one another and the labels we'd applied when we first met.

What an irony, I thought: a secret society was teaching us to be more tolerant and open-minded. For the first time, I began to understand what Tim meant when he'd said that this experience would open me up.

Just before Thanksgiving, when we'd worked our way through half the audits, it was Maxey's turn.

The first thing that surprised me was that he had made notes. The second was that he seemed nervous. I don't know why I hadn't expected Maxey to be anxious: most of us were before our audits. But Maxey had carried himself with such swagger that I assumed this would be just another boisterous performance, like the story of his road trip to Cancún. I was braced for a cavalcade of track meets, wrestling matches, and keggers, with lots of barfing in between.

Instead of bouncing around the hall as he usually did, Maxey had spent the hour or so before dinner in one of the big leather armchairs, cradling a beer. Afterwards, we settled into the sofas and the chairs that surrounded them. Maxey rested his arms on his legs, looked down at the floor, and began.

Maxey started by telling us about his biological father, whom he never knew. Maxey's parents had married young. His father had been a naval officer who had grown up in Allentown. His mother, whom everyone called Big Red, had also grown up in Pennsylvania, where her father blew holes in mountains to bring highways across the state. When Maxey was born, his parents lived in San Diego. Maxey's father was finishing up a successful tour of duty and about to transition to civilian life and pursue his passion for landscape architecture. But when Maxey was still a baby, his father was diagnosed with a cyst in his brain. Maxey's paternal grandparents wanted the operation to be done in Allentown. After an apparently successful surgery, Maxey's mom was told she should go home and get a few hours of rest, which she did only after she saw that her husband seemed alert and fine. While she was gone, Maxey's father died; they'd forgotten to put a shunt in. He was twenty-eight.

After that, Maxey said, his mother wasn't entirely sure she wanted to live. Many years later, she told him about driving alone on the Pacific Coast Highway and wondering if it wouldn't be easier for everyone if she just turned the wheel sharply and ended everything. But she couldn't make her infant son an orphan. Eventually, she met a man who loved her and, just as important—and Maxey smiled when he told us this—loved her son. Everyone's favorite picture from his mother's second wedding was of his new father emerging from the church cradling toddler Maxey in the crook of his arm.

Maxey told us that when he talks of his father, he's speaking of the only father he's ever known, the man who would go on to adopt him and give him his family name. He then explained that his mother and father had three kids after him—a brother and sister, who were twins, and then a younger sister—and that he found his calling in being a big brother. He said that the best day of his life was the day he welcomed the twins home after so much anticipation. In fact, he said, his mother thought it was weird how much time he wanted to spend with all three of his siblings. He was constantly leading them on expeditions. Of course, they worshipped him and he liked that.

We heard more about Maxey's childhood. He grew up on the Main Line, outside Philadelphia. His dad was a successful advertising man who commuted every day to Madison Avenue. His mom sold real estate. He told us about the Maxey code, drilled into him by his mother: look people in the eye, be respectful to elders, and leap up to help with the dishes when you are at someone else's home. We also got a hint of all the sports triumphs to come (track, lacrosse, wrestling) and an earful about the various girls on whom young Maxey had crushes: Maxey was indeed as girl crazy as I was boy crazy.

It surprised me that there weren't *more* stories about actual girls. As it turned out, Maxey had always craved relationships as much as sex: there were only two girlfriends in high school, first Carmen and then Kumari.

Next, Maxey talked about swimming, bodies of water, and how he always had his most mystical and meaningful experiences in the ocean. He said he could swim before he could walk.

"The connection to the ocean is the only spiritual force in my life. I guess I'm an agnostic. But as a teenager I remember swimming one night, with the stars reflected on the surface of the ocean and bioluminescence firing up from the depths below me, and saying to myself, 'Wow, this is beautiful, there must be a God.'"

The minute Maxey started talking about bioluminescence and God, I thought, *I wonder if Maxey did a lot of drugs.* As if he were reading my mind, Maxey went on to say that he didn't do any drugs in high school. He was far too serious about sports. His body was a temple. After this remark, he flexed in a cheesy way and smiled.

Then Maxey paused, as though he wasn't sure he wanted to go through with what he had been planning to say next. I'm guessing someone got him another beer. He stared at the floor for a bit longer and told us he was going to tell us about the worst day of his life. It was when he was a teenager. Strangely, it featured water.

"My brother, Jack, was out visiting my mom's sister in

Napa," he began. "She and her husband were trying to revive an old vineyard, on a mountainside, and when we were kids, we would go out there for summers. Just to hang out and help if we could. There was an old monastery because when the vineyard was going strong it was run by monks. It had been abandoned for decades. It was an awesome place."

There was also a large swimming pool on the property, and whenever Maxey and his siblings were there, they would spend their lives in the pool with their cousins. The year he turned fifteen, however, he needed to stay home in Pennsylvania and work, painting houses while training for lacrosse. His sisters were also busy at home that summer.

"So Jack had gone out alone to visit my aunt and uncle, and he loved that pool. My brother was a breath-holder guy: he liked to hold his breath and spend a crazy amount of time underwater just to scare everyone. This pool was deep and had a filter about eight inches off the bottom. And one day Jack was swimming with our cousins, and he decided to dive to the bottom and put his hand over the hole for the filter. Well, there was no cap on the filter and my brother's arm got sucked into it. He was a little guy, probably like ten or eleven, and there was no way that he could get his arm free. He was trapped at the bottom of the pool, just trapped.

"It took a long time for my cousins to realize he wasn't screwing around like he always was. And by the time they realized that, they just started screaming and it seemed to take forever for my uncle to run down from the barn. My uncle dove to the bottom of the pool, and by this time my brother was starting to turn blue. He tried to pull Jack out and he couldn't. My uncle is a strong guy, but he couldn't free my brother. He later told us that he thought to himself that he should get out of the pool and turn the pump off, but he didn't know if there was time."

Maxey then explained that there were some seasonal workers at the vineyard who rushed over when they heard the commotion.

"One of the workers jumped in, and he and my uncle were able to pull against the suction and free my brother's arm and get him to the surface. Jack was blue and wasn't breathing. My uncle tried traditional CPR. It didn't work. And he thought, 'I've got to call an ambulance.' So he ran up to the house and left my brother with the guy who helped pull him out and the other workers. My cousins were freaking out. My brother was dead."

Maxey paused again. He held himself very still. His eyes twitched a little. But otherwise, he was like a rock. What seemed like a full minute passed. But maybe it was only a few seconds.

"I was with my mother and my sisters in our kitchen in Pennsylvania when my uncle called from the vineyard on the coast. My mother told us sentence by sentence what her brother-in-law was telling her: *He'd found Jack in the pool. Jack wasn't breathing. He couldn't get him to breathe. He called an ambulance. The ambulance was coming. He would let us know as soon as he knew what was happening. He had to run back to the pool.* And then my uncle hung up. I remember my mom was just—I couldn't even hold her up—she just collapsed. I went out into our yard—and I was punching trees and crying. I didn't know what I was going to do without Jack."

Then, strangely, Maxey smiled.

"But while my uncle was calling us, those workers didn't give up. They decided they would hold my brother upside down. Which makes a lot of sense, right? CPR on someone whose lungs and stomach are full of water is not going to work. So they held him by his ankles and were pushing his stomach in and out and pounding on him—and then he just started to vomit and began to breathe. Those guys got him breathing. They brought my brother back from death.

"We almost couldn't believe it when my uncle called back. But he told us that he didn't know what kind of brain damage Jack had suffered. I mean, my uncle was a straight shooter and I don't think he thought Jack would come through it. I knew Jack would. I mean, I think the other thing that saved him, other of course than those frickin' awesome guys, was that he was like a freak because he could hold his breath for seven minutes.

"We flew out there right away and went right to the hospital. I'll never forget that as soon as we got there, Jack was awake and he made some dumb joke—like he shouldn't stick his hand in stray holes—and he just kind of smiled. And they'd told us that humor is one sign your brain is going to be okay—I mean, your brain has to be in good shape to make jokes. Then I hugged him."

We were all quiet. After a minute or two, someone asked Maxey how that experience had changed him. He thought about it for a bit.

"Well, I knew there had been a time when I was really sad that I didn't have a dad, even if that wasn't really part of my conscious memory. When I was two or three, before my mom remarried, we lived in a little house by some train tracks. All the other kids I played with—their dads would come home on the train. I knew I didn't have a dad and I didn't understand why. I also knew I couldn't ask my mom because it would make her sad. So I would constantly ask her best friend. Only years later did she tell my mom that I used to ask her why I didn't have a dad; and that I used to ask her if it was because I had done something wrong and that was the reason."

Maxey realized he hadn't answered the question and clearly wanted to try.

"Then all of a sudden, I had this dad, which was really cool, and then I had these siblings. The siblings were even more special to me because they came not *just* from my mom but from my mom and this miracle dad. When I thought I lost Jack, it felt like I was headed right back to where I started—that once again I could lose everything I had, and that maybe I didn't deserve any of it. Maybe I *had* done something wrong. It was painful—like a physical pain. I mean, I can take a lot of physical pain, but this was the worst pain I'd ever felt. When Jack survived it made me even more grateful, but I'll never forget that fear and that pain."

Maxey continued after that with a host of sports stories. He talked about wrestling and the coaches who had mentored him. About winning the league track competition at ten o'clock one morning and captaining his lacrosse team to the state championship that afternoon. We then heard more about his high school girlfriend Kumari, still the love of his life, and their tempestuous ongoing relationship, which involved constant trips between New Haven and Mount Holyoke, where she was at college. He also told us about the frat he belonged to in addition to our society and the stupid things he and his frat brothers did. There were lots of tales of drinking—he'd made up for lost time once he got to college.

"Now I know I haven't talked much about schoolwork," Maxey said with a smile, before becoming more serious. "But I really *am* interested in academics. It's just that I've always been insecure about my ability, and this dates way back to second grade when my slightly dyslexic brain was struggling to learn how to read. My teacher only added to my insecurity by calling me her Pokey Puppy because I was the slowest reader in my class. My reaction to Ms. Finley, a name I'll never forget, was to shut down even more.

"One day, Ms. Finley called my mom and said she thought I was mentally deficient. Big Red went crazy in defense of her firstborn and had me take an IQ test, which I must say made me feel more insecure. But I scored fine, and my mom made sure I was moved to another homeroom.

"Still, I'll always have Finley on my shoulder, sometimes motivating me to prove her wrong and other times making me insecure. I gave Finley a major victory my freshman year when I acted like a complete idiot. I'm guessing some of you have now heard the infamous Circa story?"

Maxey paused and looked around the group. "If you haven't heard it, you are totally welcome to laugh," he said, his mood lightening. "But, yes, I'm the guy in Vincent Scully's art history course who thought that Circa was the name of an Italian painter and not simply what you wrote before an approximate date if you didn't know exactly when a piece of art was created. In my defense, when I wrote the now infamous paper comparing a painting of a crucifixion that was labeled '*Circa* 1500' to a landscape by Frederick Turner, I'd left the assignment to the last minute, something I've been known to do. But I had never studied art history before and really didn't know what *circa* meant. So in the paper I wrote about the different styles of the two artists: Turner and Circa. I was truly humiliated when I got the paper back from the teaching assistant, and all it said was *Are you a moron?*

"Then I did something *really* stupid: I told a friend, who laughed so hard while he was explaining to me what I'd done that he fell out of his chair—and then told everyone about his friend Circa." Maxey, smiling broadly, decided to end his audit there. He said we were welcome to call him Circa, though he preferred Maxey. Or Chris. Or even Dickhead, which is what most of his rugby friends called him. (I learned then that Maxey played rugby whenever he had the chance.)

By the time we locked up that evening, it was close to midnight, and there were just a few of us left. When we were outside the hall, I told Maxey how moved I'd been by what he'd told us about his family, but he didn't seem to want to hear it. He made some stupid joke and then added, "I'm sorry I got so emotional."

Later that night and for days after, I wondered why he'd felt the need to apologize. Maybe he thought it made him seem weak. Or maybe he, too, was worried about letting down his guard.

DAYS BEFORE WINTER break, Maxey and I found ourselves aimlessly killing time in the hall.

"My whole family is going to be together for Christmas, Schwalbs," he said. "It will be great, but my folks are a bit worried about me. I mean, I'm at the big turn, heading down the home stretch, and I don't know what I'm going to do when I graduate. I know my parents will back me up, but they aren't used to me being indecisive."

Maxey paused for a second, collecting himself. Then he asked, "What are you going to do?"

"I'll spend Christmas with family. I'll put in some hours on the Gay Men's Health Crisis hotline. Maybe temp a bit. See friends. Sleep. I'm really excited about sleeping."

"No, I mean after you get out of here, with your life."

"Maxey, I really wish I knew."

It struck me in that moment more powerfully than it ever had before that I didn't know what I was going to do next. It felt good to share that with Maxey. And he seemed glad to share it with me.

PORNOGRAPHY AND LAUGHTER

"I hate that we aren't going to be able to spend that much more time together," Maxey announced the first day we were all back from Christmas vacation. "I guess senior year is all about savoring time when you know your back is against the wall and the sand is running out." Someone told him to get a grip. Someone else challenged him to shots. Wrestling ensued.

A feature of our time together was challenges, both mental ("Can you name that tune in five notes?") and physical (hopping on one foot or balancing objects on our heads). Maxey couldn't say no to a physical challenge—it was how he connected with others—and I always sat them out. A few days later I was in the hall and heard the bell to the front door. When I opened it, I found Maxey and Molly, the girl who had lived in Leningrad, standing there shivering. Both of them were dressed only in sweat-clothes. Molly, two-thirds Maxey's height, was grinning broadly. "She whupped my ass," Maxey announced. "Challenged me to race up to the top of the rock and beat me there by a mile." The rock was East Rock, a mountainous ridge on New Haven's north side.

"I did," Molly confirmed. Then they headed straight to the kitchen to get warm and rummage up some food.

In the early weeks of 1984, following our return from vacation, many of us started to voice how much we enjoyed being together. Almost all the audits were finished, and, while the time each of us spent at the hall varied greatly, everyone seemed increasingly at ease while there.

The Sunday dinners had settled into a familiar and familial rhythm. Singer would pontificate. David Kelly would challenge his arguments. I would try to change the subject. Maxey would eventually tell Singer to shut the fuck up. Often, Maxey wouldn't leave it at that. Singer would be arguing a point and Maxey would just ridicule him. They would wrestle. Something would be knocked over and would, or would not, break. Renata would drink and do dance stretches and ask funny provocative questions that would have been intrusive coming from anyone else but never from her because she was delighted with whatever you said in reply. Tom would hang on the periphery, grinning, and occasionally join in by making fun of Maxey; they had a humorous football-versus-wrestling rivalry that found its way into most conversations. Julia, the runner who volunteered as a Big Sister, would smile, taking it all in. Molly would laugh and inquire, wide-eyed, whether anyone believed what they were saying. It was an honest question. Others would choose to engage or not.

Maxey and I talked more in January than we had all fall. Most of his stories were about his wrestling career, punctuated by tales of epic nights of drinking that almost always started with tequila shots in his room and then continued when he was "forced" to go drink beers in a dive bar called Rudy's, usually referred to as "Rude Bar." The wrestling stories involved him goofing off, underestimating his opponent, but managing to pull out a victory anyway. The drinking stories almost always ended with vomit, waking up somewhere unexpected, and the crazy antics of a supposedly lovable group of knuckleheads. Frequently mentioned was a python that lived in the room of one of the knuckleheads; if you stroked its belly, it could be induced to shit on the rug.

Occasionally, Maxey talked about Kumari. Their relationship was filled with ups and downs—tearful phone calls, and almost monthly breakups and reunions. "It would be great if we could just have a good time, laugh, and not cry," Maxey once said to me. Every now and then he would also talk seriously about the pressure to do well in wrestling tournaments and how sick he was of having to spend every waking hour worrying about making weight. For almost as long as he could remember, Maxey was constantly having to slim down dramatically or pack on pounds to keep himself in a narrow range.

"I hate always having to think about everything I put in my mouth," he said one day. I had just come from a long shift on the AIDS hotline, so I said, "Me too," but I don't think he got the joke. Maxey also mentioned how much his shoulder was bothering him: he'd ripped it up in practice before Christmas. "I just have to keep focused and not mess up, Schwalbs," he told me, but I can't remember if he was talking about Kumari or wrestling or both.

Maxey never talked about his teachers, with one exception: a classics and history professor named Donald Kagan, whom Maxey always called the Great Man. Kagan taught a course on the origins of war that began with a close reading of Thucydides's *The Peloponnesian War* and went right up through the Cuban Missile Crisis. Maxey was a self-described Kagan groupie and took a class from him every term he could; his senior thesis under Kagan's tutelage would be on the showdown between John F. Kennedy and Nikita Khrushchev in 1962.

When Maxey was a sophomore, he'd struck up a conversation with Kagan after class as they were walking across campus. Kagan was on his way to visit Yale's president, the relentlessly urbane Renaissance scholar Bart Giamatti, and on a whim asked Maxey to come along. Maxey told us that he'd kept fairly quiet as the two friends spoke, but did manage to make some comments that weren't entirely stupid. At least, as he put it, he didn't feel he'd let the Great Man down. "The guy's a maniac," he told me one day, speaking admiringly of Kagan. "He thinks we should have invaded Cuba."

I shared with Maxey my own stories about my daily life and activities. My best friend—a guy named David Baer, whom I'd met freshman year—and I liked to go to the Anchor Bar; it was across from the Taft Hotel, where generations of Broadway stars had boarded during out-of-town tryouts. I would describe our evenings there. I was part of other close tribes as well, including a cluster of friends who had roomed together since sophomore year and met several times a week over pitchers at Naples Pizza. Our beer-fueled conversations often lasted until the floor was mopped and the employees were closing out the register as we debated the relative merits of San Francisco versus New York; rice pudding versus cinnamon toast; Prince versus Soft Cell.

I enjoyed hearing Maxey recount his adventures, and he seemed to enjoy mine. Beer was our lingua franca. I kept my stories light: it was fun to hear Maxey laugh.

We also began to spend the occasional evening together outside the hall along with others from our group. Late in January, Renata had a party in her dorm with her dancer friends and invited everyone to join. Most of us showed up, and it shouldn't have worked but did. Maxey had a massive head cold and brought a jug of fruit juice, which minutes later was spiked with vodka. Everyone started dancing with everyone else, and for once when Maxey's night ended with vomit and lovable knuckleheads, we were the knuckleheads in question.

AFTER MOST OF the audits were done, we invited speakers into the hall every week or so to have dinner with us and talk after the meal. This was another tradition of our society. Some of those we asked were former members; most weren't. It was up to us to choose.

One of our speakers would be the president of Yale, Bart Giamatti.

Campus remained tense: negotiations between the university and the clerical and technical workers seemed to be at an impasse. Most of us decided we wouldn't cross picket lines for classes, and some of the professors were planning to hold lectures off campus if there was a strike. (My anarchist sociology professor came up with the unique solution of preemptively canceling class for the remainder of the term and giving us grades more or less at random.)

I was still working on the New Haven AIDS hotline. I had also recently gone with a group of students to meet with President Giamatti to discuss various lesbian and gay issues, including why Yale's nondiscrimination policy didn't specifically include us. Students, faculty, and staff could be fired without cause solely for their sexuality. He was charming and promised nothing. When I mentioned this to the group, Maxey proudly told us of his tea with Giamatti two years before.

President Giamatti didn't join us for dinner, only for drinks after. He quickly learned all our names, and he was happy to be reminded of Maxey's and my visits—and to greet the few of us he already knew well. He talked about the university and scholarship, and about baseball, a passion of his. Finally, as he was just about to head out into the winter air, I decided to pose the question I'd been wanting to ask all evening.

"Excuse me, President Giamatti," I said, my voice cracking a bit. "But can I ask again about the nondiscrimination policy? Why doesn't the university have language that says that it won't discriminate against lesbians and gays? I mean, the policy names age, sex, race, creed, color, marital status, disability, and religion—but not sexual preference. Why not?" I tried to keep my voice even, but I was nervous, so I spoke more quickly and with more volume than usual. Strident.

I could sense most of the others nodding around me. Maxey was leaning forward, but I couldn't tell if I was making him uncomfortable. I remembered the Maxey code: I suspected that by grilling the university's president I might be crossing some kind of line.

Giamatti didn't look perturbed. He explained that Yale was a private educational institution incorporated in the state of Connecticut, and therefore had a nondiscrimination policy that mirrored Connecticut's. Should the state change its policy to include gays and lesbians, so would Yale. Immediately.

I could sense some relief in the room. Civilized question. Straightforward answer.

"But, President Giamatti," I continued, "don't you think Yale has a responsibility to lead the state and not simply follow it?"

"Interesting point, Mr. Schwalbe, interesting point," Giamatti said affably. He chatted for fifteen or so minutes more, then shook hands with all of us and headed out into the cold.

Later, while playing pool and drinking beer in the basement, Maxey told me that he'd been worried. "I mean, the guy, it's like he's a visitor in our home." But he was glad I'd challenged him.

"So, do you think they're going to change it?" he asked me.

"Not a chance," I answered. "Or at least not anytime soon."

"Yeah, I don't think so either," he said.

As the night drew to a close, against the sound of crashing pool balls and popping beer tops, I remember thinking: *Maybe I can let my guard down even more around Maxey.*

FOR OUR NEXT speaker, we had a soap opera writer come talk to us about the world of daytime drama. I peppered him with questions until late into the night. A gay children's book writer came to speak; when I drove him home, he marveled at the size of Maxey's arms. We also had a Navy SEAL turned property developer, a man who had seen combat and then traveled all over the world building hotels.

We all knew from Maxey's audit that his father had been in the military. Recently, Maxey had started confiding in us that he wanted to enlist. Partly for the physical challenge of it all, but also to serve and to be useful.

The night the former SEAL visited, Maxey was on fire— none of us had ever seen him so voluble.

WE HAD A few speaker slots to fill, so I offered to invite someone, and immediately drew a blank. Then I thought of my family friend Bob Chapman, a playwright and Harvard English professor. Over the course of my childhood, he had become a friend and confidant, and when I reached drinking age, we would meet in New York or Boston for martinis and burgers. Chapman had stories of working in naval intelligence in Morocco and Paris during World War II that I thought would interest everyone. I decided that I would do a quick overnight trip to Cambridge for a dinner with Chapman; that way I could invite him in person and tell him about the group. He was not much for phone calls.

At the time I had two very odd college jobs: one was breathing in cotton dust for a few hours a week, which paid handsomely; this was for a study funded by the cotton industry, so I had been assured they wanted to prove that breathing cotton was harmless, but I didn't really care if it wasn't. The second was a brief acting gig that involved insulting law school students in role-playing sessions so they could get experience dealing with incalcitrant youth. I managed to squeeze in a cotton-breathing session before the trip.

Chapman and I had a few martinis at his apartment, which was furnished with Berber rugs and rows of books that stretched floor to ceiling, and then got a cab to a favorite restaurant. We had a few more there. I remember that at one point Chapman declared that the meal had been absolutely delicious and asked for the check. The server gently reminded us that we had yet to order. Late in the evening, we decided to jettison military intelligence during World War II as the topic for Chapman's talk and settled on a new subject we both agreed would be much more interesting, but by the time I woke up I couldn't remember what it was. That morning I had to rush back to Yale first thing to be on time to abuse some wannabe lawyers. Chapman's door was closed, so I didn't disturb him before I left.

THE DAY CHAPMAN was due to speak at the hall, I got a nervous phone call.

"I've been thinking about it, Will, and I can't imagine anyone wants to hear me talk about this topic. I've prepared something but it all strikes me as very odd. If I were you, I would cancel my visit and take everyone to the movies instead."

"I'm sure they'll love it," I reassured Chapman. "But can you remind me what it is? I've completely forgotten."

" 'Pornography and Laughter,' " Chapman said glumly. "I've actually gone and prepared a scholarly talk on pornography and laughter. I think we both thought it was a good idea at the time. I'm going to stop drinking. I mean it." Chapman periodically swore off booze, a resolution that lasted anywhere from a few hours to a few days, but never longer.

I'd promised the group a speaker. Chapman had prepared something. I suspected the evening would be a disaster. But I decided that if everyone had enough to drink maybe it would seem as amusing as it had seemed to us when we thought it up. I reassured Chapman, hung up the phone, and raced over to the hall to make sure the keg was full and there was a spare on hand.

When I got there, Maxey was ranting about his day. The class he'd just attended had been an absolute joke, and he'd spent the entire time doodling pictures of the professor. He was definitely ready to get out of the academic world, he said. He had gone to college for the people and he would miss his friends. But the lectures? No.

That evening, Chapman arrived with a slide carousel. There was much discussion over how and where to set it up. My anxiety grew by leaps and bounds, but there was nothing for it but to plunge ahead. We sat down on the sofas. Chapman was in a chair next to the carousel. We turned the lights off. He cleared his throat and began. The first slide that came up was a Victorian postcard. A thoroughly ridiculous tableau vivant of portly gents and ladies, scantily clad, reenacting an ancient Greek frieze. Everyone burst out laughing.

That was the introduction—this image, so erotic more than a hundred years ago, was now thoroughly ridiculous. But was it also, perhaps, funny at the time?

What followed was an exploration of Victorian mores— with reference to the earliest days of photography and litera- ture. Chapman cited writings of the time but also stretched back to the poems of the Earl of Rochester, who had been active (to say the least) in the court of King Charles II.

As soon as I'd heard people laugh, I'd realized everything would be alright. Several slides in, I'd known it was far more than fine: everyone seemed to be enjoying Chapman's talk, so I was able to do the same. But it was during the question-and-answer period that it had become completely clear that the evening was a success—people were asking questions not just of Chapman but of one another, drawing on books, movies, and scholarly papers read in various Yale classes. When the formal part of the evening was over, almost everyone lingered. Only then did I realize how much it mattered to me that they all liked Chapman, and how happy it made me that they did.

Chapman stayed late into the night drinking and talking with the group. At one point I saw that he and Maxey were deep in conversation. I went over to join them. Naval intelligence? No, they were talking about Restoration poetry. Maxey was as engaged as he had been when the Navy SEAL had come to speak with us.

The next day, Maxey told me that he thought maybe he'd made a mistake earlier. Maybe he'd made a mistake over the last four years. Maybe he should have paid more attention to academics.

FOUNDERING

New Haven in February is a place no one wants to be. The beautiful fall campus becomes a series of wind tunnels that can blow books right out of your hands and pierce multiple layers of down. Beneath your feet lies either the treachery of black ice or deep puddles of cold slush that penetrate even the highest, most generously waxed boots. Perhaps the climate contributed to the fact that we were all getting a bit glum as graduation approached. Many of us knew what we were going to do with our lives. Most of us didn't.

Maxey told us that he was going to retake the navy test after graduation. I didn't know he'd failed it. It was an aptitude test he'd taken spring of junior year—and was far more math and science than he'd anticipated. Turned out the navy wasn't particularly interested in most of what he'd spent his time studying. That made two of them. A lot was riding on it. If he wasn't able to pass the test, there was no way he could become a Navy SEAL. And if he couldn't do that, he didn't know what he would do.

"Well, that's life," he said to me philosophically one particularly cold day as we were lounging in the hall. "If you are going to ride the crests, you have to ride the valleys. So much for laid-back, easygoing Maxey." He then confided that he'd sucked at practice the day before. "Fucking Kenny knows all my moves and I lost my shit and got frustrated and that put me in a really bad mood." I didn't know who Kenny was, but I nodded sympathetically. And then there was Kumari: more drama.

The next week Maxey had a bit of his psych back. The Yale team had won their match by a point—the score was 19–18—and that put them one win away from the Ivy title. All they needed to do was beat Cornell and they would come out as Ivy League champions. He said he was also determined to ace the navy test when he took it again.

"It still eats at me that I failed that fucking test," Maxey announced to a group of us. "And I hope I don't fail it again. I guess I just have to count on a little luck. I have to keep telling myself that I'm young so if I fall on my face a few times, it's not the end of the world. I've always searched for confidence from achievements, women, sports, or looks. I have to start looking for confidence from within. Where it really counts. And I have to work harder and get more serious."

Maxey delivered this as a little speech. It sounded rehearsed, as if he was trying to convince himself that he'd find his way, no matter what. We were sort of listening to him and sort of watching television. Singer was there and for once didn't make fun of him. Brooke, our president, was there, too, and smiled sympathetically. I nodded in agreement.

As it happened, I was counting on a little luck myself; I still had no idea what I was doing after graduation. Morris, the wiry runner, had a job at the *Miami Herald*. Julia, track champion, was off to medical school. Huei-Zu was going to become a curator; she'd been offered a paid internship at a museum in New York. David Kelly had been recruited by a New York bank. Others had applied for graduate programs in science or the humanities. But I hadn't applied to any graduate schools. I hadn't taken any tests.

I wanted to be a playwright. I figured I would work as a temporary secretary while writing plays. In New York? Probably. Or maybe I would head back to the West Coast. But I had applied for some random things and would continue to do so, just in case a great opportunity presented itself. One possibility that had caught my eye was a teaching fellowship in Hong Kong offered by the Yale-China Association, a rich foundation affiliated with the university but not part of it. I had applied for that. I was taking a course in modern Southeast Asian history and had begun to think that maybe, just maybe, my future lay in East or Southeast Asia.

Huei-Zu, who had spent time in Hong Kong, was skeptical; she didn't think I would like Hong Kong at all.

YALE-CHINA HAS ITS own handsome building near the heart of the campus. This was where my interview took place. The materials said that Yale-China had been founded in 1901 as a missionary society, that Chairman Mao—at the time Mao Zedong—had worked for Yale-China from 1919 to 1920, and that the foundation's role had grown after relations with China were reestablished by President Nixon. The centerpiece of the organization was the Yale-China Teaching Fellowships, which sent recent Yale grads to Changsha, Wuhan, and Hong Kong and paid a handsome stipend.

You could request a location. Wuhan was known as one of the three ovens of China, so that was out. Conditions at the school in Changsha looked rough, so that wasn't appealing either. But Hong Kong seemed fascinating. The more I'd researched the city, the more I'd realized that I really did want to go there. To apply, you had to write an essay explaining why you wanted to live and teach in Hong Kong. I went from "I don't" to believing it was my destiny. I could go to Hong Kong and be a playwright. After sending in my application, I wanted it as badly as Maxey wanted to be a Navy SEAL.

At my interview, I found myself in an elegant parlor, standing before the two people who would decide my fate. They both had copies of my application, résumé, and transcript. I sat down in a chair opposite them. I'd prepared all sorts of things to say about teaching and Hong Kong. My hands were annoyingly sweaty. I tried to wipe them discreetly on my gray flannels.

The interview began with the kinds of questions I'd anticipated, so I started to relax. Then there was a long silence as they studied the paperwork in front of them.

"I'm very sorry, Mr. Schwalbe," said one of them. "But I have to ask about something on your résumé. We see you've been working with AIDS victims. Don't you think it would be irresponsible of us to send you to Hong Kong or China?"

I remember feeling startled and confused: they seemed to be implying that I would bring AIDS to China (where no cases had yet been reported) and that I would spread the disease there and it would be the fault of Yale-China. I didn't answer the question—but instead changed the subject. Soon the interview was over. They pointed to the door.

I nodded, thanked them cordially for their time, and found myself seconds later outside the building, in the cold, as one of those fierce New Haven winds threatened to whip my copy of my résumé right out of my hands.

It was only then that I let myself realize what had just happened: I wouldn't be seriously considered because I had volunteered for AIDS organizations, and there wasn't a thing I could do to change their minds. I hadn't counted on getting the fellowship; it was highly competitive. But it had been something to hope for. I was back to square one, with no clue as to what I was going to do with my life. And now I had something else as well: a feeling of deep misgiving about the way I had been trying to live in the midst of the plague. Maybe they weren't wrong; after all, we really didn't know how AIDS was spread and I was pretty sure I must have it. Maybe I had been spreading it already. For a year I'd been practicing what people were calling safer sex, but no one could agree on what was truly safe, other than abstinence, and maybe not even that. On the hotline I would tell caller after caller that there was no evidence AIDS was spread by sweat, or spit, or tears, and that was true; but there was also no proof, other than common sense, that it couldn't be. I went into the building excited to go on a big adventure. I came out diseased.

Minutes after that door closed behind me, I became enraged and thought about going right back inside to give them a piece of my mind. But I didn't: I thought I might burst into tears. And I worried that once I started sobbing, I wouldn't be able to stop.

WE GATHERED AT the hall soon after Maxey's wrestling match at Cornell.

"We choked," Maxey told us. "Lost the Ivy League title. They were a better team, but we could have won if we'd sucked it up. I won both my matches, but I did it with no class. Still, none of it matters. We got demolished."

Maxey was dispirited. I was, too. A few of us filled a pitcher from the keg and settled down to talk. Pizza was ordered: not the good New Haven pizza, just Domino's. We needed cheese, bread, and grease, and it had all three. There were long silences. Someone brought up movies. Maxey said that he had just watched *The Deer Hunter*—the long and brutal Michael Cimino film about the toll that our involvement in Vietnam took on the Americans who fought there and on the country. I asked Maxey about the Navy SEALs—why he wanted to enlist, and what his chances were now.

"Flunking that goddamn test really hurt me," he said. "I really believe the navy could be the right move for me. But even if I pass my second try at the test, my chances look like shit. I had a shitty conversation with a navy recruiter who didn't seem to know anything about the SEALs, and that made things even worse. I don't know if I want to go on with this process."

Someone asked me how things were going with my Yale-China application.

I said nothing. I wasn't sure how everyone would react to the story of my interview gone awry. I feared that some of them might see some logic to the rejection, just as I myself had.

OUR NEXT SPEAKER was Jack Downey, a fellow Yalie more than twice our age who had joined the CIA during the Korean War in 1951, right out of college, and been shot down over China a year later on his first mission. He had spent twenty years in Chinese prisons, the first two in solitary confinement.

As soon as Downey was finished speaking, Maxey went over to talk with him. We all wanted to ask him more questions but instead let Maxey meet with him alone. After he left, Maxey told us that he'd learned Downey had been a wrestler and that the older man had been following Maxey's wrestling career. "Too bad I had to tell him about the end of it," Maxey said, referring not just to losing the Ivy title but to an even more recent defeat. The season was now officially over, save one match. His wrestling career wasn't ending in triumph; it was fizzling out. There was just that one last chance to go out on a high note.

Then Maxey smiled. "Well, as much as my wrestling season sucked, it sure doesn't compare to spending twenty years in a prison in China, huh? And can you believe he's been back to China to visit?" Maxey paused. "Maybe I should stop whining like a little bitch about the navy, my wrestling career, and the fact that I don't know what to do next year."

Something about Maxey's public soul-searching, and the way that he was able to put his recent failures in perspective thanks to Jack Downey, inspired me to share a story of my own. So I told the group about my Yale-China interview. Renata was particularly outraged on my behalf. Singer thought I should sue.

But it was Huei-Zu who had the best suggestion. "Why don't you just go to Hong Kong on your own?" she asked. "It's not expensive to live there. You can work over the summer and save up enough for a ticket. Find a job when you get there. I still don't think you'll like it. But what do you have to lose? Why do you need their fellowship anyway?"

"Yeah," agreed Maxey. "Fuck them. Just go."

Everyone was emphatically on my side, and no one more so than Maxey. They were all as angry as I was at the way I had been treated—actually, more so. In that moment, I realized I'd taken for granted that no one in the group had ever wiped their hands after I shook theirs; nor had anyone suggested segregating my cutlery, glasses, and plates, even after I'd told them that some of the people I'd visited were covered in lesions or coughing their lungs out. The media was fueling hysteria with headlines like GAY PLAGUE SPREADING TO

GENERAL POPULATION, and with opinion pieces applauding restaurant patrons who refused to be served by any waiter who seemed gay—but nobody in our group treated me differently from anyone else.

For the first time since I agreed to join, I felt I finally could be totally myself. And that I had a protector in Maxey. Maybe he would indeed beat the shit out of anyone who gave me grief.

HOMOS

As March began, the weather stayed hideously cold and it felt less like a new month and more like February had jealously stolen some of its days. It seemed like spring would never come. After the team wrestling disappointments, there had been the one more contest that Maxey had hoped would allow him to end his wrestling career with a win: the Eastern Championships. Maxey screwed that up. I didn't know whether he had simply not won—or whether he'd done really badly and humiliated himself. He told everyone in the hall that he didn't want to talk about it.

Maxey was now an ex-athlete who wasn't sure what he was going to do with his life and who cared very little about his classes. He had no plan. Still, he had ten more weeks of college, two wheels of his own—and no longer had to worry about making weight. So he was going to ride his motorcycle, drink, do mushrooms, and goof off. He still needed to write his Cuban Missile Crisis senior thesis, which he had yet to begin, and try to make the Great Man proud of the work. Other than that, he announced, he was planning to enjoy his freedom.

No one reminded him of the vow to be more serious that he'd made just weeks before.

I, too, was spending more time drinking, though only half the time with Yalies. The rest of the time I drank in New Haven's local gay bar, Partners. Unlike Maxey, though, I wasn't done with school. I still spent a few hours at the library most nights before my friends convinced me to join them in search of pizza and beer. Often, I would wake up in a cold sweat in the middle of the night, victim of the classic student nightmare— the one where you show up for an exam only to realize that it's for a course you've neglected to attend all term. As for that cold sweat: Were my glands swollen? Was I wheezing? Did I have AIDS?

SUNDAY, MARCH 5, WAS a particularly dismal day that began below freezing and stayed that way. The sun was occasionally visible through the clouds but could do nothing to warm the pavements, the metal bannisters, and frosty air. That evening, one by one, we gathered in the hall for dinner and wished that someone would make a fire in the great stone fireplace, but no one could be bothered.

A constant, calm presence was the David from Texas—we were from the David generation, born at a time when it was the most popular boy's name in the country. This David was just an inch or so taller than Tom, the football player, but so thin he looked far taller. He was soft-spoken and knew it, so he would nod his head down toward you when he wanted to say something, although maybe this gesture was just to make up for the difference in altitude.

On this night, we all headed downstairs after dinner to the pool table and television. David Kelly turned the channel to MTV, and he and I sat transfixed, waiting for our favorite videos to come. At some point, Maxey hefted Molly over his shoulder and carried her around the room. Then Texas David and Maxey played some pool. I noticed Maxey was becoming increasingly drunk. He kept interrupting the game to chase Brooke, our group's president, around the table—and she kept interrupting the game to chase him around.

I was enjoying being with everyone. I had long since warmed up and was pounding back ice-cold beers, which kept me even warmer.

"You fucking homo!" I heard Maxey shout. I snapped my head around. He was directing the insult at Texas David, who, towering over the table, had managed a legendary pool shot. I paused. Old habits die hard. Maxey can't have meant anything by it. I decided to ignore the remark and turned my attention back to the television. Then, minutes later, "Oh my god, you are such a fucking homo!" This time I wasn't even sure whom Maxey was talking to. I caught his eye. He looked sheepish, as though he knew he'd done something wrong, but he didn't apologize. Someone—not me—told him to cut it out. I can't remember if he acknowledged it or not. I do remember that, minutes later, he let out a big whoop and called someone else a fucking homo.

We still had some business to take care of that evening—it was time to narrow down our choices for the juniors we would ask to join for the following year. Morris called us to order. He was one of the quieter and gentler people in the hall, unless a particular argument engaged him; then he would calmly win it through the sheer force of his logic. The group had some difficult decisions to make, but Morris, ever the journalist, was able to frame them in a way that suddenly made them seem relatively simple, and we found ourselves done earlier than anticipated.

At that point, someone decided we should all go out to a bar—there was the general sense that the freezing night air was a necessary tonic that would allow the night and drinking to continue. We left the hall together, but then I peeled off for the long, cold walk back to my dorm. I don't know if anyone noticed that I wasn't with them until I was gone. I was angry with Maxey and even angrier at myself—for not saying anything, and for letting down my guard.

I remembered the promise Maxey had made to me right after my audit. How he said that he would kick the shit out of anyone who gave me a hard time. I was wondering what would happen if I asked him to kick the shit out of himself.

Spring break was a few days away. Maxey had loudly announced that he was driving down to Washington, D.C., to play some rugby and then heading to Daytona Beach with a few wrestling buddies. They were going to go wild, he said. I was going to spend the break in New York, working on the Gay Men's Health Crisis hotline. I wouldn't need to see Maxey until I returned, and then, after graduation, I would never have to see him again.

AFTER THE BREAK

When we all returned for the sprint to graduation, it was finally spring. The trees were in bloom and kids were littered across every patch of grass—reading, chatting, being whacked in the head by errant Frisbees. I put off heading back to the hall, but when I did, the first person I saw there was Maxey. He gave me a bear hug and thumped me on the back. I asked him about his break. I didn't want to be hostile; it would be easier just to keep up a façade.

"It was okay," he said. "Daytona Beach was cool. A lot of partying, but the kid who beat me at the last wrestling meet was there and it kind of sucked to have to look at his stupid smirk. Everywhere I went, there was that kid with his dumb face. And I also kept thinking that I really need to finish my senior thesis. I've wasted way, way too much time."

The more Maxey talked, the more he seemed not quite like Maxey. He seemed distracted. Even a bit discouraged. I got a sense that the time he was worried about having wasted wasn't just the time he should have spent writing about Kennedy and Castro.

Maxey then asked me about my break and when I started to tell him about it, he listened in a way that almost no one else had when they'd asked me the same question. Whether despite his "homo" remarks or because of them, I decided that I wouldn't keep it light—and would describe my evenings on the hotline. I told him about a man who was sobbing on the phone because he needed to see a doctor but was worried that he'd be deported. I told him about the calls from men whose parents wouldn't talk to them. And about the man who couldn't find a funeral home to take away the body of his lover who was lying dead next to him in the bed that filled their studio apartment.

"I'm sorry," Maxey said.

Did he remember what he had said that March night around the pool table? I wondered.

I decided Maxey just meant that he was sorry about the suffering of the people who had shared their stories with me on the phone, people hoping I had some real help to offer, which I almost never did. That he was sorry I'd spent my break on those calls. I decided it was the kind of sorry you write in a condolence note: "I'm sorry about your loss" just means that you're sad that someone you know is hurting. It doesn't mean you did anything wrong.

Yet I also decided to take it as an apology. Not for what was said so carelessly around the pool table before the break, not just for that. As an apology for everything. For the fact that gay people were dying and straight people didn't care; for the fact that our president Ronald Reagan had never even said the word AIDS; for the fact that kids in cars thought it was fun to throw beer bottles at my head; for the fact that Yale didn't have a nondiscrimination policy that included my people; for the fact that a kid at my boarding school told me that pink was the wrong color; and for the fact that I went in search of an angel with a rusty knife because maybe I wanted to die, maybe I was already dying, maybe I thought I deserved to die.

And in that moment, I realized I couldn't stay mad at Maxey. Because I didn't want to be mad at him. I wanted him not to hate me—and I didn't think he did. I wanted him to like me—and I was pretty sure he did.

Maxey asked me to continue. To tell him more.

I told more stories from the calls I'd taken, including some funny ones, which made him laugh. Like the young woman who called panicked about a mosquito bite she'd received on Fire Island and how she kept referring to gay mosquitoes.

After I finished and we had moved on to other topics, almost as though he had read my mind, Maxey said, "You know, I'm realizing a lot these days. And one of the big things is that I've got to stop saying so much stupid shit."

UP ON THE ROOF

The last pleasant afternoon before graduation found most of us on the roof of the hall. While we weren't really supposed to be up there, on any even remotely nice days we were. The roof stretched the whole length and width of the building and was covered with gravel. When it was hot, you would crisp on it; but in the spring whenever there was a cooling breeze, we would spend hours there, looking out over low-lying New Haven: the campus behind us, the brownstones around us, factories in the distance.

There was a ladder that went straight up to a hatch, and you then needed to make something of a leap from the top of the ladder to the surface of the roof. You also had to make sure that the hatch didn't slam back down on your fingers. But with practice we all came to manage this with ease, even when toting six-packs of beer.

We'd been through a few six-packs that day, and now the sun was setting. Maxey had just gone down the ladder to fetch another but emerged instead with an entire case balanced on his arm. Our last case.

The beer was now on our dime, so it was no longer Rolling Rock but PBR: Pabst Blue Ribbon. "God, this stuff is awful," I said as I grabbed another.

Maxey motioned me over to the edge. Scary, but I followed. We sat in silence for a while.

"I'm going to keep trying for the SEALs," Maxey said. He'd retaken the aptitude test and was pretty sure he'd passed this time. That, however, was just the first hurdle.

"And if that doesn't work out?" I asked.

"I don't have a frickin' clue." Maxey grabbed another beer himself. "You?"

"I'm going to go to Hong Kong. I mean, as you all said, fuck them. I don't need their stupid teaching fellowship. I'll stay at home this summer, work as a temporary secretary, save up enough for a one-way ticket, and just go."

"Do you know anyone there?"

"I met a friend of a friend at a party in New York. He just moved to Hong Kong. I think he'll let me stay with him for a few days until I find a job. Huei-Zu still thinks I'm nuts and tells me I'll hate it there. But if I don't go, it's like they win. So that's what I'm going to do. Unless I can't save enough money. Or unless I chicken out."

"And what then?" Maxey asked.

"I don't have a frickin' clue," I said in my best Maxey accent.

We sat for a while, drinking beer after beer. Then I moved around the roof talking with the others. Singer joined Maxey for a while. They had gone from giving each other endless grief to one of the strongest friendships in the hall.

The sun disappeared entirely. I found myself back on the ledge with Maxey.

"What if this is it?" Maxey asked. "What if it's all downhill from here? What if we just fuck up from now until we die?" Maxey was smiling, but he sounded more serious than I'd heard him since his audit. "You know, when I began wrestling, I had these incredible opportunities. I surprised myself when I started wrestling varsity even though I was only in eighth grade. That was crazy. It was beyond amazing to be on a great team as this little kid with an awesome coach and these high school men teaching me and encouraging me. I was even more shocked—and they all were, too—when I kept winning. I mean I was always the first guy out on the mat because I was ninety-eight pounds. I had to set the tone. And when I won, which I always did, I got this awesome reaction—like I was bear-hugged by all these heroes of mine, they were so psyched that I'd gotten us off to such a great start with a win. But they also hugged me when I lost. I mean, these were the big brothers I'd always wanted and never had."

Maxey grabbed another beer. I think it was his fourth, at least.

"I worked so hard at being strong and keeping my weight down and learning. There was a kid named Andy Nipon who was my mentor, and he taught me everything. If I let my head drop, he smashed it into the mat. If I reached back in practice, he threw me on my back and pinned me. As I learned and improved, he was proud of me—he didn't say it, but I knew he was—and that gave me confidence. I only lost three matches that whole eighth-grade year and pinned at least a dozen opponents. I was the surprise new kid on the block—not even in high school yet—thirteen years old. Andy went on to win the Nationals his senior year. I was so proud of him, and so proud that he was proud of me. I knew that nothing would stop him. He was going to Penn, and I knew he would beat every top wrestler from Texas to Maine to Virginia.

"But I also was getting more and more anxious, even while I was continuing to overachieve. In my freshman year, wrestling at a hundred and twelve pounds, I made it to Nationals—all the way to the semifinals. It was a big surprise getting that far when I was just fourteen. Everyone was talking about me being the next Andy Nipon—or even better. I had twice the points he had at the same age and now it was my turn to be a mentor and lead the dynasty. For the next three years I never lost a match during the regular season—three years of winning. But there was one big problem every year. When I got to the tournaments that followed, I would choke. I shined all year long but after freshman year screwed up at every postseason championship tournament.

"Still, by the time I was a senior I was on fire. I didn't just win; I crushed the competition at every regular meet. And I was captain of the team, just as I had been junior year. We were coming off another sensational season, again winning our league. The coach was loving it. Everyone expected me to go on to win the Nationals just like Andy Nipon had when he was a senior.

"There was no way I was going to let the pressure and spotlight get to me this time. I knew I could win the thing. I cruised my way to the semifinals of the state independent schools championship. No problem. So, there I was—matched against a kid from a rival Pennsylvania school. And the very first thing he did was pick me up and pile-drive me into the mat. I'm lying there and I can hear everyone in the stadium gasp—they were watching the great Chris Maxey get his butt kicked. I took an injury time-out and looked over at this guy. He was tough and I was going to have to reach really deep down to beat him."

"So, you did, right?" I asked.

"No. I was in shock. After my injury time-out, I looked over at him again and realized that he was even more confident and even more hungry to kick my ass—me, Mr. All-Year-Undefeated. I could have dug down deep and gone back out there, but I didn't. I went down with an injury. I threw the match, making the excuse that my bell was rung. The next weekend at the Nationals, I lost to the same kid—but at least that time I went the distance. I ended my high school career with a third-place finish. Not a first. I was no Andy Nipon after all. And I did the same thing here. But worse. Wasn't elected captain. Didn't make it through the Easterns to the Nationals."

"Yeah, but you were injured! You ripped up your shoulder, and you were still undefeated during the regular season and ranked second in the Easterns at a hundred and fifty pounds, right?"

"In the end, what really matters is that I didn't win. I choked. In my final match, I was wrestling this army guy. I was just one win away from to a ticket to the Nationals. I had trounced this same guy in the qualifiers earlier in the tournament, but then my spirit was gone and my head got in the way. I got out front in the match but this army guy never gave up. He just kept coming at me—and then with seconds left, he took me down for the win. So, that was it. The end of my wrestling. Cool Maxey, fun-loving, great wrestler Maxey, became history in one swift takedown."

I was touched by how Maxey was confiding in me. I thought back to when Maxey had felt he had to apologize for being emotional; clearly, he no longer felt that need. Had Maxey really lost his confidence? Or was this just a temporary crisis of faith? I didn't know, and didn't think Maxey did either, so I said nothing. We just sat there, on the roof, staring out at the dim lights of New Haven. After a while, Maxey told me that he was really glad we were friends. I said the same and told him I was sure he was going to be a Navy SEAL.

"If I am, and they send me to Hong Kong, and you're there, we'll have some beers and look back to this night," Maxey replied. "And we'll laugh about when we sat on the roof and didn't know what would become of us."

THE NEXT MORNING, I woke up with a dreadful hangover. In the days that followed, parents arrived, and soon it was graduation—a sodden mess as it rained torrentially all weekend long and the ceremony was held outside and unsheltered as always. Some of us brought our parents to the hall. I'm sure I did, but I have no recollection of that; all I remember is my drenched clothes. Then college was over. The fourteen of us had eaten dinner together twice a week for a year and shared our lives and thoughts. On our final day in the hall, we promised to keep in close touch and spend all sorts of times together. I was certain we all would.

Maxey and I would talk on the phone a handful of times and even exchange a few letters. But it would be a decade before we saw each other again.

CHAPTER TWO

Twenties and Thirties

BACK ON THE ROOF

When Maxey and I were in our mid-twenties, a show was launched on television called *Thirtysomething*. When it first aired, thirtysomething seemed unimaginably old: it might as well have been called *Ninetysomething*. Here was a program about people getting married and divorced, having children, quitting jobs, starting companies, and paying mortgages. These were adults. I didn't feel that I would ever be among them. I simply couldn't imagine their problems belonging, ever, to anyone I knew. At our tenth reunion, in 1994, we were ourselves thirty-something, even if just. Yet those of us who assembled at the hall that spring seemed to me to be far younger than the characters featured on the by-then-beloved program. Maybe that was because the show was written by people older than us, or maybe I still saw myself and my classmates as the recent college graduates we'd been when we were last all together. Or maybe we were just plain immature.

I'd arrived before the ten or so others who were coming

to our planned secret-society get-together at the hall and was hanging out on one of the sofas with a book that everyone was then reading, *Like Water for Chocolate* by Laura Esquivel. As always, I carried a book both to give myself a way to pass the time and as a kind of security blanket. This particular novel told the story of a woman who suffers a series of cruel disappointments; it seemed an apt thing to have with me in case the reunion didn't live up to my hopes for it.

I was excited to see everyone again but anxious. My concentration was soon interrupted by happy voices. We fell into easy conversations, as though we'd never left. There was a lot of catching up to do. I'd kept in very close touch with a few people from the crew who lived in New York or passed through and had been in sporadic contact—calls and letters, but no visits—with others, including Maxey. With some, there'd been no contact at all.

Maxey had said he was going to be there but had yet to arrive.

Then the buzzer rang annoyingly—again and again and again—and I broke off from a conversation and went to open the huge wooden door. There was Maxey, grinning goofily and hefting three cases of beer.

He put down the cases and gave me a bear hug.

"Schwalbs! It's good to see you. Been a long time, man. Hey, this is Pam."

That's when I met the woman who had married Maxey. She'd been inspecting the hall from the street and now joined him on the doorstep. They'd met in San Diego after Maxey finished his Basic Underwater Demolition SEAL training (BUD/S) in 1986 and had married in Subic Bay, Philippines, months later.

Pam's eyes were almost as intense as Maxey's, but amber

brown. She was definitely the California surfer Maxey had described to me—sun-bleached auburn hair, easy smile—and yet she had a vaguely military posture. She didn't hunch over the way Maxey did but instead carried herself four-square, shoulders back. She pushed Maxey to the side to say hello to me, and when I reached out to shake her hand, she, too, gave me a big hug.

The beers were here. The reunion proper could begin. Maxey picked one case of beer up off the ground; Pam grabbed one: I struggled with the third.

"To the roof!" shouted Maxey.

"I don't know," I said, "I'm pretty comfortable down here." Soon, I was climbing the steep ladder that led to the roof.

Maxey had monkeyed his way up already, balancing a case on his shoulder, whereas I was trying not to drop the bottle of beer I'd already started to drink. When I got near the top, I realized I was stuck. You needed both hands free to heft yourself up over the edge. I considered trying to cradle the beer in my armpit but instantly realized that wouldn't work. So I just hung there.

"Do you need help?" Maxey asked me, peering down through the hatch.

"Nope," I said.

Pam was coming up behind me, with a six-pack. "Give me your beer," she said. I wasn't sure how she would be able to manage mine without risking a fall and serious injury, but then I saw: she'd looped her arms around a rung so she could balance the six-pack on one hand and hold my bottle in the other. Simple engineering solution. I scampered up onto the roof, painfully scraping my knee as I did so, and then reached down to retrieve my beer from Pam. She followed effortlessly, and others from the group joined us. No one else needed help.

I hadn't remembered it being such an ordeal to make it up. But I also had been thirty pounds lighter the last time I'd tried.

Someone asked Maxey how he'd met Pam.

"You mean, how on earth did someone like Pam agree to marry a dickhead like me," Maxey replied. "I met Pam at the place you always want to say you met your soul mate: a dive bar in Mission Beach, California—the kind where you go upstairs and there's so much beer spilled that your shoes stick to the floor. It was right after BUD/S. I was a SEAL team officer living in San Diego and was pretty impressed with myself."

"Very true," Pam added, smiling, but it was clear that she was going to let Maxey tell the story. I think she wanted to see what version he would share with all of us.

"Our meeting was kind of funny because we literally bumped into each other. The first thing she said to me was, 'What happened to your face?' Which is a good pickup line. Then I remembered that I had this big bruise on my cheek—jumping out of a plane the week before, I'd gotten too close to the guy in front of me and been kicked in the face. It looked grim. I said, 'Well, I was parachuting as part of some special forces training exercises.' I tried to play the macho thing. She looked at me and said, 'Oh, you're in the service?' I said, 'Yeah, I'm in the navy. Have you ever heard of the SEALs?' She said she'd never heard of them—and then added, 'But I've got to tell you that if you're in the service, I want nothing to do with you.' Then she turned her back and walked away."

Maxey told us that he followed her. He learned that it was Pam's sister's birthday, and that that was the only reason she'd come out—she'd wanted to take it easy at home on her one night off from waitressing, but her sister had insisted.

Someone asked Pam: "Where was your sister when you met Maxey?"

"She was ready to go home, but after I met Chris, I decided to stay on," Pam said.

Maxey continued. "We hung out a bit more at the Pennant— that was the name of the bar—and then went across the street to another bar and had a drink there. Then we went out to find my car, which was right in front of the bar—except it wasn't, because it had been towed. And she said to me, 'You fucking idiot, you parked in a no-standing zone. Didn't you know they'd tow you?'"

Maxey used a pay phone to find out where the car had been towed and then asked Pam if she'd mind driving him to his car.

"Is this thing about your car being towed and your needing a ride some kind of pickup line?" Pam asked. "Because it's really bad if you are making this up."

At the impounding lot, Maxey spotted his car right away: "But it's behind a metal gate next to a trailer with a light on, and inside the trailer I see a guy talking on the phone. I decided to do my SEAL team thing; I said to Pam, 'I think I can get my car out of there without having to pay.' I thought this would impress her, but she just looked at me like I was insane—I think she wanted to see me get arrested. The gate to the pen wasn't locked, so that was easy, but I then realized that the tow truck was between my car and the gate, blocking the only way out. I thought maybe I could push the tow truck out of the way, and had actually put my shoulder to it, but it must have had its parking brake on. By that time, I'm making so much noise that the guy comes out of the trailer and says, 'What the fuck?' "

Fortunately, Maxey had been able to talk him down.

"And that would have been it," Maxey continued, "with me paying the fine and driving back to my place, and Pam driving back to hers, and the two of us probably never seeing each other again! But before she left, she wrote her phone number on a scrap of paper and left it on the windshield of my car."

After he got Pam's number, Maxey tried to play it cool, but he lasted only two nights before he broke down and gave her a call. "I said, 'Let's go out—let's have dinner.' " She said, "Well, I'm really busy this week.' So, I said, 'All right, I'll call you on Saturday and see what's up.' It was then that she said, 'Well, I kind of have a boyfriend.'

"I thought she was really cool, but that was that. And then I had to go away on an extended cross-training exercise with crazy Canadian special forces. I guess when I was gone, she lost interest in her boyfriend, and there was a message when I got back saying I could ask her out."

"I think I would have broken up with that boyfriend anyways," Pam added.

"Yeah. It was not the Maxey charm. Not *just* the Maxey charm," he added. Their first real date was on Valentine's Day, 1986, when he invited her to a military banquet, a formal event where everyone would be in Dinner Dress Blues. Maxey had never gone before because he'd never had anyone to bring. This time, an admiral would be giving a keynote speech.

Maxey was thrilled that Pam agreed to come but also a little bit worried. "I knew my commanding officer would be there—the whole command, in fact. I told her everyone would be dressed up, hoping she would understand, but I thought she might wear cutoffs or a prom dress. But when I went to pick her up at her apartment, she looked amazing, beautifully dressed. When we got to the banquet, my buddies were all like, 'Who's that?' What they really meant was, 'Maxey, you loser, how did you get a girl like that to agree to come to dinner with you?' "

After the dinner, Maxey's captain told him and the others that they were supposed to go up and introduce themselves to the keynote speaker. "We were near the front of the room, so Pam and I were among the first people to go up and greet him. I saluted and then shook his hand, and said, 'Admiral, thank you for your talk. My name's Ensign Maxey and this is my date, Pam Less.'

"The admiral looked at Pam and asked, 'Is your dad Tony Less?'

"Pam said he was indeed. There were about thirty guys with their dates standing behind us and we must have talked to the admiral for a full twenty minutes as he told us one story after another about Pam's father. He told Pam about meeting her father when her dad was commanding officer of a squadron, and how they caught some huge rattlesnake in Arizona, and then the admiral had all sorts of stories about when Pam was a little girl, before her father became commanding officer of the aircraft carrier USS *Ranger,* and then an admiral.

"And all the time," Maxey explained to us, "I was standing there thinking, 'What the hell?' I mean, I just thought Pam was some surfer girl I met in a dive bar. After we respectfully broke from the conversation, I pulled Pam aside and said to her, 'You didn't tell me your dad was an admiral,' and she said to me, 'Well, you didn't ask.' "

* * *

A FEW BEERS later, I had a question for Pam about one part of Maxey's story.

"I was just messing with him when I said I'd never heard of the SEALs," she admitted to us. "He was so full of himself. And the SEALs weren't as well known then as they are now—they were just these sailors who blew up things. So it was totally plausible that I wouldn't have known anything about them. Still, I really *didn't* want to date anyone in the service because I didn't want to marry anyone in the service. I grew up with a father who had to be away from home eighty percent of my childhood, and I wanted more for my kids. Then I married this guy anyways, Service and all."

"And how *are* your kids?" I asked, hoping Pam wouldn't notice that I couldn't remember their names.

"Really good," she replied. "Brittney just turned five. Brocq's going to be four in November. And now that we're at Lawrenceville, it's all so much easier." Lawrenceville is a prep school in New Jersey, where Maxey had settled into life as a housemaster, teacher, and wrestling coach. "It was insane when Brittney was a newborn and we were stationed abroad and all hell broke loose and we had an hour to evacuate. It also wasn't so easy when Chris was working for Ross Perot's company in Texas doing tech sales and trying to see if he could become a regular working stiff. He hated it—getting dressed up every day, sitting at a desk, going to meetings."

"I could never really see Maxey as a nine-to-five office guy."

"Yes, it wasn't for him." Pam added. "He was so stressed out in Texas that one day he got a massive attack of vertigo. He had to lie down in a closet in his office until everything stopped spinning. His mom was very scared because Chris was exactly the age his dad was when he died of a brain cyst. It was good we were in Houston because of all the hospitals. They did every test and couldn't find a thing." Then Pam said, "Chris won't admit that he was at all stressed by the office job. He still insists that it was just an ear infection."

AS THE EVENING was winding down, Maxey told me that he and Pam had started to take groups of students from the school on trips to the Caribbean so they could be immersed in the environment and have a completely different sort of academic experience. He'd even convinced the school to fund some scholarships for the trips.

I looked at Maxey and thought about the kid who couldn't sit still in the hall and who would drink himself to oblivion with his frat pals whenever he didn't need to make weight for a wrestling match. He'd gone from the Navy SEALs to corporate life to teaching high school. How surprising was that? Certainly, his students saw him as an adult. Married. Two kids. Maybe people did change. Maybe Maxey was thirtysomething after all.

What about me? I had a steady job in book publishing. I'd been with my boyfriend, David, for a decade now. (David hadn't been keen to come to my college reunion, and I couldn't blame him; he was home in New York.) For years we had been sharing a one-bedroom with a friend who slept on a futon in the living room, but now had our own apartment. Maybe I was thirtysomething, too.

I never thought I would make it this far. I would find out decades later that Maxey hadn't thought he would make it either.

When we were leaving the hall that night, I remembered that there was something major about Maxey's life that I didn't understand: why he'd left the SEALs. I knew he'd re-upped once, served for almost six years, fulfilled his commitment, and been honorably discharged. But wasn't it his life's dream to be a SEAL? Singer had once told me that something bad had happened and he didn't think Maxey wanted to talk about it. I decided it best to wait until Maxey brought up the subject. I didn't want to pry.

Certainly, a lot had been going on in the world when Maxey was deciding whether to continue in the military: the Berlin Wall came down; the *Exxon Valdez* spilled millions of gallons of oil and destroyed a good chunk of Alaska; and George H. W. Bush had invaded Panama and deposed General Manuel Noriega. I knew Maxey had been in Panama, so I had thought he might have been involved in that campaign but figured he probably hadn't. After all, that was on land, and he was a Navy SEAL.

Once back in my room that night I started to think of all that had happened to get us from graduation to thirtysomething and the decisions we'd both made right after we graduated. We were very different and we always would be. Still, we seemed to share a determination to take the long route home. And surprisingly, as we shared stories with each other, we were starting to find that our lives had more in common than we could have imagined.

THE SUMMER OF '84

After graduation, Maxey and a few friends had taken the great American road trip on their motorcycles while he was waiting to hear if the navy recruiters would recommend him for officer training school. Becoming a SEAL was a more grueling process than I had realized. Maxey had passed the aptitude test, but most candidates were still rejected, even after that phase. Plus, his math and science scores, while acceptable, weren't stellar. The final hurdle involved an interview in D.C.; if he cleared that, he would then be sent off to BUD/S to learn underwater demolition. It wasn't unusual for the entire acceptance process to take months, or even a year.

We'd spoken when he returned from the road trip. I told him I'd saved enough for a plane ticket to Hong Kong, but I continued to waffle. I knew only the one friend of a friend, whom I had met exactly once; he'd offered to put me up for a week but no longer than that as he had a full house. If I *did* decide to go, I'd be flying to a city where I had no job or even a lead on one, and with only seven days of lodging before I'd be on my own. Maxey didn't know what to tell me except to say that he was equally confused about his own plans.

"I need direction, too, Schwalbs," he confessed on that call. "I need to feel like I'm accomplishing something. This limbo is exactly what I wanted to avoid by turning to the navy. My sister Katie left for boarding school this morning. My other sister, Lizzie, and my brother are both at college. As for me, I just lie in bed until noon." Maxey said that he wanted to be a SEAL more than anything, but that the waiting was driving him crazy. "The house is empty all day. My thoughts are out of control." Then Maxey laughed to let me know that he wasn't falling completely apart.

"What do you do after you get out of bed?" I asked.

"I drive around town. The scenes of my triumphs!" Maxey laughed again. "All those memories of wrestling, lacrosse, and track meets. I was the guy who definitely seemed to have it all, and yet it looks like I screwed up what I had. I know I should be making use of this time and stop wallowing. I could be writing and reading. My dad told me that everyone has to wait in limbo for a while. I said to him, 'Yes, but you forget, Father; I am Chris, your impatient son.'"

I'd never heard Maxey sound like this. He seemed to sense it.

"I guess it's all right to melodramatize your situation as long as it helps make you feel better—right, Schwalbs? You know, all of this self-reflection is thanks to my sister Lizzie, who suggested to me a few years ago that I write my thoughts down every day as a way to help me understand what was going on in my life."

Maxey was keeping a journal? I was intrigued, but before I could ask him more about it, he brought the conversation to a close: "Mom is home. Gotta go. Oh, and let me know when you decide what you are going to do. You sound even more lost than I am."

While Maxey had been bombing around the country on the Bitch, I'd been in New York City, temping to save money for my ticket to Hong Kong and putting in several nights a week at the Gay Men's Health Crisis hotline, which was housed in a small room in a brownstone in Chelsea. On the nights when I worked there, I would buy a burrito, climb the stairs to that room, and steel myself for hours of calls. The horrifying truth was that we had no good information: we still didn't know how AIDS spread, we didn't know how to detect it, and we had no treatments or cures.

I was also a temporary "buddy" to a man named Victor, who was living with AIDS; his usual "buddy" was sick or away, I wasn't sure which. I would go to Victor's apartment, help him tidy it up, and pick up items from his shopping list. Afterwards, I would sit and chat, if that was what he wanted. Sometimes Victor wanted to talk for hours, and other days he didn't feel well enough to talk at all. A few times he exploded at me for something I did or said wrong.

The publishing company where I was temping offered me a full-time job at a salary of $11,500 to be the whipping boy for their most difficult bestselling author. They wanted me around full time just so he would always have a target for his rage. The publisher explained to me that it was a terrible job, but if I could handle it my career was assured.

My parents were certain I should take the publishing job and start on a career. I wasn't so sure. I'd begun to read everything I could about Hong Kong and, right after I talked to Maxey, I discovered *A Many-Splendored Thing,* a novel by Han Suyin. I already knew the theme song from the film adaptation, because my grandmother played it endlessly on an eight-track cassette in her car; that Henry Mancini ballad had been the soundtrack to my visits with her in Westport, Connecticut.

Han Suyin was a doctor and writer; she was born to a Chinese father and Flemish mother in China in 1917, and the novel is based on her romance in Hong Kong with a married Australian foreign correspondent who was killed while covering the Korean War. When I finished reading it, I was so moved I couldn't quite catch my breath.

AIDS was a war of sorts and people all around me were dying violently and suddenly. I thought of Victor, who longed to travel but couldn't make it to the end of his block most days. Maybe simply being *able* to go to Hong Kong came with an obligation to do exactly that. And I also must have known that to travel was to flee. New York—along with San Francisco—had the highest concentration of gay deaths in the world. Nobody knew how to cure AIDS, but maybe I could outrun it.

I did worry that I would be lonely in Hong Kong, but I recalled something a freshman-year boyfriend had said when he left everyone and everything he knew (including me) and moved to Japan. When I'd asked him if he was going to be lonely, he said that that was exactly why he was going: to be lonely.

HONG KONG

Two days after I finished reading Han Suyin's book and less than a week after I spoke to Maxey, I went ahead and bought the ticket. I got a nonrefundable one because it was cheapest, and because it would keep me from chickening out. A few days after that, I was on a plane heading to Hong Kong. I had a Sony Walkman and a tape of Elton John's *Greatest Hits* loaded in it, and I played the song "Daniel" as the plane took off. As I heard Elton sing about the "red taillights" and the "clouds in my eyes," I asked myself in the way that only a twenty-something can, "Where on earth are you going and what on earth have you done?"

I was "melodramatizing my situation," as Maxey would have put it, but at least I was on the move.

After a week at my acquaintance's apartment, I found my own in a part of Hong Kong called Wanchai, just a short trolley ride or blisteringly sweaty walk from the central business district. My place was only one hundred square feet and yet miraculously contained a kitchen, bathroom, living area, bed, dining space, and office. If you sat on the bed, a desk folded down from the wall—so that was the office. If you put two chairs on either side of the desk, it became the dining table. Scrunched between the bed and the door was a two-seater sofa that faced a television and the toilet.

The night before I moved in, I met a man named David in a gay bar. The bar was called the Dateline, and you had to descend two steep flights of stairs to reach it. The only sign on the street was a small one that simply had the name of the bar. There was also a placard that had three mysterious words: AFTERNOON TEA SERVED. It wasn't. The Dateline was, to my knowledge, one of only two gay bars in Hong Kong, both of them hiding in plain sight. At the time homosexuality was still outlawed in Hong Kong, punishable by life in prison. There was a special police squad whose sole purpose was to rout out gay people; months before I arrived, they were just about to arrest a young British police officer who, they said, shot himself to death before they had the chance. Curiously, he had four separate gunshot wounds.

David had just returned home to Hong Kong after six years in England studying fashion. He had worked in fish-and-chip shops, while in school, and then, following graduation, as a designer. He was nearly twenty-seven, and I had only recently turned twenty-two, which seemed a big age gap. Appropriately while at a bar called the Dateline, he was drinking an

Around the World, not the classic cocktail but their name for a lethal mixture of just about every alcohol on the shelf. He claimed that it tasted like Coca-Cola. I was drinking a Pabst Blue Ribbon, which, bizarrely, was sold as a premium beer in Hong Kong.

I'd noticed him right away—spiky black hair that took on a tinge of blue in the bar's dim light, a dramatic broad-checked shirt, jeans and high tops, and a mischievous smile—but he'd been with a group of friends and I'd been shy to approach. By the time I went over to say hello, they had all vanished. I wasn't sure I would ever find him again, but then suddenly he was back. His friend had lost his wallet so they had all returned to look for it. We'd approached each other immediately.

I'd been warned that the police periodically raided the Dateline, something I would experience later, but was told they usually just checked that everyone was carrying an ID card, which was mandatory. It was pure intimidation, but people gathered anyway.

David and I went home together that night, to my friend's place, and kept seeing each other after that. A future together would be a logistical nightmare, and yet it was too early to start even thinking about any of that.

The first work I found was teaching English conversation in the evenings; I was paid three dollars an hour plus a juice box. On a good night, the juice box was honey lemon, which I loved. Sometimes, though, it was a beverage billed as guava juice that looked and tasted more like Mountain Dew.

My job was to chat about whatever was on the students' minds and correct their English while I was at it. Margaret Thatcher had just announced that Hong Kong would be returned to China in 1997, which came as a surprise to many Hong Kongers, so the handover was sometimes a topic. A few of the students worried that this would be the end of Hong Kong and all their freedoms, but most believed that none of it would ever affect them and wanted to talk about other things.

I DIDN'T HAVE a phone in my apartment that could make international calls, so if I wanted to keep in touch with people back home it had to be through letters. I wrote my parents and a few friends. I did hear from someone in the secret society that Maxey had finally been granted an interview with a navy captain a few weeks after we last talked; that he'd been accepted into a BUD/S class with a start date of March 1985; and that he'd reported for duty at Officer Candidate School, which you need to complete first, on October 6, his twenty-third birthday.

Maxey would be one of just a few people from our entire Yale class of more than a thousand to enter the service in the months right after graduation. He would be the only person my age I knew who was joining the military. My father had served during World War II, as had most of his friends. Older brothers of a few people I knew had been drafted to serve in Vietnam. But from my immediate generation—not a soul. No one I knew other than Maxey had ever even contemplated it.

At that time, and for many years to come, gays and lesbians were barred from serving openly and were dishonorably discharged if their sexuality was discovered. Which was only one of myriad reasons—including my aversion to physical exercise and to being told what to do—that I never considered a career that had anything to do with the armed forces. But I was glad for Maxey—it was everything he wanted. I was also proud of him, because he was following his desire to be of service, to be useful.

I QUICKLY SETTLED into life in Hong Kong, and began to feel at ease. I hosted one episode of a children's television show (dressed in a bee suit) before they discovered I had no work permit. I wrote articles for magazines and scripts for documentaries. Under a pseudonym, I became a freelance television critic for an entertainment magazine put out by the *South China Morning Post*. I continued to teach English conversation and started to study Cantonese. David, meanwhile, was working as a fashion designer doing women's clothes for the global mass market and teaching design at the Hong Kong Polytechnic. We spent all our time together when he wasn't at his jobs. The acquaintance who had hosted me when I first arrived became one of our best friends. He shared an apartment (but not a romantic life) with the most profane person I've ever met: David and I had dinner at their house two or three nights a week. We also spent endless hours at the Dateline, drinking and gossiping with his (now our) friends.

All was going far better than I had dreamed.

That January, however, I got desperately ill: one night I counted seventeen trips to the toilet. For days I could do nothing but lie around, drink tea, and pray I would begin to feel better. I was reading a collection of short stories called *Tropical Gothic* by Nick Joaquin, one of the great writers from the Philippines, which was filled with baroque symbols of death and decay. David wanted me to see a doctor, but I refused. Maybe I hadn't been able to outrun AIDS after all.

As more days went by, I felt worse. I finally agreed to go to a doctor. I took the Star Ferry, the classic boat that romantically plies the gap between Hong Kong Island and the Kowloon Peninsula, to a medical office that David said was not entirely hostile to gay people. At the ferry terminal there was a machine where, for a Hong Kong penny, you could weigh yourself. I was down to 120 pounds—ten pounds less than I had ever weighed. Hong Kong's first AIDS case, only the second in East Asia, had recently been reported with screaming headlines in all the local media. A sailor in the merchant marine, away from Hong Kong for thirteen years, had been diagnosed soon after his return home.

Was my life going to end 8,000 miles from my home? Would I be the next object of terror and scorn in every news-paper and on every television station?

But as soon as the doctor finished examining me, he said he suspected I had garden-variety gastroenteritis and that I just needed to be more careful about what I ate. After a few antibi-otics and a couple of days, he told me, I would be right as rain.

By the next day I was.

David and I talked that evening, for the first time, about whether one of us might have AIDS and might have given it to the other in the five months that we'd been together. We tried to be careful, but there was still no agreement on how it was actually spread. It was like a hideous game in which you had to guess the rules, and if you guessed wrong, you died. An anti-body test for AIDS had just been released, but it wasn't clear whether it was reliable and there was nothing anybody could do to save you if you tested positive. It also wasn't available in Hong Kong.

After our discussion over dinner, we went to a local pub

called the Bull and Bear; a friend of David's from London was in town and wanted to meet there. The pub was usually frequented by young finance types flexing their wallets, but tonight the U.S. naval fleet had several destroyers moored in Hong Kong harbor, and sailors flooded the pub. They sat in groups around the small tables, legs open, showing off their crotches to each other and to the waitresses. In the bathroom, drunk, they shoved and joked around with one another, oblivious to anyone else trying to get in and out. David's friend never showed so we had one beer each, settled up, and headed for the door. One our way out of the bar, a chalk-faced blond surrounded by five other sailors at a booth put on a "gay" voice, lisp and all, and shouted at us, "So long, fellas, thee you later." The sailors around him laughed derisively.

"Oh, thank you. Welcome to Hong Kong," David said to the group, in a friendly voice.

"You know they were making fun of us," I said to David once we were outside the pub.

"Oh, well, I am what I am. Right?"

As we walked home, all I could think about was that these sailors belonged to the tribe that Maxey had chosen to join. Would he change them? Or would they change him back to the way he had been when we first met—or worse?

The following month, the first person diagnosed with AIDS in Hong Kong died. The newscaster on the English-language channel kept calling it Anti-Immune Disease Syndrome instead of Acquired Immune Deficiency Syndrome.

A few days later a local drag queen named Fifi appeared on a program about AIDS and talked about his boyfriend: a first for Hong Kong. Soon there was something in the paper about

AIDS every day, and I became increasingly panicked that I might have given it to David. Or maybe he had given it to me? We would never know. I thought about whether I would have a test when I got home and what I would do if I was positive. Every day I felt my glands to see if they were swollen. They often were. I would later learn that I was making them swell by prodding them constantly.

The writer Andrew Holleran described living as a gay man in the 1980s as being like attending "a very nice dinner party with friends, except some of them were taken out and shot while the rest of us were expected to go on eating." Years later, when I tried to tell Maxey what my life was like in the years right after graduation, I talked about the staggering number of people I knew who died from AIDS, but I did make sure to emphasize that the decade was also like a very nice party: I was enraged and worried and grieving, but I also had fun with friends and took holidays, read books and saw movies. I stayed at the party, as it were, and went on eating; everyone I know who could, did. But there was one story I told Maxey after we reunited on the roof at our tenth that I thought was just a funny story from my life abroad during those years. He helped me see it differently.

IN EARLY MARCH of 1985, eight months after I arrived in Hong Kong, I'd received a call from a friend who was a reporter at one of the two English-language television stations. She had mentioned my work with the Gay Men's Health Crisis hotline to a British television host; now he wanted me to appear on his popular English-language current events show to talk about

AIDS. I had agreed and then called to tell David, who was not happy. "You don't know Hong Kong," he said. "There could be big trouble." I tried to joke about it, but that made things worse.

David and I finally agreed that I would appear on the show but wouldn't say that I was gay. And I would bring my journal and address book to a friend's apartment for safe keeping—in case the police searched my home.

On the day I was scheduled to tape the interview, I showed up on time at the television studio, but the host arrived an hour late. No apologies. As he told me about his show, its audience, and its importance, I studied him: a tall, crow-like man in his forties with sweat dripping from the top of his nose. When he paused, I reminded him that there could be no questions about whether I was gay, something we had agreed upon in advance. He nodded, to indicate agreement, but then tried to convince me that I should talk about my sexuality. With David's voice in my head, I told him that I would leave the studio that second unless he confirmed his promise to me.

"Many people think I'm soft on homosexuals," he then told me, "because I have had so many on my show."

I asked him how many he'd had. "Four." In how many years? "Seven."

"My wife thinks I'm soft on them," he continued. "Some people even think I am one. But that doesn't bother me. I'm used to people thinking I am *anything*."

I asked him if he was gay. He answered with a sharp "No."

He told me I shouldn't be scared to talk about my sexuality, as I have a U.S. passport. I told him that was part of the problem: I was in Hong Kong on a tourist visa and was working there illegally. I didn't mention David. After more haggling he proposed that he ask me, "As an American homosexual, how do you feel . . .". I told him absolutely not. (I kept cringing because of the oily way he had of saying "homosectsuelle.") I finally gave in and agreed that he could ask me whether I was a homosexual but he would have to treat my answer as final, with no follow-ups, and then we would move on to talk about AIDS. I had come up with a plan for how to field that question without breaking my promise to David.

I needed to use the john before the taping. He said he would show me the way and then accompanied me down a long corridor, talking all the while about how he has nothing against homosexuals. Happily, he didn't follow me in.

I emerged and found my way back to the greenroom. A man there greeted us; clearly nervous, the next guest after me. The host dismissed him and then said to me in a loud stage whisper: "He thinks because he knows my wife, he will get off easier; he wants me to know he is in my circle. Not a chance: I'm going to tear him to pieces."

They applied some makeup to my face. Then the host and I took our seats and the taping began. He introduced the topic of AIDS with a dozen mistakes, including mentioning the risk to hemophiliacs of becoming infected while getting blood transfusions when he should have said clotting factor. He talked for a solid ten minutes, and I thought for a while I might not have the chance to say anything.

Finally, he turned to me and asked: "Are you a homosexual?"

I told him that, especially in a place where it's illegal to be gay, it's incredibly important that people are able to talk about AIDS without being interrogated about their sexuality.

He then asked a series of prepared questions about AIDS that he read off a list; he didn't follow up on any of my answers. Finally, he said he had one more question.

"Don't you think AIDS makes a good case for *not* decriminalizing homosexuality in Hong Kong?"

I explained how it made quite the opposite case.

Afterward, when we were no longer taping, he said, "I almost got you to make a profession of faith on that last question, and you just about did it." He was gleeful. He didn't say thank you or goodbye. I no longer existed. I ushered myself out.

The next night, David and I drank several glasses of scotch with friends before the program was aired. The makeup they'd applied was dreadful: my neck was fluorescent white and my scarlet face floated above it. At the end, David expressed relief and told me that, even at his most paranoid, he thought it was highly unlikely that the special investigative unit would come after me or him, or at least not on account of that program.

When I told the story to Maxey, he asked me why I went on the show, especially knowing that it was a risk and David was set against it. I had never really thought about it.

"I don't know," I answered. "I guess I just had some information I wanted to share."

"I'm proud of you, brother," Maxey said.

HELL WEEK

In the spring of 1985, I got a dream magazine assignment from a Hong Kong travel publication where I'd been temping. They commissioned me to take the Trans-Siberian Express from Irkutsk to Moscow as part of a continuous train journey from Hong Kong to Berlin. They offered $360 for the piece but would also give me a ticket back to New York from Berlin. I was shocked by the level of emotion I felt as I lost sight of David in the crowd on the platform when the train pulled out of Kowloon Station on its way to Guangzhou, the first leg of the journey. Within minutes I missed him so much I didn't know if I could stand it.

When we had said goodbye, we weren't sure we would be able to see each other again. I could no longer stay in Hong Kong: the government was growing wise to my working on a tourist visa, and it was hard to support myself with freelance articles and jobs that paid under the table. To get a work visa I needed to leave Hong Kong and then have an employer sponsor me before I could return; I had no prospects. David couldn't get a visa to work in the U.S.; it was impossible without a job, and if he came in on a tourist visa and was caught looking for work, he would be barred forever.

But as the train crossed the border between Hong Kong and China, I knew we would just have to figure something out.

AS I WAS sitting in a velvet wingback armchair mesmerized by the Mongolian desert framed in my train-car window and sipping a glass of ice-cold vodka I'd brought back to my compartment from the bar car, Maxey was surviving Hell Week, the first significant challenge in BUD/S training. Hell Week is a culling that comes four weeks into the six-month program; as many as half the class don't make it through those seven days. There are about two hundred people who start every BUD/S class, each hoping to become a Navy SEAL: only twenty or so are left standing at the very end.

Maxey would describe Hell Week to me right after I told him about my interview with the treacherous television show host. It was clearly a story he had told many times over the years, and he performed it like a one-man show, impersonations and all.

"At the start of the week, we were kept waiting in large, heavy, canvas tents. We sat on cots, but knew we would never get to sleep on them. We also knew that for the next week we would barely be allowed to sleep at all. The tents smelled like mildew, and inside was total darkness, except for streaks of light coming in from the entrance flaps. We were all scared shitless. But we just waited.

"It was maybe an hour. Maybe more. Then all hell broke loose: grenades and smokes going off everywhere. The bullhorn was screaming above the detonations, *'Everybody out! Muster in the grinder!'*"

I asked Maxey what a grinder was; he explained that it's what they call the exposed and unforgiving stretch of asphalt where they had to do their on-land exercises.

"All the instructors were there, helping to create mayhem. It was a beautiful Sunday afternoon, but even after the explosions stopped, our eyes teared from the smoke that was heavy on the wind, and our throats burned from the smell of gunpowder.

"*'Welcome, gentlemen, welcome to Hell'* was the next thing we heard over the bullhorn. Instructor Parker gathered us all around a small rubber boat off to the side: *'I want you to meet a friend of mine. Mr. IBS. Mr. IBS unfortunately has no arms or legs. He needs to be carried everywhere.'*"

Maxey paused to explain. An IBS is a boat, an inflatable boat that can carry seven or eight people: I for Inflatable. B for Boat. S for Small. The boats are heavy and unwieldy, and soon would be abrasive, sandy, and wet.

"There were about eighty of us in Class 134 at the start of Hell Week," Maxey continued. "They lined us up—all of us, the officers, chiefs, and senior petty officers—and arranged us in a line from tallest to shortest. They then divided the line into eight-man teams, counting off, so that you were in a team with people who were roughly your height. I was on the short side of the line, and so led a crew of seven other not-very-tall guys. But there was one group that was shorter: Senior Chief Paget would lead these guys, who instantly named themselves the munchkins. Paget and I had become good friends in the training leading up to Hell Week. It was great to have an experienced, quiet guy nearby.

"From then on, we quickly learned the IBS shuffle as we carried that inflatable boat everywhere. We were constantly ordered in and out of the water, and everything we did was a timed competition, with the boat over our heads whenever we were on land. We were never dry. The bullhorn shouted relentlessly with the rules of the competitions, and we heard over and over that it paid to be a winner. By Tuesday we had been competing against each other for more than fifty hours with no sleep. But we weren't yet full-on zombies. We still felt pain, and our minds were questioning why all of this was happening."

As Maxey was describing these first days, I tried to recall if I had ever been awake for more than two days. I remembered having pulled the odd all-nighter in college—and occasionally staying in a club until the sun came up—but never longer than one overnight and certainly not under any duress.

Maxey's third night, Tuesday, was spent almost entirely in the water, in the bay by the steel piers where the big boats docked. Instructor Parker had the bullhorn and kept them all moving quickly from the cold water to the even colder deck, back and forth. When they were finally given a moment to lie down, it was on the rusted deck, staring faceup into the darkness.

"None of us could stop shivering. There was a southwest breeze that was like ice on our skin. To make it more unbearable, they were spraying us down with a hose."

I asked Maxey what people did when they could no longer stand it.

"They made it totally clear that you could quit at any time—you just had to ring the bell mounted on a pickup truck that followed us everywhere. That third night, when we were being sprayed down with the hoses, the bell was ringing so loud and often that it seemed it might come off its mounting; more than a dozen classmates quit in a matter of hours. But then we didn't hear the bell again for a while. I was in agony, but once the quitting frenzy slowed, I felt that there was a shift toward some calm away from the pain.

"After a few more hours, they had us muster in a nearby field. We were still shivering out of control from the pier torture. We mustered by boat crew, and in the darkness, I counted my crew and there were seven of us, including me, so we'd only lost one. Next to me, I realized, there was no SC Paget. He'd rung the bell."

So now, Maxey explained, the team made up of the shortest guys needed a leader. An instructor barked through a bull-horn: *"Ensign Maxey, you have the distinct privilege of taking Senior Chief's place as the team leader of the munchkins."* A lead petty offi-cer would inherit Maxey's team.

Maxey got very animated when he told me about what hap-pened next. I recognized the college Maxey I first met, when he was back in the hall after his team won a wrestling meet:

"These munchkins were short guys, but they had huge hearts, and we started winning everything. We paddled strong together through the surf whenever we had to go out into the water; we dumped our boat on land faster than any other team; we raced back out against the current when we were told to head back out; and we returned surfing the waves to get back first to the beach. We pulled and twisted and heaved our boat and ourselves through the obstacle course and finished first again and again. By Thursday we were full-on zombies—everyone was—but we were a team of zombie maniacs. Nothing could stop us."

The success of Maxey and his team started to gain the atten-tion of the instructors. At first, the instructors laughed and made fun of the men, wondering aloud how "the little guys" could be winning everything, and using it as a way to humil-iate the other teams. But then the instructors started to get pissed off.

"Instructor Parker, who we decided was *actually* the devil, began jogging beside us as we were carrying our boat over our heads. Three days earlier, his presence would have had us all freaked out. Now we were too numb and too zoned out to care.

"'*Ensign Maxey,*' Parker shouted in my ear so loudly that I could feel his anger and frustration. But I knew that I was willing to endure whatever he had to offer. My response was: *'Whooyaaaaaah,'* which is the way candidates are trained to answer the instructors, but I had added some sarcasm in there. It was almost like I was saying, *'You bastard, you can't hurt me.'* Parker continued, *'Ensign, you know what? You are a piece-of-shit little Ivy League pussy.'* My answer: *'Whoooooooyaaaaaaaaaaaah,'* the more *a*'s the more sarcastic. *'Ensign, you and your team need to stop running and put your boat down right now.'* We put the boat on the ground. He continued: *'I have been watching you. Your guys have been carrying you and the boat. You are worthless. Your team is only winning because of them. How are you ever going to lead men into combat?'* "

Parker ordered Maxey to sit in the boat and then made his team lift the boat with Maxey in it over their heads.

"The goal was to humiliate me, and it worked," Maxey said. "It hurt more than the cold water, more than my skin, which was chafed raw, more than the pounding headaches I'd been having, more than the long, painful days that never ended. Instructor Parker, that sick bastard, knew exactly how to hurt me.

"But the amazing thing was that my team of munchkins only got stronger with me in the boat over their heads. They were screaming up to me as they shuffled forward. *'Don't worry, Ensign Maxey. We got you. You are on our team and that SOB can't hurt us. He can't stop us now.'* This was the last leg of a paddle-run-paddle obstacle course. We were so far out in front that even with me sitting like a fool in the boat, the munchkins crossed the threshold into the grinder before all the other crews. *'Put that piece-of-shit officer down and stand tall,'* Parker shouted. My team answered with the traditional *'Whooooyaaaaaaah,'* but it was all sarcasm. It said to Parker: *'You can't hurt any of us. You can't divide us. You can't stop us.'*"

"So that was the end of it?" I asked Maxey.

"Not even close," he replied. "Parker then came up to the team with a smile on his face. There was nothing more frightening than when that sick bastard tried to fake benevolence. *'Ensign Maxey, your boat crew has consistently outperformed the other crews. They have finished first again, and all while carrying your worthless ass, sir.'* When he ended a tirade with *sir,* it was like spitting at the end of a race. Parker continued, *'It pays to be a winner and you guys are dismissed to the tents for a nice nap.'*

"No team had been allowed a nap. Nothing made sense anymore and yet nobody was going to argue. We knew we were winning but none of us had really expected a reward. We left Mr. IBS on the grinder and started walking toward the breakout tents."

It was the first time they had walked anywhere without that boat over their heads. Maxey described how they had lost all sense of time: it seemed like months had passed since they were all waiting in the breakout tents at the start of Hell Week; it had been five days. They could hear Parker and his bullhorn screaming obscenities at all the other teams and telling them how worthless they were: *'This is by far the most pathetic class in BUD/S history. So we decided to add another day to Hell Week so that we can get all of you SOBs to ring out. Do me a favor, the bell is right here. . . .'* Maxey and the munchkins listened and yet sheepishly ignored the rest of their class; they let the tent flap close out the noise and the lights.

"We all fell instantly onto the cots," Maxey continued. "Holy shit, how good did it feel to be not moving, to not have someone yelling in my face? I went quickly into another world. In my dream, there was soft light and trees and grass; there was a girl with long legs playing Frisbee. . . .

"And then I was jolted awake, totally dazed. It had only been fifteen minutes that we were allowed to sleep, and now Parker was in the tent with the bullhorn and two other instructors, who carried buckets of water, *'Get your lazy asses up. Mr. IBS needs to go for a swim. Get your boat and get your asses over the berm and down to the beach.'* It hadn't been a reward at all. It was just another form of torture. As we were coming out of that deep sleep, we had ice-cold water thrown into our faces. Moving again was painful beyond belief—much more difficult than it had been when we were on autopilot—and yet we managed to regain the zombie-like state that allowed us to keep breathing and ignore the pain and exhaustion. I loved every one of those munchkins and was proud to be one of them.

"Hell Week somehow ended the next day. And I started to think that I just might make it through the next five months of training."

When Maxey was finished with the story, I asked him how he managed to survive that week. He answered without hesitating, "It was really just thanks to one big thing: realizing that you don't become a SEAL, you become a member of a SEAL team. I didn't make it through; those guys pulled me through."

CATCHING UP

After meeting up on the roof at our tenth reunion, Maxey and I talked more often. Neither of us ascribed any meaning to the fact that we had only recently reconnected. During the years after college, we hadn't *not* talked; we just hadn't talked. And that was true for most of us in the secret society, and for most of the people we'd befriended in school. Partly, it was the times in which we lived: with no social media, no email, no cell phones, and with many of us itinerant, the logistics of keeping in touch were daunting, involving phone calls or letters to parents or mutual friends just to track one another's whereabouts. But it was also partly time itself, as we scrambled to establish ourselves in jobs, or finish graduate schools, or start relationships.

I had quickly filled Maxey in on the other major events of my life. I'd told him how I'd returned to Asia after a few months in New York, following the epic train trip; how I'd stayed in Hong Kong for two years on staff at two travel magazines; and then how David and I had decided to move to North America. I explained that David and I had spent five years having to commute between New York and Toronto, only able to spend every other weekend together; Canada had granted him immigration when my own country wouldn't. Once David had become a Canadian citizen, then he'd finally been able to move to the U.S. and look for work.

Maxey and I both marveled at how soon after graduation he had met Pam, and I David, and how lucky we were. We discovered more in common, too.

I told Maxey how I was still grieving the death of David Baer, my best friend, who had been hit by a bus and killed while riding his bicycle by Lincoln Center, and how I'd flown back from Hong Kong for the funeral. Maxey volunteered that he'd lost a good friend, too, and was still suffering. He didn't say more and I didn't ask; I assumed he would tell me when he was ready.

We always talked about other members of the group. I'd kept in closest touch with David Kelly, now a banker working with musicians, who had come out as gay a few years after graduation; with Renata, who was working as an associate choreographer with a New York dance company; with Huei-Zu, who was recently appointed as an assistant curator at New York's New Museum of Contemporary Art; and with Singer, who had gone into biotech. Singer had been continuously in touch with Maxey, except during the years when Maxey served abroad.

But other than telling me about how he made it through Hell Week, Maxey never said anything else about his time as a SEAL. I assumed it was secret or maybe that something had happened that he didn't want me to know—maybe something involving the friend he had lost. Besides, now Maxey was busy teaching high school and raising a family with Pam, so it didn't seem odd that it didn't enter our conversations.

I did bring up the SEALs once. In 1992, there was a huge best-seller by a fellow named Richard Marcinko who chronicled his time as the leader of SEAL Team Six. It was called *Rogue Warrior*. On the cover of the paperback was an out-of-context quote from the *New York Times Book Review* that said that the author made "Arnold Schwarzenegger look like Little Lord Fauntleroy." This first book was followed by a string of best-selling spin-offs: *Rogue Warrior Red Cell; Green Team; Task Force Blue*. Every color in the rainbow—save lavender. And it inspired a host of other books by Navy SEAL team members.

"What do you think of this Marcinko guy?" I asked Maxey.

"Not much," he replied curtly. "Remember what I said about how I made it through BUD/S—how *everyone* who makes it through BUD/S makes it through BUD/S? Well, that becomes more true once you become a SEAL, not less. It's always sup-

posed to be about the *team*. Not about the individual SEAL."
And then he added, "Most SEALs would never do a book like
that. It's not who we are."

What Maxey did work into every conversation was something about the water—his love for diving and swimming, his
need to lose himself in the waves, and his desire to give others
the experience he had when he first dove below the surface and
started to discover what he'd found there.

I was always glad to see Maxey when he came to New York,
and he must have been glad to see me or he wouldn't have
called. But our conversations generally stayed within certain
parameters—we would catch up on where we were in our lives,
trade information on the others in our group, maybe talk about
a book or movie or television show, and then say how much we
were looking forward to getting together again.

In early 1996, Maxey called not to make a plan for an
upcoming visit but to tell me some exciting news: he and Pam
were thinking about starting a school on Eleuthera, an island
in the Bahamas. He said that it was early days and already the
most intense and frightening thing he'd ever done.

It was a crazy idea—to pick up and move to this island with
three small kids and another on the way. (The year before they'd
had their third, Tyler.) Maxey still wasn't sure if they would
go through with it, or even could; raising the money and finding the land were just two of the enormous obstacles. But they
wanted to try. In the meantime, he'd continue teaching.

At the time, I was wrapped up in my own job crisis: I had
a beloved mentor and boss who was being sidelined by the cor-
poration that owned us; I had been forbidden even to talk to
him. Ironically, I was simultaneously helping to plan a confer-

ence in Indonesia on freedom of expression—a tremendously complicated endeavor in a country under a brutal dictatorship, where possession of the wrong book could land you in jail for a decade. The first book I had edited after entering publishing was by Indonesia's most famous writer, Pramoedya Ananta Toer, a man who had been jailed for his writing under three different governments. Pramoedya had finally been released after fourteen years' imprisonment without trial but was under city arrest, and all his works were banned.

So when Maxey told me his idea to start a school, I was only vaguely encouraging: I asked a bunch of questions but didn't pay much attention to his answers, mostly because I was stretched too thin in other directions, but also because the ambitious way he described it all made it sound unlikely that any two individuals could make it happen. The school sounded like what a German friend of mine once referred to as a "Schnapps-plan"—the kind of grandiose scheme you come up with after several glasses of schnapps but abandon in the sober light of day.

Later that year, the fourth Maxey arrived: Tegan. I accused Maxey of trying to confuse me with the names. Brittney and Brocq, the first two, were easy. But Tegan and Tyler? How would I ever be able to remember which was which?

IN THE MIDNINETIES, as I approached thirty-five and David headed toward forty, we settled into a routine that revolved around our two closest friends, whom we'd see a few times every week; other great friends with whom we were in constant contact; David's pals from Hong Kong, whom he'd chat with on the phone for hours every Sunday; and a wide variety of people in New York City or around the country, whom we spoke to and saw every few weeks or months or years, alone or in groups. There were work friends, too—the ones you see for a meal when the day is over, or before or after industry events. We were lucky to have so many people in our lives, luckier to share friends with my parents and siblings, and even luckier that we enjoyed spending time with my immediate and extended family, including aunts and uncles, cousins, children of cousins.

Maxey, of course, had his own friends—from Lawrenceville, from the SEALs, Pam's family, his family, people they'd met on the islands, other teachers at Lawrenceville, the parents of their children's playmates, and a whole group of Yalies I didn't know, including a few of the jocks I'd been so careful to avoid. In addition, he and Pam just didn't have much time for socializing. They had four small kids and a school they were trying to start.

My bond with Maxey remained strong, I thought, even though we rarely found the time to talk. I was sure that if I ever was in a jam, Maxey would be there for me. And I was equally sure that if Maxey ever wanted something from me, I would give it or do it without hesitation.

HUEI-ZU

On a Tuesday morning in February 1997, I woke up, found a pair of blue jeans, wrapped myself in a parka, stepped into a pair of boots, walked down the four flights to the street, stumbled to the newsagent, and bought the *New York Times,* as I did every morning, stopping to buy two bagels on my way back. I then climbed up the four flights, put water on for coffee, shouted to David that it was time to wake up ("Five more minutes! Just five more minutes!" he shouted back, as he always did), and settled in to read the paper.

Even on pleasant days, the precipitous climb back to our apartment made the task a chore. And on days of bad weather, we wondered whether we really needed to eat or read. Can man live by coffee alone? We tested the hypothesis when it rained or snowed.

I had some leisure this day. After ten years at William Morrow Publishers, I was leaving my job. A new executive had been installed above my sidelined mentor, and he didn't think much of me or the books I published. I didn't think much of him and did little to hide it. It had been a tense and miserable workplace for months, and I was exhausted and saddened by all the office politics. I'd started my publishing career there as an assistant in the rights department and thought I would be a lifer. But I'd been forced to choose between my job as editor in chief and my loyalty to my mentor, a man who had given me my career and his friendship. Every day that I stayed and reported to someone else felt like a betrayal.

So I was going to go work for a new publishing company, one that was just a few years old, but they couldn't bring me on board until their new fiscal year began, six months later. This meant I had a sabbatical of sorts ahead of me. David and I were talking about renting out our apartment and going to visit his family and our friends in Hong Kong, maybe travel a bit. We had enough saved to manage it, and I could take on some free-lance editing. I was particularly excited that I was going to be allowed to start a new line at the new firm, publishing Asian fiction in translation; I could also use the trip to scout authors. And when again would I have a break like this and know that I had a job waiting for me? David was willing to quit his job designing children's wear and look for another one when we returned.

The paper this February day carried stories about a jury award in a civil trial against O. J. Simpson, subway ridership skyrocketing, and morale in France sagging. I made my way through page after page, ending in the final section, D. It wasn't really my habit to spend too long on the obituary page. But that day, I glanced at it. A food writer I admired had died. I had seen her byline, but we'd never met. And then I saw a name below it: Alice Yang. Curator and Historian. 35.

I put down the paper. Walked around the apartment, back into the kitchen. Maybe I had misread it. Maybe there was another Alice Yang. But when I was able to look at the paper again a moment later there was no escaping the fact that Huei-Zu—Alice—was dead.

The first line read:

Alice Huei-Zu Yang, an art historian and curator, died early Saturday morning after a hit-and-run accident at Canal and Varick Streets in Manhattan. She was 35 and lived in TriBeCa.

The obituary mentioned that Huei-Zu was born in Taipei in 1961 and graduated from Yale with a degree in art history in 1984. It said that Huei-Zu's husband, an architect, had been injured in the accident and was in the hospital in stable condition. It described Huei-Zu's prodigious success in her field.

Huei-Zu was one of those friends I saw only once every few years. She had just passed her oral exams for her Ph.D., taken a new job as a museum curator, and edited a book to accompany a show she organized. There was always going to be more time, and more reunions. We had friends in common and I would hear about her from them. And when we had met, we always laughed—about our experiences at Yale and about the fact that she told me I would hate living in Hong Kong and not only had I loved it but I'd fallen in love there.

We would also talk about contemporary Chinese art, her field of expertise, and in particular about a remarkable Taiwanese ink painter she was championing: Yu Peng. Huei-Zu had thought deeply about this artist and I was simply someone filled with a layman's enthusiasm, but she seemed happy that I shared her love for his work.

In the days following, I spoke to many of our crew. (I hope I wrote to Huei-Zu's husband and parents and brothers to tell them how sorry I was, but I don't know if I did. When I was in my mid-thirties, I didn't know how important that was.) I felt again the shock that comes from discovering that the spool has run out on a life, and that whatever time I'd had with that friend was the only time I would ever have. No do-overs. No chance to cram in one more drink, meal, or conversation. Done.

When I reached Maxey, I realized that we had gone nearly a year without talking at all. I had never called to ask him how his kids were doing. He hadn't rung to ask me about my job. I hadn't followed up on his plans to start the school. I realized I had reports from Singer, and so did he; Singer was now playing the role of Hermes, God of sports, merchants, and travelers, and the Immortal tasked with keeping all the other Immortals—and mortals, too—apprised of one another's comings and goings.

Maxey and I shared with each other memories of Huei-Zu. Each of us talked about the last time we'd seen her. There was a lot of silence. I also told Maxey that I was leaving my job after ten years and had taken another, and that David and I would be heading off on a sabbatical.

"I love you, brother," Maxey said, as we hung up.

I felt bleak after the call; the memories didn't crowd out the sadness but made it more acute. I also wondered whether I would talk to Maxey once a year or every few years, or if that might even be the last time *we* would ever talk—perhaps because one of us wouldn't be long for the world, or perhaps just from inattention.

THE SCHOOL BEGINS

The following February, the phone rang one Sunday morning, just as I had come back from the exhausting trip to get bagels and the *New York Times*. David and I were still living in the four-story walk-up but I had packed on twenty-plus pounds by gaining just a few pounds a year over the last six or seven; now I was always out of breath when I got home. Nothing a bagel couldn't cure, though.

It had been an eventful year. A few weeks after Huei-Zu's death I had had a serious bout of chicken pox that confined me to bed for several months; I had never had it as a child and this was before there was a vaccine that was recommended for most adults. Once I recovered, we visited David's family in Hong Kong and made several long stops during a circuitous route home. I was now six months at my new publishing house, and David had found another job designing kids' clothes.

"We're going to do it, Schwalbs," Maxey told me, a little out of breath (although I imagined he'd been running miles and not hunting for bagels). "Pam and I are going to start the school. In the Bahamas. On Eleuthera. For real. We are going to begin construction this fall and our first term will start next spring, in March 1999, just thirteen months from now. I'm like frickin' beyond excited."

This was the first time we had talked in a year, and he was still the kid I met in the hall who wanted to bounce all over the room, but now it seemed that he'd channeled that energy into something that fully engaged his heart and mind. He went on to say that Pam was going to do the admissions and he would be head of the school, but a different kind of principal. He'd spent enough time in the military answering to authority that he knew he didn't want to be someone giving orders—whether he was addressing a platoon, a boardroom, or a class of teens. He wanted to be guiding but not leading. The whole idea was to come up with experiences that would fully engage young people and make them partners, not observers. He was guided by a saying that he couldn't get out of his head: "What I hear, I forget. What I see, I remember. What I do, I understand."

So Maxey and Pam would start the school. He explained to me, in a torrent of words, how it all began and what they had planned for the future.

At Lawrenceville, Maxey had been tasked with teaching Conceptual Physics (a.k.a. Physics for Poets). Unable to stay away from the water and obsessed with the idea of teaching young people through experience rather than rote learning, he found a way to get funding to train them as scuba divers. This way, the students could see and hear how light and sound move through water, understand the concept of buoyancy by observing the ways that they themselves could float or sink, and learn that math can be life or death when you are calculating pressure versus volume density on your lungs.

That same year, he had met one of the founders of the Mountain School, a semester program in Vermont for high school juniors that taught them about farming and the environment while also strengthening their confidence and self-sufficiency. Maxey would model the Island School after that program. He would also use what he'd learned during a sabbatical he'd taken two years earlier, when he got his master's in marine resource management.

What he wanted, he said, was to take young people out of their comfort zone, away from parents and television and cars and stores, and away from the cliques that governed their lives.

"Cliques like jocks and theater gays?" I asked. "Jocks and theater gays love each other."

"Exactly," said Maxey.

Additionally, he wanted to create an environment that re-created everything he loved about his sports career—the family vibe established by his best coaches and the fact that everyone in the team competitions wanted to do well for one another—but none of what he liked least. When he choked in the individual competitions at year-end, he always became depressed. But now when he looked back, he realized the individual competition didn't matter; his satisfaction had always come from being part of a team.

All through high school and college, Maxey had been terrified of failing, but now knew that if he hadn't failed, he would never have found the confidence he needed.

He told me that he also wanted to make up for the damage to the ocean he'd caused as a SEAL.

"You know, Schwalbs, I became a SEAL because I loved the water. I did want to be of service. But I also wanted to get paid to go diving. I wanted to explore and be physical. And then, when I was taking my platoon across the Pacific, we wound up in the Philippines and they asked us to clear a path through a coral reef so that landing craft could get to the beach that was across from the port at Subic Bay. The way you do that is you weave tubes of explosive into a mat and then lay it out over the coral reef and detonate the thing and watch the plume of smoke rise from the explosion. Landing craft can't come in to a beach through coral reef—the boats would get cut to shreds or beached—so you have to blow up the reef to make a channel. That's what SEALs are supposed to do. Blow things up. And that's what we did.

"After the blast we waded into the water with a net, and I was laughing maniacally as me and my guys scooped up all these floating, dead fish to cook on the grill."

"And that's why you left the SEALs?" I asked.

"No," Maxey said. "That wasn't it. We blew up a reef. We ate the fish. I stayed in for four more years. I don't believe in epiphanies, but I think your worldview can change dramatically. We've already built a base camp for the school on a small island, and now my life is going to be completely dedicated to my first love, the ocean. I don't want to blow up reefs anymore. I want to save them."

Maxey told me that they had been given a site for the school on a protected cape in South Eleuthera but needed a variety of approvals from the local authorities before the Office of the

Prime Minister would give them the green light. "I have to tell you about this experience I had with the deputy director of fisheries. We were walking along the beach in front of the site and came upon two young boys cracking open small conchs for bait. The fisheries guy told them that what they were doing wasn't legal—which they didn't know—but then explained that the law exists in order to *protect* the conch fishery by ensuring that juvenile conchs survive long enough to reproduce and increase the conch population. And I saw these boys turn into young environmental warriors right before my eyes. With just a little bit of knowledge, they were all charged up to save their home. Right after that, the fisheries officer turned to me and said that he thought education was the only hope, for the Bahamas and the planet—and that they were excited to work with us."

Maxey and Pam had started small, creating a program for local sixth-graders on Eleuthera. They had an equal number of girls and boys participating, and wouldn't have gone ahead if they hadn't. He told me that girls had been shut out of way too many physical, ocean-based programs by educators who assumed they weren't as keen to explore the wilderness as boys were and so had done nothing to encourage them to apply. He was particularly excited about partnering with an educator who'd been working for years on South Eleuthera.

That was just the first step. The school itself would be only the second step. Eventually, Maxey hoped to establish an institute right on the school's campus staffed by first-rate scientists, so that the Bahamian and foreign students could work alongside them and take part in actual marine conservation research.

"I want to try to do for a bunch of young people what our life in the hall did for us. Mix things up. Get them to live and work together. Have them help build the school and be responsible for it. Push them intellectually, emotionally, physically to show them that they are stronger than they know. Turn them from consumers of education to creators. And I want to inspire young people to believe they can make a difference. Maybe then they won't turn out like the knucklehead who laughed when he blew up a coral reef."

"How do you feel about living in Eleuthera?" I asked, knowing the answer.

"Are you frickin' kidding? I'll get to swim every day with nurse sharks. And Pam and I want to raise our kids there. We've put our life savings into a small condo. It's where we want to live, retire, and die. You got to come visit, Schwalbs. You and David. It's unbelievable."

I told him we would for sure—and that I wasn't even the littlest bit surprised that he was really going to do this, especially when I realized he could be in the water every day.

He was also excited to help the economy of the island, he said, but in a sustainable way, so that it wouldn't need large resorts or ports for big cruise ships. In 1992, Hurricane Andrew had devastated South Eleuthera; none of the resorts there had chosen to rebuild, leaving hundreds of people jobless.

I then asked where he was getting the money to build the school.

"We have to raise five hundred thousand dollars," he said. "Lawrenceville is providing all the support we need for back office and other things. But I have to build a whole campus, and I want to do it with local materials and with as little impact as possible. Solar energy. Right now, the site is just a piece of rock. No vegetation. No nothing."

He asked me what I thought. I told him that I had never heard him so excited about anything. I said I was excited to help in any way I could. I don't know if he realized that I hadn't answered his question. What I couldn't tell him was that I didn't think there was any way he and Pam were going to be able to pull this off. It *still* sounded like a Schnapps-plan. No one in our circle had done anything like this, built an institution from the ground up. I couldn't imagine being able to accomplish anything like it. I didn't doubt Maxey and Pam; I doubted all of us.

AFTER MAXEY'S CALL, more months went by without our speaking again. David and I were absorbed by the routines that dominated our lives. We were both working hard at our jobs. And on top of that there was all the bill-paying, friend-seeing, family-attending, holiday-planning, thank-you-card-writing, movie-going, and book-reading that we had been doing for years and would keep doing until we were both in the grave. I had also remained involved in the freedom of expression work and other causes, including joining the board of a local community college. I was now thirty-six; David forty-one. As a friend of mine often said, "We will all have time enough to catch up on our sleep when we are dead."

Every day, when we came back from work, we would be greeted, as we had all our lives, with a pile of mail. The occasional gem but mostly bank statements, flyers from local businesses, and appeals from various worthy causes.

One day an envelope arrived from the Island School on Eleuthera. I opened it, excited to hear from Maxey. But it wasn't a personal note; it was a form letter.

November 15, 1998

Dear Friends,

Thanks to the continued support from Lawrenceville School and an amazing group of colleagues we are feeling like we have a plan to make the Cape Eleuthera Island School happen. We broke ground in September to build three buildings that will house and feed our pioneer students. We are fortunate to have John Norris Carey, known to all as the Giant, leading his construction team, all local residents and our neighbors. It is especially challenging to build in the out islands and our seven-month construction schedule is ambitious even for a Giant.

Thanks to the generous support of Bill and Sally Searle and the Searle $100K matching challenge, we have been able to raise over $250k towards our goal of $500k to complete construction. Our fantastic site was donated by Dan and Pamella DeVos. Please consider making a gift to this dream now becoming a reality. Your support means a great deal to me and Pam and to the future of a school that seeks to put young people to work in the care of our ocean planet.

We wish you and your families a glorious Thanksgiving and give thanks for all who are stretching to support our good work. Thanks to Lawrenceville advancement team, all gifts will receive a letter giving tax exemption. Please do not hesitate to call with any questions or ideas.

Respectfully,

Chris and Pam

I was feeling a bit overwhelmed by bills that month. I also thought that, while it was wonderful that Maxey was starting this school on a Bahamian island, it wasn't exactly my top priority. It was great that Maxey was so excited, but kids weren't really my thing, and neither was the environment. I would of course send something. Though if Maxey still needed a quarter of a million dollars, my $100 or so wouldn't make much difference.

Then I kept forgetting to do even that. I would remember at odd moments—at two a.m., when I was half awake worrying about something at work; in the middle of a movie that had momentarily lost my interest; or at a family dinner, when a relative was telling a story I had heard a dozen times before—and I would think, *Must send a check,* but then I would forget again. And every time I thought to call Maxey, I would remember that I hadn't sent anything, feel guilty about that, and put off calling him until I'd sent a check—which I would again neglect to do.

A few months later, I learned from Singer that Maxey had been in town but hadn't called me. That was okay—I was busy and Maxey was busy, too. He must have been here fundraising. He'd call me when he was here next. Then he was visiting New York again and didn't call me. Guiltily, I felt relieved because I was exhausted. I didn't need another night of drinking beer until the late hours. We would catch up later.

I briefly wondered if he was mad about my not sending a check. Or about my not being in touch with him. Or both. Even though I hadn't called or written him, I couldn't help feeling a bit hurt. Wasn't it the responsibility of the person coming to town to call the person who lived there? Wasn't that just one of those unwritten rules of friendship?

CHAPTER THREE

Midlife

FLOYD

When I'd first heard Prince sing about 1999, the year seemed impossibly far in the future. But soon enough it was here, and it was college that seemed unfathomably distant. Still, David and I lived like people just out of school, with no encumbrances: no kids, no pets, no houseplants—except for one hardy African violet we never seemed able to kill.

In late spring, Maxey and I spoke for the first time since he had told me that he and Pam were going to go ahead and start the school. I had called him one afternoon for no reason I could name; I think I just wanted to test our bond and see if I noticed any change. It had been more than a year since we'd talked. I missed Maxey.

"How are the kids?" I asked. I didn't say anything about his coming to town without calling me, and he didn't mention it either. I remembered that I hadn't yet sent a check but was determined to do so right after the call.

"Awesome. Of course, we don't sleep at all. But it's crazy and great. Having kids is the best thing in the world. Britter is stepping up and being a great big sister to the little girls. Brocq has a huge heart. Ty is so beautiful that sometimes Pam and I feel like she's not real, like she's an angel, and we get scared. Tegan is still in diapers. She has the cutest pug nose. The other day was nuts. Ty snuck out onto the dock because she wanted to be Brocq's first mate—Brocq was in the little skiff getting ready to go to sea. Ty reached down to pull on the bowline and Brocq didn't notice as he was also pulling the boat close to the dock. Ty held on tight and when Brocq pulled the line, he pulled Ty right into the water. We didn't see any of this—we just heard Brocq screaming for help. We arrived and there he was holding on to his sister with one arm and clinging to the four-by-four piling with the other. But Ty was so mad at him for pulling her into the water that she wasn't helping at all—she was punching him in the head. And I swear that Tegan—who almost never smiles—was grinning in her crib during all of this."

I could have sworn that it should have been Ty in the crib—that Tegan was the older of the younger two—but then again, I knew I could never remember which was which, except when Maxey reminded me, which he'd had to do every single time we talked. Maybe that was because when Maxey was telling this story, and every time he had told this kind of story in the past, I found my mind wandering—to work or to the ongoing to-do list that was ever scrolling through my head.

I asked Maxey about the school, now in its first term. I assumed that it was breathtakingly demanding: twenty-two students, their parents, the teachers. Not to mention forging relationships with local government, building a campus, and the fundraising, always the fundraising. All Maxey said was that everything was going great: they'd already built a dormitory, a place to have meals all together, and a shaded deck for sharing ideas. The students had made paths across the limestone moonscape, he told me. They'd cleared and planted. And Pam? Great, too.

"And what about you, Schwalbs, what are you up to?"

I probably told him a story about office politics, or a restaurant, or a show, or about someone we had in common. I know I didn't tell him about my friends, or about David, or about the books I was publishing, or about anything that really mattered to me. That year I'd helped organize (with two friends) the first-ever visit to America of Pramoedya Ananta Toer, the Indonesian author I published and revered. I said nothing to Maxey about that.

I do remember hearing, as I talked, screaming in the background on his side of the call, indiscriminate squeaky voices demanding parental adjudication for one outrage or another perpetuated by a sibling. I thought I sensed in Maxey's voice the need to end the call—to get back to school, or get out onto the water, or stop his kids from arguing, or just do something else.

It was on that call that Maxey first asked me if David and I ever wanted to have kids. I replied the same way I always replied when people asked me this: "Nope, we are in fact the last gay men in America who do NOT want children." Then I added, as I almost always did: "We're way too selfish. We can barely keep our one houseplant alive. And we like to go where we want to go when we want to go there."

Usually, I didn't really mind the question. But I felt like Maxey was judging me. As though he thought my life, without children, was more trivial than his.

I'VE ALWAYS DREADED Labor Day weekend because it's the only thing that stands between a perpetually squandered summer and the grind of the rest of the year spent dreaming about everything I'll do, read, and eat when summer weekends come again.

In 1999, David and I spent Labor Day moping at a friend's beach house before returning grumpily to the city. In the coming days I started to see reports of a tropical storm forming: Floyd. This was followed by news of massive evacuations throughout the South.

It usually wouldn't have occurred to me to worry about Maxey in a storm; he'd been a SEAL after all. But the school was just starting its second semester that fall, and its twenty-eight students and seven faculty members, along with everyone on Eleuthera, were right in Floyd's path. I also knew that Pam and their four kids—whatever their names were—were all with Maxey on the island.

On September 15, I saw in the *New York Times* that Eleuthera had been hit directly with 110-mile-per-hour winds; that the streets were flooded; roofs had been ripped from buildings; and the population was living in shelters.

I couldn't reach Maxey so I called Singer, who had managed to find Maxey. He told me that, two days before the storm was due to hit, Maxey had made the decision to wait for the next day's five a.m. National Oceanographic and Atmospheric Administration report and only then decide what to do. The initial report had predicted a category-five direct hit over South Eleuthera, but Maxey had wanted to stay if it was at all possible; he was particularly worried about abandoning the campus and his neighbors and the message that would send to the students. At the same time, he was receiving a constant stream of calls from frantic parents. Eventually, the U.S. embassy rang and told Maxey that they needed to evacuate all U.S. citizens. A school parent, who was a senior State Department undersecretary, had asked the embassy to get involved.

Still, Maxey had waited for the early morning NOAA report before evacuating everyone. He had become friends with the woman who owned the only airline with direct flights between the island and Florida, Twin Air, which had four or five puddle jumpers; she had assured him that there would be time to get the students and faculty out. Maxey, Pam, and their kids had been the last to leave and were now reunited with the others in Florida. Singer told me that the school was probably destroyed.

I reached Maxey a week later. He sounded very glad to hear from me.

"It was frickin' nuts," he said. "I'd been on the phone with my friend at Twin Air when we got the word from NOAA. It was worse than anyone thought; Eleuthera was going to get a direct hit. We sent the students and the teachers to Florida first. I realized that the embassy's request made sense." I didn't let on that Singer told me the embassy hadn't just asked: they'd insisted. "Pam and I had stayed behind for a bit to make sure we did everything we could do to help the school and our neighbors weather the storm. Besides, we owed it to the parents of our students to make sure that every one of their children was off the island before we left with our own family.

"But my friend at the airline told us not to worry; she was

committed to getting us all out. She had given her word and she never went back on her word. It was about three hours after the first plane left that it was able to return for Pam, me, and our kids. On the way to the airport, Tony—that's our medical director, who would stay behind to help our neighbors—was driving me and the family in our old Suburban to get this last plane out. As we rounded the bend into Rock Sound there was a loud boom. The atmospheric pressure was so low that the back window of the car had imploded and shattered inside the car. We were all covered in glass, although no one was hurt. As I said, nuts."

By the time Maxey and his family caught up with the rest of the school in Florida, the southern part of the state was under mandatory evacuation, and the school that had offered to host them was itself shutting down. They found some vans and headed north but got stuck on Interstate 95 behind everyone else doing the same thing. Eventually, they were given shelter at the Archbold Biological Station in the middle of Florida. They slept on the auditorium floor. "But here's the cool thing," Maxey said. "I brought my copy of *Omeros* with me, so I had the students read Derek Walcott to each other and we became this awesome team. One kid flew home to Cleveland yesterday, but everyone else is going to go back to the school no matter what." The students' loyalty was inspiring, but the prospect of their return was also daunting. "I don't guess a single building will be left standing," Maxey added.

Maxey and I talked about how fitting it was for all of them to be reading Walcott's epic poem set on St. Lucia and inspired by Homer's *Odyssey,* just after they had been buffeted by the elements and were now trying to figure out how to return to a place that might be gone and that was, for some of them, home.

A few days later, a Twin Air pilot who had flown over the school brought the news that all four buildings were intact, but one had lost its roof in the storm. What the pilot couldn't have known was that the roofless building was under construction and hadn't yet been given a roof. Miraculously, the school seemed untouched.

No planes were allowed to land because the airport was flooded and full of debris. Maxey kept the students moving from one temporary home to another. Eventually, they all wound up sleeping in the wrestling room at a high school in Miami, studying aquaculture by day and continuing to read Derek Walcott's *Omeros*.

WHEN WE SPOKE again a few weeks later, Maxey sounded more subdued. The island was devastated: the vegetation was gone; the ocean, usually a fan-deck of dazzling blues, now looked like chocolate milk. Worse still, families had lost their houses, their shops, everything. A quarter of the buildings on the island had some kind of damage; one out of a hundred was totally destroyed. No one on Eleuthera had been killed, but one person died on Grand Bahama Island, and there were more than seventy deaths in the United States.

Maxey, Pam, their kids, the students, and the faculty had returned as soon as they were allowed and were sure it wouldn't interfere with relief efforts. There was no gas or electricity at the school, so they did all of their cooking over an open fire. While he was pleased that his students had come together, Maxey had never been more aware of all the disparities between the school and the community. If he could possibly keep from doing so, he wouldn't evacuate again unless the entire population of the part of the island that was in the storm's path was able to leave. They also needed to step up what they were doing to contribute to the life of the island, he said.

Maxey told me he was really glad that I'd called him when he was in Florida—that it had meant a lot to hear from his old friends—and that he was excited to see me when he was next in New York. I realized that Maxey hadn't had a problem with me; I had a problem with me. I thought about all the times I visited various towns and didn't call friends who lived there, assuming they would understand that I was busy and would not read anything into my failing to schedule a get-together.

The power of our experience senior year was that we all had to see each other twice a week. Now that we spoke far less frequently, it was easy for paranoia and doubt to enter our friendships. I realized that I needed to take a breath before I decided that Maxey or any other friend had dropped me—a suspicion that in the past had sometimes led me to dropping that friend so I wouldn't get hurt. And that I also needed to be more aware of friends who might be feeling that I'd dropped *them*.

I wondered, briefly, if there was some reason why I didn't feel I deserved Maxey's friendship—some way in which, deep down, I still saw it as tenuous and was almost waiting to be proven right. Maybe it had to do with my being gay, and believing at my core some of the prejudices that had surrounded me. Or maybe it just had to do with my being me, and worrying that the more people knew me, the less they would like me. Those were strange and unwelcome thoughts, so I buried them.

We ended the conversation with Maxey letting me know how much work lay ahead: at the school, in the community. He was going to go all in and work around the clock if that was what it took. Almost losing the school during its second semester, Maxey told me, made him aware of how important the school was to him. It meant everything. Absolutely everything. Soon after the call I finally remembered to send a contribution to the Island School.

ARGONAUT

Maxey next came through NYC on a school fundraising trip in 2000, and we met up. We talked about the usual things—my job, the school, our secret society friends—but I was also furious about the passage of Proposition 22 in California, making it law in that state that the only marriage that would be recognized was between a man and a woman—even if a same-sex marriage had been legally performed somewhere else in the country. Maxey shared my outrage. A few weeks later I received a letter from him:

Hey Will:

It was great to see you. I have to share a story from last spring, where I was able to support and navigate a journey for our first openly gay student. In January, I got a message from a mother asking if we could talk. On the phone she explained how happy she was to learn that her son Andy had been accepted and yet she wanted me to know that he was openly gay and even a little angry, aggressive about sharing. She asked me whether or not I believed that we would be able to welcome and support her son through The Island School

Semester. My answer definitely was inspired by your audit and a desire to make our community the place I dreamed it would be for all different kinds of young people.

The first night we all gathered in the common room. I remember Anthony Francis was facilitating the community meeting. After telling the students the importance of conserving water and staying hydrated, it was time for us all to share. Ants started: "I am Anthony and you can call me Ants. I am from Jamaica and I love to bake bread." Most faculty and students followed this lead and shared something they liked to do. It was now time for Andy to share. In truth, the first time I saw Andy, his appearance reminded me of you when we first met. Andy had his hair spiked in all directions and the back was dyed pink. He was wearing some kind of collar with what looked like rhinestones. That first night, he made a point not to wear his Island School T-shirt uniform like the rest of the students. He sat on a table with his back against the wall. He was nervous like everyone and took a moment to look around the room and let some silence frame his statement. "My name is Andy and I am from New York (another pause). I am queer and I think everyone is a little queer." There were some shy chuckles, and the girl next to him laughed maybe a bit too loud. I think everyone admired Andy for his courage. I wanted to somehow let Andy know that I was here to support him; that I had a close friend who is gay. Then I realized how absurdly shallow and even selfish that was; the connection had to come across a real experience; had to have some depth. The semester starts with a 3-day kayak expedition where everyone learns how to live out on the seascape wilderness. The 3-day makes the rustic campus feel more comfortable.

Andy was not excited about kayaking. I heard him say, "Why the fuck do I want to take a shit out on a beach like some kind of dog?" Like you, Will, he was great about being real and calling shit out. He was even more vocal about the kayaking when he returned from the 3-day: "I hate fucking kayaking and I hate camping and I hate those goddamn bugs that you can't see, and yet you feel them eating you alive." As it turned out, it was not just the kayak that Andy hated. His advisor Susan pulled me aside and had Andy's place-book on her lap. "Hey Maxey," she said, "I know this was for my eyes only and yet I feel that I need to share with you." She opened the page and there in huge block letters Andy had written: "I Fucking Hate Chris Maxey."

Luckily, I seemed to be the only person Andy hated. He loved the community and his peers and most of the faculty, too; and everyone loved him. He created fun and excitement wherever he went. In the boys' dorm he organized a shower ritual where they would rinse from a water tank, soap up, and run one lap around the building chanting some crazy version of Yellow Submarine. On Sundays, with one of the girls, he opened a hair salon and over the next month everyone went to get a haircut. There was talk of Cindy and Andy opening a salon in LA when they got back to the big US.

It was now seventy days into the semester and time for the 8-day sea kayak expedition. Andy, of course, started bitching and was even less happy when he found out I was going to be his kayak guide. Now, we'd had some time at meals to talk, and yet I knew that he was still stereotyping me as an old, clueless, homophobic jock.

He was surprised that I told him that I was psyched to have him on my team, that I knew he would find the 8-day better than the 3-day. Andy looked at me like I was a complete idiot. Will, you looked at me like that many times.

It was time to tell him about you and to actually tell him about our friendship. I told him about your wild hair and clear reservations about having much to do with me and yet how we managed to become close friends and learned to try not to stereotype. Andy listened and was unusually quiet. When he got up, he smiled and said, "The only thing I am psyched about for this stupid"—he was keeping it clean as we'd instituted a ten-pushup punishment for swearing—"kayak trip is the chance to get to know people better."

It felt like there was a small breakthrough. Kayak trips are always set up to socially engineer across friend groups. It's often a time when students realize that being different is awesome and you might find that your best friends after kayak are people you never took the time to meet earlier.

We left campus and began paddling down the coast. Andy was strategically placed in the front of a double with a strong paddler in the back. It was impossible for him not to complain and it was also impossible for him not to engage with this new pod of people. He would randomly start singing and tucking his paddle under the straps so that he could use his water bottle like a microphone. Everyone laughed and he made some of the long, hard paddle days a lot of fun. This girl named Joanna who paddled with Andy in the double was constantly teasing him and reminding him that she was not there to be his engine. Of course, that just gave him more material and he started making up a song about Joanna, the love engine in his life.

After four days of paddling and camping and working

together, we were becoming a close family. Nights around the fire were spent cooking and telling stories, roses and thorns, highs and lows from the full adventure days. Andy started to have more roses than thorns and some were not even sarcastic. Like: "When that eagle ray jumped right in front of my kayak, I thought I was in a Disney movie."

We arrived at the southern tip of the Island, Lighthouse Point; it's a spectacular experience to be paddling together with confidence as you pass through the narrow gap that separates the main island from a string of large rocks that spill down to the southwest. Andy had an undisguisable look of pride as he helped carry his double kayak up above the highwater line. He even took the lead as others came in to help. "Lift on three," he shouted, and the team came together with the rhythm that comes from practice and teamwork.

It was now time for the 48-hour solo where each student is positioned along the spectacular seascape that winds up to the north. Most everyone is nervous as we brief the team. Lena, who was guiding the trip with me, is a teacher at the school. She uses the image of an hourglass to tell the story of how each of them came from a big world with family and friends and later came to this small island and over time built a community here. Then it came time to break into even smaller groups, the kayak pods, and *now* we had reached the moment, at the apex of the hourglass, where it was time for each of them to celebrate being alone and for each of them to reflect on how far they had come. They would each be doing that, solo, for two days, before rejoining the larger group and then returning home. This time alone was the perfect chance to ask themselves some important questions: *What have you learned about yourself? How are you going to set goals for the rest of the semester and the rest of your life?* Not even Andy was joking around. Lena asked that no more words be spoken. It was time to walk together along the beach—but every 400 meters a student was chosen to stay behind the group until all of them were planted alone along the shore, with four football fields or so between each of them. Lena and I walked back the almost two miles; solo was launched.

The two days pass slowly in both a beautiful and painful way. After lunch on the second day, it was time to regroup and retrace our steps. We walked together as the pod grew bigger and the smiles were almost bursting as we traveled in respectful silence. The end of solo has us climb together to the top of the ridge and sit high up on the rocks in a circle with ocean in all directions. It was later in the afternoon; the sun was beginning to swing low to the western horizon; we sat together looking deep into each other's faces wanting so much to share and hear the sound of voices. Lena looked up and took the time to smile at each of us with patience and gratitude, and then she spoke: "Welcome back to the pod; solo is now officially over." A flood of laughter and greetings and story-telling spilled out across the circle and down the rocks to the sea. I imagined that the people on Cat Island might feel the energy from our pod as we erupted in celebration.

There would be no end to the sharing but it was time for an important announcement. I interrupted the excitement with a short blast of the conch horn. "Hey, argonauts!" That is what we named ourselves. "It's now time for you to lead on your own. Lena and I will stay in the distance ready to step in if there is a safety issue. You have two full days and a waxing

gibbous moon rising tonight." You could feel the excitement
and some anxiety as Lena and I stepped back from the circle. Joanna, Andy's kayak companion, wanted to start making plans for dinner, and then a boy named John suggested a
conversation about goals. He asked, "Can we go further than
Cotton Bay? We're strong now and it would be so cool to
paddle north further than any other kayak group in the past?"
This led to a lot of conversation and Andy stayed quiet. A
kid named Sam jumped in and reminded everyone, "We are
a pod and we can only go as far as the weakest member of
the group." Several others followed Sam and even mentioned
Andy as someone they needed to think about. "Andy isn't a
strong paddler, and we need to respect him." John came back
and shared that during the last leg Andy and his double were
out front pushing the pod towards Lighthouse. Andy smiled
that dangerous and unpredictable, sarcastic smile: "Thanks
everyone for being so thoughtful and sharing how you think
I might be feeling. The good news is I am here and somehow
I'm beginning to love what I once dreaded. Yes, I now love
fucking kayaking and shitting on the beach; I even love those
crazy ghost crabs and those fucking insects." Everyone was
smiling and I didn't have to tell Andy to give me 10 push-ups
for swearing: He got in a prone position and started counting
out 10 of them, and we all got down and joined him. It felt
so good to be there seeing this team come together. "OK,"
Andy said, "It feels like you've all identified me as the weak
link and therefore it's my honor to set the course. Let's make
a feast and, as the moon rises, let's launch onto the sea. The
night is calm and it will be beautiful paddling in the sparkles
of the night ocean."

The argonauts paddled all the way to Half Sound and there was so much to celebrate as we gathered for a surprise banquet. It was then that Andy came up to me and put his hand on my shoulder. He said, "Maxey, thank you for putting up with me; thank you for believing in me." I didn't have to say anything. I was so incredibly proud of Andy and his argonauts.

Respectfully,

Maxey

When I finished reading Maxey's letter, the first thing I felt was a bit of pride myself. Maxey wanted to show me the effect I'd had on him and had taken the time and care to put it all in a letter. Though the story was a testament to the courage of these remarkable young people, it was also a testament to our friendship.

The next thing I felt was how proud I was to know Maxey: the school and community he and Pam had created were changing lives.

I thought about the ways Maxey changed my life. The first example that came to mind made me wince a bit: Maxey had helped me realize that people you don't like aren't always who you think they are, even when you are quite sure—and what's more, even if they are, they may want to change. The wincing was because it was a lesson I still so often forgot.

I called Maxey right away to thank him for the story, the letter, and for being patient with my taking so many years to figure out what Andy the Argonaut had realized in less than one hundred days.

After the call, I felt Maxey and I were closer friends than

we'd ever been, and probably as close as we would ever be. But I was wrong about that, too.

THE ISLAND SCHOOL

I was at my desk on a breathtakingly cold day in January 2005, trying to find a piece of paper I'd lost or misfiled, when the phone rang.

It was David Singer. We talked about his work (sequencing the human genome, whatever that was) and the book I was reading, and his life in San Francisco (even though he was rarely there, constantly flying around the country for his job) and mine in New York. We caught up on spouses and Singer's three kids. Before too long we were talking about Maxey.

"I'm a little worried about him," Singer said. "He and Pam are still having problems."

"That sucks." I realized it had been years since I spoke to Maxey. Nothing had happened between us: we had just let a few weeks without calling turn into a few months and then years. I was spending more time with fewer people and knew Maxey was, too.

"Let's go see him—fly down to the island—cheer him up," Singer suggested.

I told Singer I would love to do that but couldn't spare the time.

"Call in sick," Singer told me. "We'll just go for two nights. We'll leave on a Friday morning and be back Sunday night."

I waffled. On such short notice, the tickets would be a fortune. "I'll take care of your ticket," Singer said, reading my mind. "I've got so many frequent flier miles I could never use them in three lifetimes. Plus, we won't spend a cent when we're there because we'll be staying with Maxey. He won't let us pay for anything."

I waffled more.

"I'm flying in tomorrow. I'll have your ticket. We'll meet at the airport. I won't take no for an answer. Just promise me one thing," Singer said. "That you won't forget your passport."

BY THE TIME the wheels of our plane touched down in Rock Sound Airport in Eleuthera, I was already two rum drinks into holiday mode. We stepped off the plane into blinding sun, and there, on the tarmac, was Maxey. He gave a huge hug to Singer. I put out my hand. He brushed it aside and gave me a huge hug as well.

"I really hate that, you know," I reminded him.

It took us a good half hour to make it the fifty yards from the tarmac to Maxey's jeep because Maxey stopped to chat with everyone in our path. Was the baggage handler's mom on the mend after surgery? Would Maxey mind if a group from the local school came by that Thursday? Did he catch any grouper he might want to share—that last one was crazy delicious? How were his kids? How were their kids?

"What are you, the mayor?" Singer said.

"Man, I love it here," Maxey said. "And no, I'm not the mayor. They don't have mayors. We have our local Rock Sound administrator. If you were staying longer, we could go hang out with him—he's awesome. The school wouldn't exist without him. But since you buttheads are here for only a day and a couple of nights you just get me."

Singer called shotgun (what were we, twelve?) but then gave it to me, after Maxey threw our overnight bags in the back of his jeep. The side was emblazoned with THE ISLAND SCHOOL logo.

The ride from the Rock Sound Airport to the school is about forty minutes, through a landscape that varies from lush to arid and is dotted with settlements consisting of a few houses with a small general store. When we would come to these, Maxey would slow down so he could exchange greetings with whoever was gathered outside. I remembered Pam's descriptions of the job Maxey had had working for Ross Perot, when he'd had to wear a suit, and go to an office, and sit in conference rooms, and create reports: how the pressure had caused him to get so dizzy that he passed out. Seeing him in shorts and flip-flops behind the wheel of a jeep, shouting pleasantries to friends who shouted them back just as loudly and exuberantly, made me realize how out of his element Maxey must have been.

Yet at the same time he was a little less exuberant than usual. When none of us were talking, there was silence in the car—not the ridiculous bursts of song Maxey usually produced to fill up every moment of airtime.

After about a half hour, we came to a simple, squat white building with a bright blue door. There was a sign out front: DEEP CREEK MIDDLE SCHOOL. This, Maxey explained, was the other school they had started.

Service had been part of the program right from the beginning of the Island School, and some of it involved the older students—from abroad and the few from the Bahamas—working with the sixth-graders in South Eleuthera, helping them with their studies and even teaching them how to snorkel and swim, skills many of them didn't have. But then it became clear that the older students were getting far more out of it than the local kids they were tutoring. This was especially true for the overseas mentors, who would form bonds with the local kids only to return home to their regular lives; the sixth-graders who had been tutored would feel abandoned. At the same time, these younger kids were graduating from small, neighborhood primary schools to join a few hundred other students in a school that went from seventh to twelfth grade, where they would be the littlest ones, and where most of the oxygen was taken up by the high schoolers.

A board member had challenged Maxey to ask his neighbors what they really wanted for their kids and the answer was overwhelming: they wanted a local middle school where the kids in Deep Creek could learn with other kids the same age and have access to a first-class program built around the kinds of learning Maxey was offering at the Island School.

An educator who had been helping run the Island School's service outreach program became the middle school's first principal, convincing the board to fund it. The Bahamas Ministry of Education loved the idea, and gave Deep Creek Middle School full accreditation. Maxey's daughter Brittney was in the first class of students.

The two schools were intertwined, Maxey said. But if he could have only built one, it would have been Deep Creek Middle School.

EVENTUALLY, WE DROVE past the Island School—Maxey would show us that later—and then over a small bridge toward a little spit of land sticking out into the ocean where he and

Pam lived. In front of us was a cul-de-sac, and Maxey pulled the car in tight outside an open garage filled with bits and pieces of boat—sails, motors, life preservers—and with bicycles, boxes, and dry goods. He then led us across a few pavers into the house, a small, two-level townhouse attached to identical houses on both sides, that looked out at boats, moorings, a marina, and the wide ocean in the distance.

The house was clearly decorated by Pam—teal and cream walls, blue wicker chairs, a sea-green couch with a bright assortment of pillows, and a tile coffee table decorated with shells and plants. In fact, there were shells and plants everywhere.

"Pam sends her love," Maxey said. "And the kids, too. It's just us guys." This struck me as odd, but I said nothing.

He then showed me to one of his kids' rooms and Singer to another. Next he told us there were some house rules we needed to follow:

"If it's brown, flush it down; if it's yellow, let it mellow. I'm not kidding. We don't have much water. So, don't be city kids. Oh, and navy showers. That means you get wet; you turn off the water. Then you soap up. Then you turn on the water just long enough to get the soap off you."

"Anything else?" Singer asked.

"Yeah, we don't drink alcohol before we go to the school, and we never drink in front of the students."

"Anything else?" I asked.

"Oh, yeah, just one more thing. Morning exercise is really important to me. It's part of what makes us a community. It grounds us. Everyone does it. It would be really meaningful to me if you both took part tomorrow morning. Really. It would mean a lot to me."

Singer—mountain climber, soccer player, marathon runner—didn't hesitate for a second before saying, "Of course, Maxey." So I followed suit. "Morning exercise" sounded kind of appealing. Stretching a bit while it was still cool. There might be a breeze off the ocean. Building up a little appetite before breakfast. How bad could it be?

"I'm parched—a beer?" I asked.

"First, the tour."

We piled back in the jeep and went over to the school, now just over five years old. They had added several buildings since I'd last seen pictures. Maxey drove us past THE ISLAND SCHOOL sign down a long dirt road to a small, covered area where a few cars were parked. There wasn't much in the way of landscaping—Maxey said that a recent storm had taken out most of the plants, so they had just replanted. All the planting needed to be local, of course.

"Awesome school," Singer commented. "Shame you don't have any students."

"Yeah, where are the students?" I asked.

"They have to go off every afternoon for a few hours—they are supposed to wander—explore—get lost. Before they arrive, we have them read Barry Lopez's *Rediscovery of North America.* The idea of having them wander on their own every day comes from that. They're in this amazing place and I want them to see it for themselves, every day. And I want them to come back and have things to tell each other. And things to tell me. I want to learn from them and I want them to learn from each other. I want them to have adventures. But it's not just about wandering; at the start of the term, we tell each student to find a quiet place, their own place, and they have to go there for several hours every week—to read, draw, sleep, I don't care. But each one has to choose a special place to be alone for those hours, a *querencia.* That's also inspired by Barry Lopez; he explains that *querencia* is a physical place where you go to seek safety and gain strength. So that's why you don't see anyone—they are either exploring or in their quiet place, their *querencia.*"

We walked through the school's kitchen and the large pavilion where every meal is served; we saw the building that housed the school's offices and a few of the classrooms; we went into one of the boys' dorms. All of the buildings sat along a sandy beach and beyond them the ocean stretched from side to side and out to the horizon. The dorm we entered was set back a bit from the dining hall, and was spare with rows of bunks. I left Singer and Maxey and wandered over to the far side of the room, where there was some heavy netting hanging from the ceiling at eye level. Inside there seemed to be a large bundle of clothes. As I went over to examine it, something that looked like a human arm shot out from the bundle. I screamed as a small person leaped out of what I now realized was a hammock, landing at my feet.

The little human greeted Maxey, with a shy smile, and then apologized for scaring me.

"So now," said Maxey, "you've seen one of the faculty kids taking advantage of the empty dorm." Maxey then turned to the lad. "As you were!" The lad gave Maxey a high five and climbed back up into the hammock.

"Do you do the military thing with all of them?" I asked.

"Never," said Maxey. "Just messing with you."

As the last stop on our tour, Maxey brought us to a boat-house that jutted out over a small cove. Several kayaks were suspended overhead—and life preservers were neatly stacked like little skyscrapers, creating a small cityscape. There was a closed area at one end, and inside I could see scuba tanks and gear, piles of flippers, and assorted tubs of suntan lotion and bug repellent.

While Maxey was showing Singer the scuba stuff, I walked to the side of the boathouse. Beyond the cove, the water stretched out in gleaming bands of emerald, sapphire, and aquamarine. In the distance there were some fishermen in a small boat. I found myself almost dizzy from the brilliance of the sun on that expanse of water.

"Nice, huh?" said Maxey. "We still have everyone read *Omeros* during the three months they're here. I love that when Walcott writes about a conch fisherman, and they read about him, they can come to this spot and see the conch fishermen for themselves, and they can meet them, and talk to them. I love that they read someone who grew up in the Caribbean, who is sharing with them the most meaningful stories his home has to offer—any place has to offer—about being human. I love that when they get here that epic poem makes them think about home, what home is, and that the earth is our home. And about the weight of history."

Maxey recited a few lines he'd memorized:

> *Oh open this day with the conch's moan, Omeros*
> *as you did in my boyhood, when I was a noun*
> *gently exhaled from the palate of the sunrise.*

As Maxey continued to talk about *Omeros,* Singer and I both stood quietly, listening to him, and looking out at the stillest water I had ever seen create an ocean. I was certain that Singer was going to stop him, make fun of him, or just ask if we could go back to the house and finally have a beer. But Singer didn't. Maxey talked about the conch shell's invocation and discussed the light that gave the fisherman Achille happiness, the same light right before us. He talked about the way Walcott wrote about wounds and afflictions.

I suspected this was a talk he gave to the students to introduce them to the poem that meant so much to him, but I also felt that it was important to him to share these works with us during our time with him; Maxey was clearly wounded in some way and wanted me to know, even if he wasn't ready to talk about it directly.

Finally, Maxey stopped talking and just stared at the ocean. There we were, three friends on the wrong side of forty, with our eyes fixed on the horizon, which was growing harder and harder to see as the sun was melting behind us.

"Let me show you one more thing," Maxey said. He took us down to the boats to point out one that was named *Dave and Di*. When that letter came from Maxey those years before, Singer and his wife, Diana, had sent a check—and now had a boat named after them. I was even more sorry than before that I had waited so long to send a check or give my friend support of any kind when he was building the school of his dreams.

"NOW WE CAN toast your arrival," said Maxey as soon as we were home.

First up were the Kaliks, the beer of the Bahamas. At some point, Maxey produced a bottle of rum. He also came up with some spiny lobsters and some grouper that he'd either caught or had been given to him. We grilled those. A bottle of wine was opened and drunk. After dinner, we found ourselves sitting outside, the three of us, dangling our legs over the edge of the dock. Maxey pointed a flashlight beam at the water so we could see the bull sharks and nurse sharks swimming right below our feet. We talked almost nonstop, but when we were quiet, I listened to the sounds of the water slapping up against the pylons, regular as a heartbeat, and the occasional grinding of a boat against the planks. It was a hot night and I felt as though I could happily slide into the water—but for the sharks.

"They won't hurt you," Maxey said, able to read my thoughts.

"I'm good," I assured him.

It was then that Maxey decided to share with me a wound that wasn't healing: he told me why Pam wasn't there. Singer already knew the whole story, but he hadn't informed me because it wasn't his story to tell. Over the years, Singer and Maxey had become much closer than Maxey and I had. I wondered if perhaps it was because Singer, like Maxey, was straight and had kids, whereas Maxey might have thought that I wouldn't understand all he was going through. But Singer and I had grown much closer over the years, too, so maybe it had nothing to do with kids. Perhaps Singer was better at this kind of long-distance friendship than Maxey or me. He was certainly less self-absorbed than either of us.

"Pam is a really beautiful person inside and out, and we're both totally comfortable with each other. Right from the start, we loved having fun. And we both love the ocean. I mean, when we met, she even tried to teach me how to surf and that was pretty funny; I couldn't even sit on the board, and every time a wave came it would sweep me off and wash the board back to the beach. After a few hours of that, she told me, 'Maybe you should just bodysurf.'

"We loved the ocean. We loved each other. We both wanted kids. Pam really wanted to be a mom, and I knew she would be a great one. Right from the start, we were a team; it was the two of us against the world. When we got married in Subic Bay, when I was on that first Pacific tour in the navy, it was this super small wedding: the ship's captain married us, my assistant platoon officer was my best man, and the base commodore's wife was Pam's maid of honor. Then we came back and had a small family wedding in San Diego, just a party in the backyard of the Admiral's house with our families and a few buddies, and started our life."

"Yeah, thanks so much for inviting us," said Singer.

"We only invited a few local friends, butthead," Maxey said.

"Then we went to the Defense Language Institute in Monterey to learn Spanish together—that was one of the reasons we were eager to get married. Pam found an apartment for us in Pacific Grove and we moved up there. It was an awesome way to start a marriage, and we were still a team, but it became really challenging because we were literally in school together. We were even in the same class together. We were basically together 24/7. We had this wonderful teacher from Spain who became kind of a surrogate mother to us. She knew the tension that exists in a new couple. Pam and I also have such different personalities. Pam is super smart and doesn't have to be onstage, and I'm always struggling to feel smart and always have to be onstage.

"So, I think at the end of the day, even though I did all the homework and was more engaged, Pam did as well or better in the class than I did. And I wasn't good about that. There were also times at the end of a class when Pam would say to me, 'You were an asshole in there. You've got to shut up.' After a while we got really out of sync. I mean, literally. Our diurnal phase is very different, and sometimes that's great and sometimes it's really challenging. Pam can stay up all night long. I get up early in the morning. It's not necessarily that I'm a morning person, but I override whatever fatigue I have with just crazy singing and jumping around; the more tired I am the more I act like an idiot. I want to turn music on—and she is like: 'Do not talk to me. Do not say anything. Do not turn on music. Shut up.'

"After that, we were stationed in Panama and had Britters. So, once again, it was us against the world. There was that crazy time when Pam and Brittney had to evacuate back to the U.S. in the middle of the night with only a few hours' notice—but even that brought us closer together."

I realized I still didn't understand what had happened in Panama during Maxey's deployment and why Pam had to evacuate, but now was not the time to ask.

"Then we moved to Texas, where I had the office job with Ross Perot, and then Brocq was born and then Tyler five years later in Lawrenceville and then Tegan while I was in graduate school and then we started the school. During all those years, we never had much conflict. But we never really talked either. We weren't really a team anymore. Just two people in constant motion.

"After Tegan started to walk, it was the end of our bringing life into the world. That hit us pretty hard, but it hit Pam really hard. There was some postpartum depression and

I mostly ignored it. I was focused on the school, only on the school, and working like a maniac. That was true before Hurricane Floyd, but a million times more so after. My mind was always elsewhere—with the students, the faculty, raising money, dreaming up new buildings, research, conservation, and everything that goes with being the leader of a school. It's a massive ego trip and I loved it. And the more depressed Pam was, the more time I spent at the school.

"So here she was, really depressed and kind of just shutting down, and she also had to deal with the loss of her husband—because I was married to the school at that point and not to her—and the loss of her ability to bring more kids into the world. I mean, she could have continued to have kids, but I made the move to get snipped and we both came to recognize the reality that our last child was Tegan, which had been our plan. But none of this was anything we ever really discussed, and I poured fuel on the flames because I wasn't willing to talk. I just was like, 'You should go get help.'"

I noted that Maxey had said "you" and not "we."

"The way I said it to Pam it was like an accusation: *You. You're the problem.* I wasn't that direct, but that was the message she was getting. Then it got really bad. Really bad. Eventually she just needed to go for a while. So, the first thing she did was pack her bags and return to New Jersey to get some space. And I stayed here with all four kids."

"I'm so sorry," I said. And then added, "I wish I'd known." But I regretted saying that. It sounded like I was criticizing Maxey for not telling me. Maxey said nothing for a while and then continued.

"Brittney was in eighth grade at Deep Creek Middle School and the other three kids were in the local primary school. We found a great Bahamian lady who came in and helped. It was so hard for Pam. I mean she needed space for herself away from me, but to get that meant literally giving up, for a little while, what was most important to her, our kids. While she was back in New Jersey, she was running admissions for the Island School and she lived in a little apartment that was also the office for the school. Pam was handling the school's finances, too. Pam talked to our kids every day. After three months, she came back to Eleuthera for the first time, and after that, she would go back and forth. When she was here, she would live in the house with the kids and I moved to a neighbor's house. She was very clear. She told me, 'I need space away from you and I want to be with our kids, so when I'm here you need to get out.'

"After a while she came to me and said she didn't want the kids growing up down here without her. She told me that I never gave them enough time before and she didn't see how I would be able to give them enough time now.

"The two older kids had been away at camp when she told me this—my parents had spent some money to have them go to this rawhide camp out West—and they'd had a great time. Brittney was thirteen and Brocq was eleven. When I went to pick them up, I said, 'Your mom and I are getting separated for real, and Mom's going to move you guys up to the States along with Tyler and Tegan, and I want you to tell me how you feel about this.' Brittney was very matter-of-fact and was like, 'Yeah, I'm ready, I've done the Island School thing; I should go up there and work toward getting into Lawrenceville,' and Brocq was the opposite. He said, 'Dad, I can't leave the island. I'll die up there.' I convinced Pam that it was okay for Brocq to stay, and that's what happened. Brocq stayed here with me for two years while Brittney and the little girls went back to the U.S. So we became a ripped-apart family, and I just have to handle the fact that it's my fault.

"Still, we made sure the kids talked all the time and got together a lot during those two years, and Pam and I have stayed connected on many levels. Pam still does the admissions for the school. Brocq's now back in the States for good with Pam and his sisters. He's in eighth grade and will go to high school there, too. I'm not going to get Pam back, but we're doing our best for the family. A friend has loaned me a garage apartment in New Jersey, so I can spend lots of time with our children. We know we are so damn lucky because we have the greatest kids."

I counted the years—David and I had been together for seventeen years. We didn't have children. We hadn't started a school or company together. We had our share of arguments, some major and some trivial. I didn't feel I had any good advice to give Maxey. I just said again that I was sorry, that it must be difficult, especially with the kids.

Singer had much more to say, and I noted how nuanced his thinking had become since our school days. This wasn't the pugnacious, argumentative guy who had entered our lives all those years ago—this was a different David Singer. He started by saying that, yes, it sounded like Maxey did screw up, in a big way—but that we all screw up in different ways, that life is just screwing up again and again, but maybe we can learn each time something about ourselves and the world. He didn't hold back, either, with his admiration for Pam. Not in an accusatory "She's right and you're wrong" way, nor in a wistful "You had something great but you blew it" way, but rather to acknowledge that Maxey's sadness was justified: that Singer recognized that Maxey had every reason to be sad. He would be happy again, of course. But the loss was real.

I think that's when the bottle of rum reappeared. The last time I looked at my watch it was one a.m. We had been drinking steadily for nearly eight hours.

I WOKE TO machine-gun fire. Or maybe it was fireworks in my ear. Or maybe it was someone hitting my head with a mallet.

"Wake up, wake up, wake up—time to exercise!"

It was Maxey. Pounding on the door.

My heart was racing. My head was throbbing. I was pouring with sweat. My sheets were bunched up around my legs. I didn't quite know where I was.

"Wake up, wake up, wake up—coffee's on—we leave in ten minutes."

Maxey kept banging.

"Oh, Maxey," I groaned. "I can't, I just don't think I can do this. I need to sleep."

There was a pause. The banging on the door stopped. Then silence.

I lay in bed for a minute and replayed in my mind the conversation from the day before about how morning exercise wasn't just exercise, it was part of what made the school a community. I thought about how Maxey had said how much it would mean to him if Singer and I took part. I thought about how I knew Singer would do it, and then I would feel like a real schmuck: the friend who didn't. I thought about all Maxey had shared with us just a few hours ago. And I thought, again, *How bad could it be?* A little jog, a little stretching, and then I could blissfully go back to bed for a few hours.

I shouted that I was coming and to wait for me, threw on

some shorts, a T-shirt, some sneakers, had some aspirin, chugged coffee Maxey had left for me, and met him outside the house, where he and Singer were stretching in the dark. I stretched, too.

A few minutes later, we were off. We jogged at a modest pace and I had a little trouble keeping up but felt good. My head cleared. It was going to be a beautiful morning. Before I knew it, there was the school sign, signaling the end of the run. Waiting for us were a group of students and the faculty, though I could barely tell the one group from the other, partly because the sun hadn't yet risen, but also because they all looked about twelve to me.

Then, disturbingly, the group started jogging away from the school, down the road, in the direction of the airport.

"Where are we heading?" I asked Maxey.

"We are going off on our run," he answered.

"I thought we just did the run!"

"Oh, no, that was just how we got to the school. Now we are doing the run."

I didn't ask how long the run would be. I knew I wouldn't like the answer. I started sweating profusely. I thought I was going to vomit. After about twenty minutes, I started to fall way behind. Maxey fell behind with me, saying his knee was bothering him. I don't think his knee was bothering him. After an hour we were still running. My legs were cramping. I didn't think I was going to make it. We did, however, seem to be running in something of a loop. I figured we would eventually be back at the school. The sun was rising and it was already getting hot.

"Almost there," said Maxey, not at all out of breath.

"How far are we running?" I asked, gasping for air.

"Just five miles," Maxey answered.

And then, finally, at last, we were done. The rest of the group was by the side of the road, shifting from foot to foot. Curiously, they seemed to be perched on the edge of a cliff. Not quite back at the school, but close to it. I walked up to them, clutching my side.

When I looked over the cliff, I saw some of the runners swimming.

Suddenly I realized that, one by one, the runners were jumping off the cliff. They were going to swim back to school. "Oh, hell, no," I said.

I looked at Maxey, who laughed.

Maxey, Singer, and I walked back. Singer didn't seem too winded; I was still struggling to fill my lungs and my legs were starting to stiffen. But soon we were approaching the circular courtyard in front of the school. The sun had risen quickly, and there was no shade to be found where we were standing. In the distance was the dining hall; I saw eggs and a lot more coffee in my future. Maybe some tropical fruit?

"Whoa, where you going?" Maxey asked me.

"Breakfast!" I replied joyfully.

"Well, if you must. But we've already missed most of morning circle; that's the ritual we do every morning. We circle around the flagpole at six thirty before the sun comes up over the water. Every day a different student leader calls us all together; then the students count off so we make sure everyone is accounted for; and then there are announcements. Then we all sing together the Bahamian national anthem, which is actually a beautiful song—not about war, like ours, but about lifting your head to the rising sun, pledging to excel with love and unity, marching sunward even though the weather may hide treacherous shoals, and finally reaching your God. Love that it says 'your God' and not just 'God.' Then we do some stretching, basic yoga poses; we're just in time for that."

"Maxey, I don't have a clue how to do yoga."

"Don't worry," he said. "I'll walk you through it. I do yoga every day now. And meditation, too. The key is breathing. Just follow me. And just do your best. It's not a competition. But remember to breathe."

We joined the dusty, sweaty circle. The student leader was guiding us all through the stretching. Child's pose. Downward dog. Warrior. Sun salutation. I looked over at her but was constantly back to front, or stumbling forward or backward. Maxey kept looking over at me, and when he did, he would let out a big breath, reminding me to breathe. I kept forgetting to do that. My muscles were screaming. Sweat was pouring down my face. I found I couldn't hold any of the poses—it was like everyone around the circle was made of wire and I was made of dough. Then I would catch Maxey's eye. He would breathe, and I would breathe along with him.

Now that the sun was higher in the sky, catching gleaming, dust-covered faces, I looked again at Maxey and almost didn't recognize him. Something about him was different, but I couldn't put my finger on it. It was him, but it wasn't him. Maxey and not-Maxey.

Then I realized what it was. That kid I had met who bounced around the hall, who leaped from sofa to chair, who couldn't sit at a table for ten whole minutes, who interrupted silence with loud snatches of song: that kid had learned to be still.

Could a Maxey who wasn't in motion really be Maxey? There was another Maxey I was going to need to get to know.

This was the first time I'd ever really visited Maxey in his world. At college, our secret society's hall was so exotic and preposterous that it belonged to all of us together but to none of us in particular; maybe that's part of the reason we could all be ourselves there.

After graduation, aside from reunions, we'd met entirely in my New York City neighborhood's bars and restaurants. I'd known Maxey for more than twenty years but until that weekend had never been in his home.

What surprised me was how much I liked Maxey's world: I'd barely had an awake moment to myself since I'd arrived, but I'd enjoyed being part of a boisterous group; my muscles were sore from the run and the yoga, but that felt good, too. Granted, I couldn't ever see David and me living by the ocean, surrounded by kids and teachers, greeting the sun and swimming with sharks, but I could certainly picture us visiting often, and perhaps even bringing a bit of this world back into our own each time.

It was no accident that Singer had brought Maxey and me back together time and time again; he straddled both our worlds and was equally comfortable in each. Plus, he was like an Australian sheep dog, compelled to keep the herd together.

But with this new perspective came regret: Maxey had four kids I'd never met. I'd missed a whole chapter of his life. It was no one's fault; it was just a fact. We were in our forties now. I wondered if we could make up for lost time or if, instead, we'd missed the chance to be closer friends.

TRIALS

In fall 2005, nine months after our visit to Eleuthera, Singer was in town for business, and we went out for dinner and drinks—except that Singer was hardly drinking. He was now a vegan and ridiculously trim.

"How's Maxey?" I asked.

"Not well. You know how he said he didn't think Pam would ever come back. Well, he really hoped she would. But he says it's now pretty clear that she's not coming back. I just talked to him. They're getting divorced. They go before a judge in a few weeks."

"Should I call him?"

"Yeah, I think you should," Singer said.

But I didn't.

I did consider it but decided I had best not. I thought: Maxey hadn't confided in me, he'd confided again in Singer. If he wanted me to know, then he would have told me. Maybe he found the whole thing embarrassing. I knew how much he loved Pam and how much he was hoping things would work out. Would he really want me to know they didn't? Better not to call. I thought back to the Maxey I'd seen during morning yoga: calm, quiet, in control. He would reach out to me if he wanted.

Weeks later, the phone rang.

It was Singer.

We chatted about this and that. Singer's kids. I told him more work woes. This time he cut me off quickly.

"You didn't call Maxey, did you?"

"No, I thought maybe he didn't want me to know what was going on. I mean, he told you first, not me."

"He's hurting. A lot. Just fucking call him."

So I did.

The call started awkwardly. We chatted about the school a bit. I got the lowdown on all his kids. Brocq was longing to get back to Eleuthera. In the two years he'd spent there with his dad, when he wasn't attending classes at Deep Creek Middle School, he'd spent every spare second in or on the water, surfacing only from time to time to eat, sleep, and prepare to get back out to sea.

Maxey then said things had been really rough for a lot of reasons. I told him I had heard from Singer that he and Pam had given up on getting back together and were now getting divorced.

"We just did," he said. "It was nuts. The whole thing. I started out by meeting with Pam's lawyer. And this lawyer was going on and on about the school, and how beautiful it was, and how a neighbor on her street had sent her kid there and all, and how many boats we had. I was thinking, 'Wow, I know this is Pam's lawyer, but she seems really cool.' Then, all of a sudden, it was like her head twisted around, like the girl in *The Exorcist*—"

"Blair, Linda Blair—played Regan," I offered.

"Yeah, whatever." Maxey continued. "And this lawyer gets right up in my face and asks me, 'How much is the school worth?' I told her that I didn't know, because it's a not-for-profit, all built through donations, a 501c3. Pam told her the same. This lawyer just could not get it—she had to call an accountant to find out what a 501c3 was—and then she realized that I have no money—that I have no savings—that Pam and I barely pay ourselves a salary—just enough to live on—that it all goes into the school. The whole conversation was awful for Pam—she kept trying to step in and kept saying to her lawyer, 'He's telling the truth, he's not lying,' and I was like, 'Holy shit,' but then it dawned on Pam's lawyer that I truly have no fucking money. You could see the lawyer's face fall. I mean, to be fair to her, she was just trying to do right by Pam. And she must have been thinking, 'This poor woman has four kids and she's divorcing a guy who got so obsessed with his work that he basically took her for granted—and he doesn't have shit except a pathetic salary that could disappear any second and not even a military pension, which would have been great, but he would have needed to stay in for twenty years to get it, and he was only in for six.'"

"So what did your lawyer say?" I asked Maxey.

"Here's the thing: I don't have a lawyer."

"Maxey, I love Pam, but are you serious? You didn't have a lawyer represent you in the divorce?"

"I went to one of my lawyer buddies, and he said the same, said I shouldn't go into this alone, and he referred me to a guy. I called him, but within minutes I had to say, 'I'm sorry, I've got to get off this call.' I mean, this guy did what any divorce lawyer does. He said, 'Tell me a little about your wife, is she dating someone, does she drink a lot, does she do drugs?' And I said, 'Dude, she's going to be my ex-wife soon, but she's the love of my life and the mother of my kids. What the fuck are you doing?'"

There was quiet. Maxey said nothing. I said nothing. I wondered if we'd lost the connection.

"Sorry," Maxey continued. "I get emotional. So, I figured fuck it. I went into the divorce proceedings without a lawyer.

In the courtroom, the judge said, 'Are you sure you don't want to be represented?' And I said, 'Yes, Your Honor, I'm sure I don't want to be represented.' She asked me three times and had me answer three times. Just so it would be clear and on the record. Then I said to the judge, 'Just give her whatever she wants; she deserves all of it and more.' But since I don't have anything, the best thing Pam's lawyer could do was maximize my contribution based on my salary. We agreed on a sum and that's for life. She can marry a gazillionaire and she still gets it, every month, for life."

"And custody? The kids?" I asked.

"That was classic Pam. She never wanted anything but joint custody. That's what she asked for. We're going to do what's best for the kids. We're also going to continue working together for the school. She's going to continue doing admissions and all the other stuff she does. So, yeah, there was a lawyer on her side and there wasn't one on mine, but she didn't beat me up. She didn't ask for anything that wasn't more than fair."

"And how are you doing, Maxey?"

"Other than the fact that I just fucked up my whole life? Great."

I thought Maxey was crazy for not hiring a lawyer, but I admired him for it. And I was glad that I had called him and that he felt he could share his wounds. I didn't know what I could do or say, but I wanted to be a better friend—without Singer needing to prod me. Maxey and I agreed we would talk much more often. I was looking forward to doing that, and to visiting Maxey again in Eleuthera and as soon as time and money allowed. David was also eager to see the island and spend time there. After two years, we finally made plans. But they were almost immediately scuttled.

*   *   *

MY MOTHER WAS diagnosed with stage four pancreatic cancer in October 2007. For months before, we'd allowed ourselves to believe that she had hepatitis, that she just needed to rest, that all would be fine. But while I was out of the country for work, she had called to tell me her diagnosis. I read on the Internet that most people with pancreatic cancer that had spread to other organs survive only for three to six months.

Two months later, I quit my job in order to start a cooking website. I had been doing the same work for more than twenty years and worried that if I didn't try something different, I would wake up at sixty-five or seventy and wish I had. I also wanted the flexibility to spend more time with my mother, for whatever time she had left. David had his salary and I would do freelance editing.

When Maxey heard from Singer that my mother had cancer, he called me and told me he was there for me. I remember I was really glad to hear from him and grateful for the call. I knew he would be. I told him that.

As much as I wanted to keep in touch with Maxey, Singer, and friends who lived in other places, I found myself unable. Mom's illness narrowed my focus. It was hard to make plans, especially ones that needed to be set far in advance. It was also hard to brief friends on the phone because Mom's treatment was a roller-coaster; relatively good days were followed by dreadful ones, so someone who wasn't up to date would come away thinking things were much better or worse than they were. This meant I constantly needed to explain or correct, which I found exhausting. I started posting updates on my mother's condition to a blog I'd created for that purpose, but I included almost nothing about myself—other than to mention some of the books we were reading together. I simply didn't have the energy to reach out to people who weren't immediately at hand.

During that time, as I would only later find out, Maxey's life was also spinning out of control. He and Pam had both been dating people they really cared about. The woman he'd been seeing lived in Princeton, which allowed him to spend more time with his kids: Brittney was studying in Argentina, but the younger three were all still at school in New Jersey. Then his new girlfriend tossed him out. She told him that he was clearly still in love with Pam and that wasn't fair to her.

As Maxey would eventually tell me, "That's when I really got adrift. I mean, I just felt I didn't have any ability to get back with Pam so I started dating another woman, a much less serious relationship than the one I'd had in Princeton. Then I drove my motorcycle off a road and crashed it. I wasn't trying to hurt myself—I just crashed it the way I was crashing everything in my life. You start messing one thing up, and then you start messing everything else up, too."

BACK ON THE ROOF, AGAIN

In the spring of 2009, we had a twenty-fifth college reunion. I wasn't at all sure I wanted to go. Although it was miraculous that my mother was still alive, almost a year and a half after her diagnosis, now she was dying more quickly: it seemed likely that she wouldn't live to see the end of the year. Leading my life day to day took all my energy: the last thing I wanted to do was to be forced to reflect on it. Also, my new business was in desperate shape.

Then I changed my mind and decided to attend, just for a day. I love seeing what happens to people over time: who looks old, who stays young, who tells you they've changed completely when obviously they haven't changed at all. Mostly, though, it was because I ached for the me who had just graduated and was heading off into the world. True, that boy had yet to meet David, the man with whom he'd spend his life, but he also was yet to have a failing business and a dying mother and the feeling that whatever work he'd already done was the best he would ever do.

I made a plan to hitch a ride up and back with two friends: a classmate and his wife. We would go to a lecture in the morning to hear reflections from people in our year who had distinguished themselves enough that they could describe their accomplishments with ostentatious self-deprecation, then would attend the big class lunch. After, I would peel off to visit my secret society and see who was hanging out there. I would then meet up with the rest of my classmates for drinks and dinner and head back to New York City, with the two-hour drive to compare uncharitable notes.

By the time I got to the hall, I was hot, sweaty, and cranky. Too much bonhomie, too much forced nostalgia, too much sitting in uncomfortable chairs listening to classmates I had never met. Maxey was already there, perched uneasily on the sofa, beer in hand. When I entered, he stood up but winced. He didn't bound toward me to give me the usual uncomfortable hug. I stuck out my hand for a handshake.

"Great to see you, Maxey," I said.

"You too, Schwalbs."

"Where is everyone?"

"Up on the roof, I think. Let's head on up."

This time, Pam wasn't there to help me climb up to the roof. I didn't even try to carry a beer with me; someone else would have to supply the beverages. I yanked myself up the steel ladder, a rung at a time. Happily, someone had brought up not only beers but a cooler as well. And the beers themselves were Heineken. We weren't just getting older; the beers were getting better.

Maxey climbed up after me but didn't sit, instead looming awkwardly over me. After a while, I stood up again so we could talk. He seemed very uncomfortable.

"How are you doing, Schwalbs?" he finally asked.

"Not too bad," I said. "You?"

"Not too bad," Maxey said. "How's your mom?"

So I told him. How it looked like she didn't have many months left; about the books she and I had read together; and about the way she always described herself as lucky. I then launched into a litany of complaints about my start-up, how drained I was, how it was failing.

Finally, when I'd talked myself out, I told Maxey, "I've got to sit."

Again, I saw that pained expression on Maxey's face. Had I been too frank and too verbose and too much of a downer?

I plopped myself down on the roof. Maxey lowered himself awkwardly next to me, resting his full body weight on his hands, like a gymnast on a pommel horse, so that he could stretch both legs straight out in front. Odd.

"New hips," he said. "The old ones got completely ground down, so I got them replaced in March."

Maxey wasn't uncomfortable with what I'd shared with him. He was just plain uncomfortable.

"Wow. Painful?"

"Not at all. I just have to remember not to cross my legs or they'll pop out of their sockets. I did that once. Now *that* was painful."

"I guess that's the price of being in shape, huh? You're the one who's falling apart."

"Nice," Maxey said. "But true. Maybe I should have taken a page from your book and not been such a lunatic with all the physical fitness." He paused. "Actually, things are a bit hard these days. I don't know."

"You mean about Pam?" I said.

"Yeah. But when the kids go on vacation, we all go together. People always say, 'This is super fucked up that you go on vacation with each other, aren't you guys divorced?' But it works for us."

"And the school?"

"It's amazing. The students are amazing. It's growing like crazy. Pam and I still work together on that, but you know, she's in Lawrenceville with all the kids."

I saw Maxey wince again, but this time the pain wasn't physical.

"Something terrible happened a few years back. I never told you about it, but I want you to know," he said. "Brocq had this awesome best friend. They took one of the boats out fishing. They were twelve. The engine cut off when they were in the deep; the wind was blowing offshore and so the boat was being swept quickly out to sea. When they first tried the radio, it wasn't working. They thought they would swim for shore. But it was much farther than they thought. Brocq's friend was struggling. Brocq tried to help him. He couldn't help him. Brocq made it back to the boat. His friend didn't. As soon as he was back, the radio started to work. Brocq immediately called for help. But it was too late. They had life jackets on the boat but they'd felt they could swim better without them."

I didn't know what to say.

"Brocq was crushed. I was crushed. His friend's family are devastated. It's all my fault. Everything is my fault. I can't make this right. I can never make this right."

My mother had just turned seventy-five and it was clear she wouldn't see seventy-six. But she was going to die before her three children. I thought of the parents of Brocq's friend, whose son drowned while he had decades of life before him. I thought of Maxey. I wanted to ask him if he felt responsible so I could try to reassure him, as I would do with any friend, and say that bad things happen and that this wasn't his fault. But I knew he knew that really terrible things happen, and I also think he would have argued with me that it *was* his fault.

"You know, I also can't help but think back to that terrible night on the airfield in Panama," he said. I nodded, even though in fact I had no idea what had happened there. It still didn't seem like the right time to ask.

Dusk fell. We climbed down the ladder and left the hall, with the huge wooden door slamming shut behind us. I remember noting Maxey's slow, painful steps as he walked away from me and rounded the corner toward campus. I didn't see him again before I left New Haven after the class dinner.

On the ride home with my friends we talked about our classmates—lingering on those whose annoying tics had grown more extreme. All the while, I was distracted; I kept thinking about the family of the child who drowned, and Brocq, and Maxey, and my sense that I'd failed him. I wondered if there was something I could have said that might have given some comfort.

I was supposed to be the words guy, and I'd always believed that I could find the right ones. More and more, I was discovering that, just as Maxey's body was failing him, words were starting to fail me. I was beginning to think that, no matter how much I trusted the power of language, there were situations in which nothing I could say would make things any better—and that what I said might even make things worse.

ON SEPTEMBER 14, MY mother died of pancreatic cancer at age seventy-five. We'd had almost two years to say goodbye and spend time together, but it still came as a shock, an untethering. I told everyone I was fine. I wasn't.

I was also struggling with my cooking website. We owed money to our developers. We owed money to our designers. We were being audited by New York State because we used so many freelancers. I was desperately trying to get funding from venture capitalists.

I was worn out from the months of sleepless nights worrying about my mother before her death but also from being woken up at two o'clock in the morning when the website crashed. We'd made a few big deals for the website content and they were our lifeline, but they required that the site be up and running every second of every day. If the site went down, I would get a blaring alert on my cell phone. I would then have to scramble to find one of the developers and convince him to leave whatever bar he was in to fix it. David didn't like our mealtimes interrupted but was an extraordinarily good sport about the middle-of-the-night alarms.

And on many nights, when I did finally sleep, the angel with the rusty knife by his bed would appear in my dreams. He had reentered my life right after my mother's diagnosis. Fortunately, I always awoke gasping for air just before he plunged the knife into my heart.

In the days after my mother died, I kept up a frantic schedule, but the busyness didn't distract from my grief; it magnified it. And my usual insomnia was worse than ever; my endless sleeplessness gave me ample time for remorse and regret. I spent my hours awake at nighttime for days after her death torturing myself over things I should have said and done differently, cues I'd missed, opportunities to have been of more comfort.

CHAPTER FOUR

Forties

DRINKS WITH SINGER

It was always on the coldest winter days that I heard from Singer. On this particularly brutal January day in 2010, four months after my mother's death, his email was short: "Old man," it said. "Coming in from San Francisco. Can you have a drink with me and the newly engaged Maxey tomorrow night at 9:30 Upper East Side?"

Newly engaged? Not something I expected—from my conversations with Maxey I didn't think he'd ever get over Pam. We had spoken once or twice after the reunion, and I knew he was fully recovered from his hip operation, but he'd never mentioned that he'd been dating seriously.

Singer had found an Irish bar near his hotel. When I arrived, I spotted them at the very back, in a booth, just starting their first beer. Maxey had a particularly goofy expression. He leaped to his feet and gave me one of his bear hugs. After I ordered a beer, I started quizzing him.

"Maxey! Wow! Congratulations! Singer said you are engaged. That's fantastic. Tell me everything."

"Well, I started dating this incredible woman and I asked her to marry me. She said yes, so we're going to go for it."

"And what about your kids? Do they like her?"

"They don't just like her. They love her." Maxey paused dramatically. "She's their mother."

It took me a second. At first, I thought: 'Wait, you mean Pam wasn't their mother?' Then I realized that Maxey and Pam were getting remarried.

"After the motorcycle crash," Maxey explained, "Pam showed up at the hospital right away, to make sure I was all right. You know, she was also there the whole time when I had my hips done." In fact, I hadn't known: Maxey hadn't mentioned this to me before.

"And Pam was like, 'Okay, I'm really worried about this guy, and he's my ex-husband, and the father of my kids, and we created a school together, so I guess I've got to fucking save him, and then I can get on with my life.'"

Pam had called Brittney in Argentina to tell her that she was going to look after Maxey, and Brittney had suggested that she come to Buenos Aires instead—simply to take a break from everything for a while. "Pam was all set to leave," Maxey continued, "because she really was freaked out—I was a mess—but instead she stayed and told me, 'You know what? I love you, and I've never stopped loving you, and we're going to frickin' figure this out.'

"And that was it. I came out of my fog. The only reason I was acting out and trying to have other relationships was that I was trying to live my life. But really there was nothing I wanted more than to be back with Pam and have our family together again."

They cautiously started seeing one another—on Pam's terms. "She decided that every month or so we would do one thing—we still pretty much lived in two places, Eleuthera and New Jersey—so one month we learned how to kitesurf together on the Outer Banks, and the next month we drove to Williamsburg and the next month we went to a play. We even did a zip line, and Pam's afraid of heights. The whole idea was that we were dating each other, doing things that would allow us to fall in love again."

Maxey had tried not to get his hopes up or to overstep. That's why he hadn't told us, he explained, because he was terrified that it all might blow up in his face.

"And then just a little while ago, I was in the school office in New Jersey and there's a young woman colleague there and she turned to me and said, 'What are you waiting for? Stop being such an idiot.' My sister Lizzie had also been on my case about this. So the next time I saw Pam, I got down on one knee again. And she said yes."

They were planning to get married in August. Brittney was making all the arrangements. "It will be our third time, because we were married in Subic Bay and then again in San Diego," he reminded us. "It's just going to be the immediate family."

"So we aren't invited again," said Singer.

"Brocq is going to be my best man," Maxey added, ignoring him.

"When are *you* going to get married?" he asked me.

For me, this question was right up there with asking when

David and I were going to have children, which Maxey had only recently stopped doing. Still, it was such a joyful evening that I tried really hard not to sound annoyed as I explained that, after twenty-six years together, I considered David and me to be more than married. While I'd been to a gay wedding in Massachusetts, I added, there was no way David and I would ever agree to have what we considered a second-class wedding: If straight New Yorkers didn't have to travel to another state, then why should we? Why would we ever get married if that union didn't carry with it all the same rights and privileges? That was clearly never going to happen in our lifetime, so we were never going to get married.

"I totally get that," Singer said.

"I do, too," Maxey said.

Now it was my turn to catch Singer and Maxey up on my life. I had a story I wanted to tell them, about my mother's final gift to me.

"I was scheduled to have lunch a few days after my mother's death with the man who edited the email book I cowrote," I explained. It was a purely social engagement—this editor had become a friend—but I'd set the lunch up months before and simply forgot it was on my calendar until that very morning. I really wasn't in the mood for a chatty lunch, but because I'd neglected to cancel, I thought I should just go through with it.

"That morning, I was alone at my website's office but too distracted to work. I turned on the computer and wrote at the top of a page: *The End of Your Life Book Club.* I wrote fifteen pages without stopping about the books my mother and I had read when she was dying, and about the conversations that we'd had about them.

"I mentioned it to my editor friend at the end of our lunch and then sent him the pages I'd written. A few days later he offered me an advance that I think will save the website—or at least allow me to keep working on it while we try to save it."

The idea of writing the book scared me, so I hadn't told many people that I was doing it. But I was excited to try—and for the opportunity to continue my conversations with my mother. Maybe I could find some of the words I hadn't been able to find before. Sharing this news with Maxey and Singer felt particularly safe because our friendships had nothing to do with this part of my life: I knew they both had confidence in me, but I also knew that they wouldn't care if the book never happened and the website went down in flames. We raised a glass to Maxey's engagement, to my book, and to Singer, for having grabbed the check on a fake trip to the men's room.

When the evening was over, we were all heading in different directions: Singer was walking back to his hotel; Maxey was taking the subway uptown; and I was taking a different line downtown. When Maxey was about fifty feet away from us, he turned and said what he always said when we saw one another: "Love you guys!"

Singer shouted the same thing back, and I turned and waved goodbye enthusiastically at both of them.

NO DRINKS WITH SINGER

In January 2011, Singer told me that he was coming back to town again and wanted to have dinner with David and me. I was greatly looking forward to seeing him as always but also quite desperate to get advice from him about my website. I was trying to get the business back on track and figure out some way to dig ourselves out of our debt. I was writing the book in the meantime and had finally finished a first draft. I hadn't slept properly in months, and now I had a new theme to haunt my sleepless hours: Why did I have to go and start a business? Why couldn't I just have been happy in my publishing job?

The day before we were to meet, we found out that Maxey would also be in New York City, fundraising for the school. Of course, we invited him to join us—we were eager to catch up on life at the school—but I asked Maxey if he would mind if I reserved a chunk of the dinner to ask Singer for advice. If he was bored, he and my David had plenty to talk about (mostly making fun of me).

But the morning of our dinner, Singer sent an email announcing he needed to cancel. "I have some weird virus that has somehow affected the left side of my face," he wrote. "I'm on an antiviral and steroids, feel ok but look pretty awkward. I am probably more conscious about it than I should be, but only my right side can smile, and I look like a camel when I chew. Major bummer."

Singer guessed that he had Bell's palsy, and a doctor quickly confirmed it. I recalled that a friend's mother had had the same condition when we were kids; at first I'd been scared by her half-drooping face, then I'd ceased to notice it, and finally, about three months later, I realized that she was totally fine again. I told this to Singer.

Maxey couldn't make dinner either, as it turned out. We both got a text from him that simply said: "Driving around Boston in the freezing rain. Where is Eleuthera?"

It was only then that I realized I'd been thinking about getting Singer's advice, but it hadn't occurred to me to ask Maxey for his.

Why hadn't I thought Maxey might have some wisdom to offer? He had been a naval officer, a teacher, started two schools from scratch, attracted millions in donations, and managed construction of a campus from the ground up.

Had I held on to my first opinion of him while he had long ago let go of his of me?

I knew the answer and wasn't proud of it. I thought back to the story Maxey had told in his audit about Ms. Finley, the teacher who called him her Pokey Puppy, and I winced with shame. Maxey showed me nothing but respect and affection, and had never demanded that I recognize how smart he was. Maybe that was because Ms. Finley was still on his shoulder, sometimes urging him to prove her wrong but often making him insecure no matter how much he accomplished.

I'd almost certainly missed out on a lot of good advice over the years; I could change that going forward. I also thought about whether I could get Maxey to ask more for himself out of our friendship. As it happened, Maxey would soon do that without my prompting.

MORE DRINKS WITH SINGER

Maxey, Singer, and I agreed that we needed to have a drink together to celebrate our fiftieth birthdays, but the challenge was figuring out where and when. A week before my birthday, in July 2012, Maxey, who had turned fifty in October 2011, emailed to let me know he would be in New York in a few weeks. (He signed that email and all his messages "Respectfully," which I found oddly formal.) Singer would be there, too. His birthday was the same month as mine. We had a date.

I chose the place: Monument Lane, a months-old restaurant near me that was designed to look like it had been around since colonial times. I was a big fan of their "cask ale," a warm, highly potent, barely carbonated beer that had been fermented in "ye olde" casks on-site. Maxey asked if he could bring a young protégé of his named Peter Meijer. Peter had been a student at the Island School, then a sergeant in an Army intelligence unit deployed to Iraq, and then graduated from Columbia University. He was now part of Team Rubicon, an organization comprised of veterans that goes wherever in the U.S. or the world it is needed to help deliver humanitarian aid following a disaster or crisis. "Clearly a slouch like us," Maxey warned.

The day we were meeting there was a torrential rainstorm; gutters overflowed, and the water seemed to come not just down but from every angle. The restaurant was only a few-minute walk from my apartment, but by the time I arrived I was drenched. Maxey got there soon after I did, so we had some time to talk, just the two of us.

I ordered us some cask beers, while Maxey tried to dry his hair with a cloth napkin.

"You know," Maxey began, "I've wanted to say two things to you. First, happy birthday. And second, you're a frickin' shithead."

I thought he was joking, but then I saw that he wasn't. My mind raced to figure out what I'd done to make Maxey so mad.

I recalled that solicitation letter for the school all those years ago, and how many years it was before I finally sent a check. Then I realized that I never congratulated him on the birth of any of his children and still wasn't sure how to spell the names of the two oldest (Brittney? Brocque?) and couldn't remember if Tyler was older than Tegan or vice versa. There was also the fact that I was such an idiot for always going to Singer for advice and never him—even when he was right there with us. I apologized for all that in a great torrent of words.

Maxey stared at me, impassive. But now he seemed amused.

When I was done, Maxey said, "I don't care about any of that. Though it *would* be nice if you could learn my frickin' kids' names, but I also know that you've barely met them. No, you're a shithead because whenever I say 'I love you, brother,' you never say that. You just say nothing or 'Bye.' You also totally freak out when I hug you."

"That's not true."

"Yeah, it is. Why is that?"

"I don't know," I said. "Maybe because when you say you love me or give me a hug, it's just like a friend, but when I do it, it might seem too gay."

"But you are gay, you frickin' psychopath," Maxey said.

I wanted to explain that I still felt anxious, even with my oldest straight friends, about their thinking that I was coming on to them if I was too affectionate. That I wasn't even conscious of it, but it was always there. I wanted to remind him that he knew perfectly well by this point that I wasn't a physically demonstrative person and never had been. (I often feel that I would have been far more comfortable in Edwardian England where a nod or bow in someone's general direction with perhaps a tip of the hat was all that was usually required.)

I was spared further rationalizing when first Peter Meijer, and then Singer, walked in.

We sat at a high-top table and signaled for more cask beers. Peter was just twenty-four: less than half our age. The only things I knew we shared were Maxey and the fact that we were dripping with water.

After we'd made the arrangement to meet, Peter had emailed us to apologize for the fact that he'd be showing up in jeans and a T-shirt instead of a suit because of the rain. I had been puzzled by his email, but it made more sense after I met him in person. He was unusually deferential: waiting until he was sure each of us had finished talking before speaking himself; leaning forward to listen; asking follow-up questions. He had what you could call old-fashioned manners. If this was how people were going to treat me now that I was fifty, well, maybe getting older wasn't so bad, I thought.

I studied Peter a bit: he had bright red hair cut short, a trim beard, and an easy, lopsided smile. He also had heightened awareness of everything going on around him. His back was to the room, but he seemed to sense the server's presence before the rest of us did.

Maxey, Singer, and I told various Yale stories—I'm guessing "Circa" came up—and Peter laughed in all the right places. Then, after a while, we asked him about Team Rubicon, and he explained that he was just about to leave for South Sudan, where he would be trying to help provide humanitarian aid for refugees. It felt good, he said, to put to work all the training he'd had in the army.

As I looked back and forth between Maxey and Meijer, I could see how someone might mistake them for father and son. I could also see a kind of brotherhood between them that I didn't think I would ever experience with Maxey—or with anyone, for that matter. Watching these two, I started to wonder what I'd missed by not doing the kind of service they did. Certainly not the chance to be bossed around, but maybe something else.

At one point I was desperate for an ice water—I had drunk too many beers too quickly—and when I ordered, the server asked me if I wanted a straw. Before I could answer, Maxey interrupted.

"Is it plastic?"

"Yes," the server said.

"Then he won't have one." I thought it strange but put it out of my mind.

The rain was now even more intense, driving from one side of Greenwich Avenue to the other and sending people running for cover. Exploded umbrellas floated by on surges of water.

"Good thing you survived Drown-Proofing," Singer remarked to Maxey.

"Well, there's kind of a story about that," Maxey said. He then called for another round of beers before launching into it, but only after I asked Maxey to remind me what Drown-Proofing was. "It comes before Hell Week," he said. "No one can be a SEAL who hasn't survived a Breath-Hold swim and then Drown-Proofing. The Breath-Hold swim is more or less what it sounds like: you do a somersault into the water and then have to swim underwater to the other end of a pool, kick off, and swim back, still underwater, without taking a breath. If you come up for air, you fail. If you succeed or pass out, you pass. So that's the first big swimming test.

"But Drown-Proofing is a whole different level of torture. They tie your feet together and your hands behind your back. You get in the water at the deep end and bob up and down twenty times. Then you have to swim the whole length of the pool, fifty meters, and back. Next you float for five minutes, do a forward and backward somersault, and grab a mask from the bottom of the pool using your teeth. If you touch the bottom of the pool at any time, you fail. You get two tries. If you fail the first and don't try again, you're out. If you fail both times, you're out for good."

"Did you pass the first or second time?" I asked Maxey.

"Well, neither. I failed the first time along with fourteen other guys. They put us in a corner and asked us who wanted to try again. Half of the guys said no; they'd almost drowned as had we all, and they rang the bell and were out. I went again right away along with seven other guys and couldn't do it the second time either. I've never been buoyant—no matter how hard I tried, I just sank to the bottom both times. So did three other guys."

You need fat cells for buoyancy, Maxey explained, and he had almost none. That he owed to genetics and wrestling: Ever since the age of thirteen, he'd alternately dieted and binged on food so he could compete in one weight class or another; but his mother had never let him pig out on junk food the way other wrestlers did. She'd insisted that he eat only the good stuff when it was time to put on pounds. As a result, he never developed fat cells, just muscle. That's why Maxey could never make the long swim into the shallow end and back without sinking and bouncing off the bottom.

I was confused. "So you failed both times?"

"Yeah, well, they gave us a really hard time but said they might let us try again if we made it through Hell Week. The other three guys didn't make it through. So I was the only one left who hadn't passed. I was hoping they forgot. They hadn't. Before I could go on to the next phase, they made me do Drown-Proofing a third time. I'd called my mom, Big Red, and she had an idea. She tied her own ankles together, clasped her arms behind her back, and threw herself in a swimming pool. Sure enough, she sank to the bottom but then floated to the top, eventually concluding that her breasts gave her buoyancy. Since she knew I wasn't going to grow breasts, she had another idea: enemas. She thought I could pump myself full of air using an enema bulb. She actually went out, got a Fleet enema and enema bulb, and mailed them to me.

"She included instructions: I was to empty my colon and then pump it full of air. She hoped she'd taught me over the course of my childhood not to release gas in public, but she did think that it might be a challenge to hold the air inside for two whole lengths of the pool plus the dive at the end."

We needed another round of beers, clearly, and got them.

"In the end," continued Maxey, "I didn't do the enema thing—though I think I told Big Red I did. I mean, she'd gone to all that trouble. When I tried Drown-Proofing the third time, and briefly touched bottom on the long swim, the examiners looked away. So I failed three times and was able to continue with training."

It was rare for Maxey to tell a story about the SEALs, and I don't think he would have done it had Peter not been there. I noted that once again the story he told was one about failure, not success; those were the kind from his entire life that Maxey liked to share. What struck me most, though, was that the story showed how much the navy must have valued Maxey: the SEALs were willing to break their own rules to hold on to him. I thought about what a smart decision it had been: he was given command of a platoon as a junior officer and ranked top platoon commander at SEAL Team 5.

I also wondered: Why *hadn't* they been able to hold on to him in the end?

Over the next few days, Singer, Maxey, and I exchanged a host of nonsense emails about hangovers and other things. Because Maxey had picked up the tab, we all thanked him. He wrote to us that it was no trouble, that he loved us, and friendship was everything. When I wrote Singer and Maxey back I still couldn't bring myself to tell them that I loved them, but I did say I agreed that friendship is everything.

CHAPTER FIVE

Fifties

SHARKS

At age fifty I decided to reread Evelyn Waugh's *Brideshead Revisited.* I had first read the novel after swooning over Jeremy Irons and Anthony Andrews, who played Charles Ryder and Lord Sebastian Flyte in the 1981 television adaptation. Other Waugh I'd read had been caustic and satirical and delightful, but this book was everything the show had made me hope it would be: romantic, melancholy, and more than a little gay. The idea of encountering again a novel written from adulthood that reckons with all the events that brought our narrator from his impressionable youth to the present appealed to me, now that I had less time ahead of me than behind.

In the book, Ryder recalls himself, Sebastian, and their friends at college: "The languor of Youth—how unique and quintessential it is! How quickly, how irrevocably lost! The zest, the generous affections, the illusions, the despair, all the traditional attributes of Youth—all save this—come and go with us through life. These things are a part of life itself; but languor—the relaxation of yet unwearied sinews, the mind sequestered and self-regarding, the sun standing still in the heavens and the earth throbbing to our own pulse—that belongs to Youth alone and dies with it."

While rereading, I stumbled across a picture of Maxey and me from the weekend we first got to know one another, stretched out languidly on the grass at that country house our group had borrowed, relaxing our "unwearied sinews" and totally absorbed in ourselves. I felt a pang: that languor had been lost decades ago, just as Waugh described. I wondered if something else could take its place, though. Could middle and old age have languor, too—even of a different sort? Or had all languor become exhaustion, pure and simple?

The cooking website returned to a state of bare profitability and was sold, allowing us to pay all our debts and return to the investors most of what they had invested. In addition, the purchaser offered me a job as an editor-at-large, which I was delighted to accept.

Still, even with a steady job and no alerts to wake me in the middle of the night, I found myself increasingly worn out.

My father had at first done remarkably well after my mother's death, but then had a heart attack, a series of falls, and a hip replacement operation. My sister, brother, and I did our best to help him navigate these challenges and a shrinking world. At the same time, friends were starting to face a variety of health problems. And there was something else: I just didn't feel well most of the time. I suffered from sinus infections, one after another, which I couldn't seem to shake. At night, when my congestion would wake me, I felt as though I couldn't get enough oxygen.

I was also putting on weight. At fifty-two I weighed 185—fifty pounds more than I'd weighed in college. The math wasn't looking good if I kept eating and drinking at the current rate.

In January 2014, I was asked to address the annual gathering of people who had been members of the secret society, an event that took place yearly at the Yale Club and included the newest members, the oldest, and everyone in the middle—which Maxey and I were almost exactly. The topic I chose was "The Future of Reading." I planned to start with a bit about the book I'd just published about my mother and the books we'd read, but talk mostly about reading in a digital world, sharing research that showed that young people prefer printed books to digital, and that no one need get hysterical about whether the physical books so many of us love would have a place in the world going forward.

Singer was coming in for the event, although Diana, his wife, needed to stay home with their three kids. Maxey was bringing Pam. Excited to see them all, I settled on a place we could go drinking after the speech and dinner. David would be with me as well.

A few days before the speech, I got a call from Maxey.

"Great news, Schwalbs," he said. "Tyler and Tegan are going to be able to be there, too."

Happily, by now I had learned which child was which. Tegan, the youngest, who was almost eighteen, wanted to be a writer and was thinking about working as deckhand on a charter boat instead of going to college—a plan her parents supported. I had told her she should never take life advice from me because I had a bad record when it came to advising others, but if she wanted to be a writer, I did think that going out into the world to work like that was a fine idea. When she and I had talked about this, just a month before, I'd asked her if she'd read *Two Years Before the Mast,* the 1840 book by Richard Henry Dana Jr. about leaving Harvard to spend time at sea on a merchant ship. She said she would read it, and I knew she would.

The recent news on Tyler, now nineteen, was simply that she'd moved to Argentina and was thriving there, studying Spanish and teaching English. "I'm psyched to see her," Maxey said on our call, "and so proud of her. It's great to see her so happy; she can really be herself in Argentina. She and her girlfriend have really made a life for themselves there."

"Girlfriend? As in friend who is a girl, or romantic partner?"

"I told you," Maxey said. "Tyler is gay; she came out to us."

"You so did *not* tell me that, Maxey. I would have remembered!"

I wondered how difficult it had been for Tyler. I couldn't know unless I asked her. Just because your parents have gay friends doesn't mean they necessarily want that for their children. I suspected that there might have been a slightly rockier patch than Maxey's description indicated. My mother, with plenty of gay friends, had been very upset when I'd come out to her—and then was upset with herself for being upset. Being gay was in most circumstances easier now than it had been when I was a teen, and then was far easier than it had been decades before. That didn't mean it was easy; gay kids were still dying from suicide in far greater numbers than straight ones.

Gay rights had been almost constantly in the news in the months leading up to our get-together. The biggest development for David and me had come when the Supreme Court overturned a key section of the Defense of Marriage Act in the case that Edie Windsor brought against the United States. This meant that the federal government could no longer discriminate against same-sex couples when it came to federal rights and benefits.

David and I had continued to say we wouldn't marry unless we had all the same rights and privileges—and this Supreme Court decision wasn't exactly that: it still wasn't clear whether one state *had* to recognize a marriage performed in another state. We decided that it was enough for us. So, with four friends present, David and I got married at New York's City Hall in September 2013. We contacted family and friends right after to let everyone know and to explain why we hadn't wanted a big wedding: we felt it would devalue the years we'd already spent committed to one another.

I'd sent an email to Maxey to let him know. He had instantly replied, "Congratulations on twenty-nine years with David; it is wonderful that you are married. I often talk about commitment and love and the life you have built together that has outlasted most marriages."

At last, the U.S. had joined France, England, Ireland, Wales, Austria, Germany, and Brazil in recognizing gay marriage—or, as we could now call it, marriage. At the same time, however, Vladimir Putin, Russia's leader, had launched a propaganda law with draconian punishments that made it a criminal offense to say anything positive about gay people. Summoning the image of a decadent America to play to his homophobic base was good politics and a great diversion from the dissent at home coming from the likes of the punk band Pussy Riot. Uganda passed an anti-homosexuality bill that included a penalty of life in prison. And at home, in the United States, it didn't take much to see that a backlash was building with the rise of "religious freedom" bills devised to claw back some of the rights that had been won. There was also a horrific increase in acts of violence against LGBT people—especially trans people of color.

After the speech and the dinner, we headed out for drinks as planned, to a restaurant near Grand Central Station that didn't mind putting some tables together and allowed us to share a whole bunch of desserts instead of ordering a full menu. They also didn't seem to mind the boisterousness that was Maxey in full form: bouncing up to the bar to get drinks for everyone, trapping Singer in a headlock, embracing Pam one minute and David the next. People at other tables were invited to join us, but they wisely declined.

My husband (it still felt odd to refer to him that way, but I was getting more accustomed to it) was entranced with Tyler and Tegan, and they seemed to be with him. David can be quite reserved with people he hasn't met, but sometimes he takes to someone instantly and he did with them. They were showing him pictures of the sharks that gather in the water right outside the condo where they'd grown up, and where Maxey and Pam still lived. David decided to tease the young conservationists with made-up recipes for shark's fin soup, which we'd long ago stopped eating. They in turn showed him pictures of themselves swimming with the sharks, which brought up stories of the first time he'd seen the film *Jaws* and various tales of people being eaten while swimming in the South China Sea.

It wasn't a night for serious conversation. I didn't get to welcome Tyler to the tribe. Tegan told me of her plans to leave school and head out on the charter boat, but there was no chance to talk more about writing or Richard Henry Dana. (I tried to bring him up once but a few drinks in couldn't recall whether he was Henry Richard Dana, Dana Richard Henry, or Henry Dana Richard, and then gave up.) Maxey wanted to talk about Wallace Stegner at one point; he had discovered Stegner from the book I wrote about my mother and was now reading *Angle of Repose*. Pam was also a Stegner fan, and she and I had exchanged messages about our love for *Crossing to Safety*. Singer loved Stegner, too, having discovered him after moving out West, but since none of the younger folk had read him yet, we agreed to park that conversation to avoid spoilers. And it certainly wasn't the evening to talk about Waugh and the languor of youth. So mostly we told stories from the past, many at Maxey's expense, which delighted his daughters.

The only moment of tension came when I ordered a scotch and soda and the server asked if I wanted a straw. I said, "Sure," before I noticed that Tyler and Tegan were frantically trying to catch my attention, drawing their hands over their throats in the classic semaphore for "cut it out" and "mortal danger." I looked bewildered, but Tegan bounded up and informed the server that I wanted a straw only if they had a *paper* one.

"No, just plastic," said the server.

"Oh, then he doesn't want one," Tegan said. She signaled me over to a corner of the bar to fill me in. "Dad goes crazy if anyone uses a plastic straw—the plastic winds up in the ocean and causes terrible damage to sea creatures, like turtles. I've seen him lunge across tables to keep straws from being handed out, and he lectures anyone he sees using one." I remembered our drinking at Monument Lane. "He loves you, but that could have ruined the evening." I thought at first that she was joking but then realized she wasn't.

Eventually we were the only ones left in the restaurant; the staff was placing the chairs upturned on top of tables and mopping down the floors. Decades after college, I was still shutting down restaurants. I signaled for the check, but Singer or Maxey had already paid it.

"You guys have to stop treating me whenever we go out for drinks," I said.

"Well, speaking as someone who has been married three times . . ." began Maxey.

"All to the same person," added Pam.

". . . we couldn't miss the chance to take you out to celebrate your wedding," Maxey continued. "We're proud of you and we love you both."

Singer gave a slightly longer toast, included how sorry he was that Diana couldn't be with us to celebrate, and then ended by saying, "You know, we're really happy for you guys. We love you both, too."

It had been a long day and night, and I was tired, but tired in a good way. I also felt an unfamiliar sense of peace. I hadn't talked about my sinuses, which ached. I hadn't asked my friends what they were going to do with the rest of their lives, nor discussed my plans and fears. I probably *had* talked too much about myself and my book and my website but didn't feel the kind of mortal dread I sometimes did after an evening where I'd been solipsistic. These were people who'd been with me for three decades and clearly were willing to put up with an excess of me, just as I had long ago reconciled myself to an excess of them in whatever form that took. More than reconciled, in fact; it was something I'd come to cherish.

At the end of the evening, I caught sight of David, his face flushed from drinking, laughing with Tyler and Tegan. He was now learning more about Tyler's girlfriend in Argentina and about Tegan's plans to sail the world. Maxey and Singer were also talking animatedly, and so I had a minute alone with Pam.

"Does he ever slow down or is he always that high energy?" I asked her.

"He's pretty much always like that, but by now he knows that if he's too loud in the morning I'll kill him. For real. So he's getting better about that. He makes the coffee and tea every day, so there's that, though you've never heard anyone bang around in a kitchen the way he does just to pour a French press."

We took many pictures that night, but none of them captured the image that's fixed in my mind: Pam and me, Maxey and Singer, David and Tyler and Tegan, all talking and laughing together just before heading out into the just-above-freezing New York night.

As we put on our coats, I remembered a line from *Brideshead Revisited* when Charles Ryder, the narrator, says, "Sometimes, I feel the past and the future pressing so hard on either side that there's no room for the present at all." Maybe this was exactly the opposite: maybe the sense of peace I was feeling in that moment was my head making room for the present, without the past and future pressing so hard. No need to regret our history—I shared too much with these people to dwell on that. No room for the future—the two youngsters would take care of that for us. Just the present.

JAMÓN

I had reconnected a few years previously with a high school friend named David Scully, known to everyone as Scully. When we first met, he'd been a diffident golden boy, the kind of kid who seems to sail through without much effort. Scully had an easy familiarity, so I thought of him as one of my better high school friends, even though I later realized, after he became a mid-life friend, that I'd barely known him when we were teens. I discovered that in the intervening years he had become a fanatical cook and pursued a passion for ocean science, which started with his childhood in coastal Maine, continued through college, and led him to becoming the board chair of Woods Hole Oceanographic Institution. It was clear that Maxey and Scully had to meet. Like my mother, I am on a perpetual quest to introduce my friends to one another whenever possible, especially if they share an interest.

So, in 2013, I had insisted they get together on one of Maxey's trips to New York. I told Scully about my Navy SEAL friend, and Maxey about my Woods Hole pal. They met and formed an instant friendship that came to include their institutions: Woods Hole and the Island School. Maxey and Scully were now always coming up with new adventures. I felt like I had done something for the environment simply by making sure they met.

In May 2015, when Maxey was in New York to consult with members of the board of his school, the three of us decided that we needed to get together.

Near Union Square in New York City there is a restaurant called Bar Jamón that serves, appropriately, wine and ham.

Also, delicious croquettes. Scully lived around the corner from Bar Jamón and I worked close by, so we decided we would all meet there. Bar Jamón is a compact space, with high eating counters in rich, worn wood, as though a grand dining table had been chopped into planks to get it in the door and never reassembled. There's just enough space around each table and bench for a person to squeeze by. Scully had staked out a corner of a table and when I arrived a few minutes late seemed pleased to see me for a variety of reasons, one of which is that it takes more obnoxiousness than he possesses to hold several empty seats in a crowded New York bar.

Soon Maxey was there giving me the usual bear hug. Within minutes, he and Scully were talking at lightning speed. The conversation bounced around from ocean swimming to jellyfish to coral reefs to submarines. The two of them were having way too much fun together, but I could also see they were energized by their passion for the ocean, and for inspiring young people to want to save it. I was happy to hear Maxey and Scully so engaged but had to fight off a twinge of jealousy. I wanted them to get along, sure. But maybe not this well.

Eventually, Scully excused himself. He was cooking dinner for his kids that night.

"I love that guy," Maxey said after he left.

"I know, you tell me that whenever we talk," I reminded him. "And he says the same." I was sure I sounded a bit peevish, but Maxey didn't seem to notice. I also realized that a straight guy could say he loved another straight guy, but had I said it I would have had to explain: platonically.

Maxey then launched into more about the work they were doing together. Our conversations had taken on a new kind of ease. I no longer worried about what I said around Maxey. I wasn't sure when things had changed, but it seemed to have been gradually and then all at once. I knew I *could* be peevish whether he noticed or not.

When Maxey paused for air, I took the moment to steer the conversation away from the ocean and asked for the rundown on Pam and their kids.

Maxey grinned. The great news was that Pam seemed to have largely forgiven him for ruining their earlier marriage—although he assured me that he wasn't taking any chances with this one. He was now doing his best to balance home life with his other great love, the school.

"Oh, and I'm now totally addicted to kitesurfing. When the wind blows, I start to sweat and shake and slap my forearm."

"What does that even mean, 'slap your forearm'?" I asked.

Maxey ignored the question. "Brittney is back from Argentina and working with us at the school. She did all the heavy lifting on organizing the event we had with Jack Johnson and the United Nations."

"Jack Johnson, like the musician Jack Johnson? The guy who lives in Hawaii?"

"Yeah, he came as part of a conference to try to figure out how to get the plastic out of the ocean and how to convince people to stop putting it there."

"I've stopped with plastic straws, I swear," I volunteered. This was a bit of a stretch. I always intended to, and sometimes succeeded, but I also kept forgetting.

"You better. I'm not kidding," Maxey replied, recognizing that I was fibbing. "Seriously, Schwalbs."

"I'll do better. Really. No more straws." There was a small

piece of ham left on the plate we'd been sharing. I pushed it toward Maxey. He ripped it in half and gave me half back.

"You wouldn't have believed what an ass I made out of myself at the conference," Maxey continued. "I thought I was being cool when I introduced Jack as the Banana Pancakes Man—that's one of his famous songs—but then he made me come up onstage and sing it in front of everyone. Fortunately for everyone there, I only know the first verse."

"And Brocq, Tyler, and Tegan?" I asked.

"Brocq's still in South Africa, diving and filming large ocean predators. Tegan is somewhere in the Mediterranean right now working on a yacht, which means she's eating beans and toast and getting disrespected and bossed around. She's an awesome hard worker but she doesn't much like being told what to do so I don't think that's going to last. But, as you know, she's writing."

I did indeed know. Tegan had emailed me after we last met and started showing me some of her work. In it, she chronicled her feelings about her family's earlier split—Brocq staying with her father. I'd encouraged her to keep going and felt ashamed that I'd spent so much time confusing her with her sister. I had finally admitted to myself that I didn't really feel comfortable around small children and therefore wasn't very interested in spending time with them. As a defense mechanism, I had refused to retain information about my friends' kids until they'd reached a certain age. Not an elegant solution, but neither was admitting to being a twenty-first-century W. C. Fields.

"Tyler is back in Argentina with her girlfriend, doing great."

"I'm so glad to hear that."

"And you, Schwalbs?"

I told Maxey how worried I was about a new book I was writing. It was both overdue and unfinished. I ran through my other family and social obligations and told him that David was planning a trip to Hong Kong to see his parents and brother. There was a lot going on, and I was feeling pretty tired and stressed.

"But you're looking great," Maxey said. "How much weight did you lose?"

I was chuffed, as the Brits would say, that he had noticed. "Twenty-five pounds." I'd finally found a diet that worked and that I loved. But I couldn't shake my sinus problems. I'd had two infections in the last few months and felt sluggish.

"You know, Schwalbs, I really have to get you down to Eleuthera. Sea air. And I'm telling you, you got to learn how to breathe. I'm not saying it will cure your infections once you get them, but I know it would help you."

I couldn't imagine finding time in my overscheduled schedule.

"It's also been a difficult time," I said. "A friend of mine, a guy named Steven Mark, has a brain tumor and is really starting to fail." Steve was the first investor in my cooking website. "He's had two surgeries and all sorts of experimental treatments. His wife tells me that he's now all but blind, in a wheelchair, and has lost the use of his right hand. He recently fell when they were trying to bathe him, shattered a mirror, and just missed slicing an artery." I didn't know Steve very well but liked and respected him enormously. "He always gave me great advice and encouragement, even when I'd made a hash of things. Even after the sale of the website, we continued to get together whenever we could for drinks. The nicest guy and it's so unfair."

Maxey was unusually quiet when I was talking about my friend with the brain tumor. He seemed to be looking past me, over my shoulder, at something in the middle distance. When I finished, Maxey was silent. As silent as I had ever seen him. I then remembered that Maxey's biological father had died of a brain tumor when Maxey was a toddler.

After a while we talked of other things and were back to laughing.

Later that night, when I was home and about to go to sleep, I wondered why I'd told Maxey about Steve. Yet I didn't regret it; I wanted to share more of my life with Maxey, and I was doing just that.

STINGRAY

At the end of February 2016, I called Maxey just to check in.

"Weirdest thing, Schwalbs. I was kitesurfing and I had the strangest feeling. And then I kind of fainted."

"I faint when I even look at someone kitesurfing," I said. "That's nuts, flying in the air on a surfboard attached to a kite."

"I actually fainted four separate times."

"Do you think maybe you should stop kitesurfing?" I asked.

Maxey ignored me. "I think I was dehydrated two of those times, but not the other two. I was semi-unconscious—not totally, but I had some tremors I couldn't control. Strange stuff. I usually only faint when Pam is nice to me." I laughed at that, a running joke.

"Are you going to get that checked out?" I asked.

"Yeah, I'm in Nassau now doing just that. I'm sure it's nothing."

I didn't hear from Maxey after his visit to Nassau. So I, too, assumed it was nothing. Then in April he emailed to let me know that he and Pam were coming to New York for an Island School benefit and was hoping we could join as their guests. A fancy New York chef would be cooking—his son had gone to the school. But I had a work meeting that night and couldn't change it. Maxey was especially bummed, he said, because he wanted me to meet the present scientist-in-residence at the Cape Eleuthera Institute—the research arm of the school— who had been working with the students to tag and study stingrays.

"They're awesome creatures, Schwalbs."

All I knew about stingrays was that one had killed the famous Australian conservationist and television personality Steve Irwin. "I'll take your word for that."

"They're beautiful—everything about them," Maxey said. "You just want to try not to step on them if you can help it."

"Noted," I said. "Still, not something I need to worry about walking around Greenwich Village."

"You know, you should come back down and visit. I'll send you a video we made of stingrays in Eleuthera," Maxey said. "It will blow your mind. Extreme stingrays."

In May, as I was doing an extreme closet clean to avoid finishing my book, the phone rang. It was Maxey. He wondered if I had time to talk. I was eager to hear how the benefit with the fancy chef went. I hadn't yet watched the stingray video, but Maxey never grilled me on things like that.

"Remember I told you I fainted while kitesurfing?" he began.

"Yes," I said. "You were getting it checked out in Nassau."

"So, yeah, I went to Nassau, to a neurologist there. He did an MRI and it was immediately obvious what was wrong." There was a long silence. I didn't know if I'd lost the connection or if Maxey had stopped speaking.

"What did he say was wrong?" I asked.

"Well, he says I have a brain tumor," Maxey replied. "A pretty big one."

I didn't know what to say, so I said nothing for a while. And then, just "I'm so sorry." I realized that the last time I had said that to him in that tone had been when he'd told me Pam had left him.

"Big Red and Dad are freaked out," Maxey continued, "though Dad doesn't show it, and he knows he needs to keep my mom calm. The first question I asked the doctor was whether it was a colloid cyst. That's what my father had. But it's not that. Colloid cysts are totally benign tumors but have to be removed if they grow too big because they can cause sudden death. I knew my mom would lose it if I needed to have the exact same operation that killed my father. They're much better now at removing them than they were then, but it's still an operation with some risk. But colloid cysts are always on the third ventricle and I have nothing growing there. My third ventricle is in awesome shape."

"Do they know what it is?" I asked.

"Well, they think it's one of the best kinds of brain tumor you can have: an acoustic neuroma. It's usually a growth on your auditory nerve. Not cancer, not malignant, nothing like that. But acoustic neuromas grow, sometimes really slowly and sometimes fast, and if they grow too big it can cause major problems. Mine's pretty big already—about an inch and a half long—and it's moved beyond the auditory nerve towards the vagus nerve, so that complicates things."

I'd remembered reading about the actor Mark Ruffalo, and a tumor he had just when his career was taking off. I was pretty sure it was an acoustic neuroma. "Is that like Ruffalo's tumor?" I asked. Maxey hadn't heard of Ruffalo, so I said I would send him some links. I remembered that Ruffalo had diagnosed his tumor in a dream. I asked Maxey if he knew anything was wrong before the kitesurfing episodes a few months back.

"I now think it might have started growing when I was working for Ross Perot in Texas back in 1991, when I got so dizzy that I had to go to a closet and lie down. I've had a few episodes since then but always thought I'd exercised too hard, or hadn't drunk enough water, or something—but all that's just hindsight. I really didn't know anything was wrong until these fainting spells. Oh, except my hearing. My kids and Pam have been telling me I've been losing my hearing in my left ear. It drives them nuts. I just thought the hearing loss was from diving—as well as all that firing of guns we had to do when I was training to be a SEAL."

I repeated what I'd said before. "I'm so sorry, Maxey." And then added, "This sucks." I thought back to Steve, my friend who'd had the brain tumor. He had died soon after I'd told Maxey about him.

Maxey was quick to reassure me. "Yeah, it does suck, but not too much. At the moment, they just need to watch and wait. If it doesn't grow or grows slowly, they won't need to do anything. At least for a while. Again, it doesn't spread to

other parts of your body. It's just a big tumor. The thing they
have to be careful about if they operate is your hearing. You can
lose that totally. And your face muscles. If they accidentally
cut a nerve, you can wind up looking like Singer did when he
had Bell's palsy, but not just for a while—forever." (Singer had
made a complete recovery.) "There's also always some risk when
they are messing about in your brain. But, you know, I'm just
hoping they'll find that I actually have one."

When I hung up, I called Singer. We both knew that the
news could have been far worse. Still, I was very worried. I realized that at this point in my life I was panicked by the thought
of Maxey vanishing from it. So many times over the decades
we had gone years without seeing each other or even talking.
How was it that suddenly I was devastated by the thought of
losing him?

As Singer and I were talking, I also thought about how,
since college, I had gradually become aware of many ways that
I wanted to be more like Maxey. I wanted to stop caring quite
so much what everyone thought about me and instead just
be satisfied when I was doing the right thing. I wanted to do
more—really, anything—for the environment and creatures.
I wanted to be bolder. Also, I sensed that Maxey held in his
mind a picture of me that was better than I really was. I wanted
to be that person. I wanted to be a better friend: less judg-
mental and less afraid. I suspected that the two were closely
connected.

I knew that the odds were good that Maxey and I would
have years more to nourish our friendship and for me to become
both the person Maxey thought I was and someone more like
him. Yet I also couldn't help thinking about Huei-Zu, about
David Baer, killed by the bus, about all the friends I'd lost to

AIDS and other calamities, about Steve, who'd had the tumor, and, yes, about my mother, whom I still missed every day.

MAXEY'S TUMOR CONTINUED to grow. He called me at the end of August to tell me that they were going to operate in December. Brittney had found them a terrific surgeon and medical team. They weren't sure they were going to be able to get all of the tumor out, but they thought they could get enough. He was going to have the operation at New York-Presbyterian. I knew that place well. That's where my mother went for urgent care when she spiked a high fever while she was being treated for her cancer.

At the end of September, I read about a tropical storm that was developing: Matthew. By October 1, it had developed into a category-five hurricane. I thought back to Hurricane Floyd, the storm that had caused Maxey to evacuate the school in its first year, 1999. On October 2, the phone rang. It was Maxey.

"Hey, buddy, can I use you as a sounding board?" I said of course. "The hurricane challenges just keep getting bigger," Maxey told me. "The storms keep getting bigger. This one looks to be a few days out, and I'm constantly on the phone with parents. I understand their concerns about the safety of their children, and I tell them that I believe we are safe here, but that I can't promise to keep their children completely safe. Even on the calmest day, the school is never zero risk. And when a potential cat-five hurricane is heading towards us, there's a heightened risk.

"But here's what I'm going to tell them. First, to trust the science. The school is sited on the inside of a protecting peninsula, and everything is built way beyond code. We have our own freshwater supply. We have our own renewable energy system and backup generators that work off biofuel. I'm also going to remind them that this is a science institute and a school all in one—totally integrated—and that we need young people to believe the data and believe that they themselves can be scientists and engineers *right now.* So if there isn't data that tells us we should leave, what does it say to our students if we tell them we're going to ignore the science?

"Second, I want to remind them that we need their children to help in the days leading up to a crisis. You know I say this to them all the time, but the problem with how we raise so many of the young people in the U.S., especially the privileged ones, is that we don't ask enough of them. We don't give them any sense of how much they have to offer others. We need our students to help our elderly neighbors board up their homes and make sure they have food and water. We need them to help us protect the animals and plants, take the solar panels down, and be available to pitch in where they are needed. We can't do that if we all run away whenever a storm comes.

"We're not just a school with fifty students from the U.S.: we're a community and a village with close to three hundred people and we're all connected. I mean, the idea of evacuating with just the fifty students from the States and leaving our neighbors, *and* the local students who attend the Island School, *and* the Deep Creek Middle School kids, *and* the primary school kids, *and* our colleagues and their families to weather the storm while we run away is . . . well . . . it's just not right. Everyone leaves or no one should leave. And if everyone needs to leave, our students need to help our neighbors evacuate safely."

I told Maxey I really admired that. I thought he was finished, but he was just picking up a head of steam.

"Third, I want to tell them that we're going to need teams of people who are willing to help get water and supplies to the communities around us after the storm clears. Young people deserve to be asked to help. Otherwise, you just make them feel helpless. It's easy for us to get electricity back here at the school, because we're self-sufficient. But we built and designed the school to weather storms not just for ourselves but so we can bounce back quickly and take care of our neighbors in South Eleuthera who don't have those resources. To do that, we need the incredible energy of young people who can really get out and make a difference. And that's not going to happen if they are back at home watching the storm on television."

I interrupted him to ask how he thought that was going to go over.

"Well, some of the parents are very rich, and they want to send a jet down to pick up their children. And those have been the parents who've been the most adamant. I need to reassure them that if the science and the government tell us to leave, we will leave that minute. Of course. But I need to make it clear to them that if there isn't an evacuation order, and they send a plane to pick up their child, then I'm sorry but I can't welcome that student back after the storm has passed."

Maxey paused to take a breath, and I was just about to tell him I thought he had explained himself well when he drew the conversation to a close. "Wow, Schwalbs, thanks for your advice. I now know exactly what I'm going to say."

Then he hung up.

Within days the storm had passed. It devastated Haiti,

causing the worst damage since the 2010 earthquake. It also hit Eleuthera hard and did a lot of harm, but the school was largely untouched. The students and faculty were able to join in with their neighbors to help in the community.

Not a single student had left the island.

EVEN THOUGH THAT particular storm had passed, there was a lot of anxiety throughout the rest of the fall. Donald Trump had just been elected president. I had been a passionate Hillary supporter. Maxey was terrified of Trump. And on December 13, Maxey would have his brain surgery.

THE WATER CURE

On December 16, I woke up early, quickly drank two cups of coffee standing at the counter in our galley kitchen, and then headed out of the apartment building toward the subway that would take me to the hospital to visit Maxey. I'd hardly slept the night before. All I'd been told was that Maxey's surgery had lasted six hours, far longer than was expected, and that he was resting well; I didn't know more.

I'd also been kept awake yet again by the most curious thing: day after day, my feet felt like they were freezing even when they were warm to the touch, and the feeling was especially intense at night—even if I had a hot-water bottle between them and was under multiple layers of wool blankets and down comforters. I was sure it was something transitory—it was winter, after all—but it made sleep elusive.

When I arrived at New York-Presbyterian, I found Maxey sitting in a chair, with his back to me, staring out the window of his hospital room. He hadn't heard me enter, so I paused just inside the door and observed him for a few seconds. He sat unmoving, like a boulder. At fifty-five, he still had a full head of blond hair. Maybe not blond, I thought—more like straw-colored, or the sisal you find on the floor of a seaside cottage. My own hair was thinning; I nervously ran my fingers through what was left of it. I had rushed to the hospital but now found myself stalling. What shape would I find Maxey in? After giving a quiet nod to Pam and to Tyler, who were sitting at a small table nearby, I slowly approached Maxey, announcing my presence when I was just a foot away so as not to startle him.

"Hey, Maxey. It's Will. How you doing?"

At first he didn't move or even turn toward me, but I could hear him take in a sharp breath. Then came the voice I'd been hearing over the last thirty-plus years, a little more gravelly than usual but unmistakably his. "Hey, Schwalbs, I'm doing pretty good, man. How're you doing?" Maxey pivoted the chair toward me and started to stand. This movement had Pam and Tyler leaping from their seats—not to stop him but to be there to catch him, should he fall.

A lifetime at sea and decades of tropical sun had deeply creased and weathered Maxey's face, but he's such an animated talker that I'd never noticed. Now his expression was rigid. Moreover, half of his face was the Maxey I knew, and half looked strangely younger. Once he was standing, Maxey attempted a smile. The wrinkled half of his face dissolved into even more wrinkles, and one eye narrowed, half of the Maxey smile. The oddly youthful side of his face, however, remained smooth and expressionless: paralyzed. Maxey's eyes were fixed in the middle distance, as if looking past me.

Maxey paused and then took an unsteady half step toward me to give me a hug. I startled when I saw his face in full. A jagged, six-inch scar now ran from above Maxey's left ear down to his neck. Painted orange with some kind of antibiotic lotion, it looked like a three-dimensional model of a snaking river, the stitches like rope bridges traversing it at various spots. I was worried about bumping into it and escaped the bro-hug the second I could.

After wobbling silently for a bit, Maxey sat down. His face became expressionless again; he was obviously fighting to keep from grimacing in pain.

I asked him how he was doing (pretty good), who had visited (all four of his kids, with Brocq flying in from South Africa; his parents and siblings; David Singer and a few other friends), and how long he thought he would be there (just a couple of days). I caught Pam shaking her head; it would be more than a couple of days.

Then Maxey clearly wanted to change the subject.

"So guess what my costume is going to be for Halloween this year?" he asked me.

I look over at Pam and Tyler, who looked pained; it was obvious they had heard the joke that was about to follow. I didn't have a clue, so I shrugged and looked back at Maxey.

"Frankenstein, of course. I've got the scar. I just need to put some bolts on my head."

Maxey stood again and then walked slowly from his hospital room, with Tyler guiding his arm, toward where his parents and brother, Jack, were waiting in a family sitting area. Maxey's sisters had been with him in the hospital all night; they had just left. It was agonizing to watch Maxey because he was so unsteady and seemed to be in great pain. Pam stayed in the room to make some calls.

Before Tyler, Maxey, and I reached the sitting area, Maxey asked me to walk him past it to the end of the hallway and back. He was eager to exercise. I took Tyler's place at Maxey's side, and he gripped my arm hard. As we walked, I tried to guide him as gently but firmly as I could for the thirty or so paces. As usual, he was moving a bit faster than seemed sensible, and I was terrified that he would fall. We didn't talk much; he clearly needed to concentrate.

When Maxey and I rejoined the group, Tyler helped him onto a firm chair; I sat next to Jack on a couch; Maxey's parents and I awkwardly shared pastries.

That was only the second time I'd met Big Red and Maxey's father, and the first time I'd met Jack. When I looked at him, I recalled the story of him almost drowning in the swimming pool when he was a little boy. Of course, he wouldn't know that I knew that. I wasn't sure what—if anything—they knew about me. It felt lopsided, and I was wary of inadvertently saying the wrong thing.

The mood was slightly giddy but also purposefully mundane. We had the kind of disjointed conversation you might have during the ad break in the third quarter of a football game when it's almost certain your team is going to win, but you don't want to jinx it by getting too excited, so you talk about other things instead. We asked one another where we were going on vacation, how we got to the hospital, where we were staying and for how long. Tyler told me she'd been back from Argentina for a few months and was teaching at the school. I already knew from Maxey that Tyler and her girlfriend would be traveling back and forth between Argentina and Eleuthera for a bit. Maxey remained largely silent as he tried to focus on whoever was speaking.

I asked about Brittney and Tegan, the oldest and youngest siblings, whom I had just missed. They were now roommates living in the city: Brittney worked in advertising, and Tegan had cofounded a company named Querencia Studio, which was working to help the fashion industry focus on sustainability and become more aware of the impact it has on the environment.

After ten or fifteen minutes, Tyler guided Maxey back to his room. I knew that the Maxeys were a social clan, so I stayed on a bit and we chatted, but quietly, in hushed hospital voices.

When I got back to Maxey's room, he was seated in the chair and again staring out the window. The hospital sits on the East River and the room's view looked out over Brooklyn's loading docks and warehouses, but Maxey wasn't looking at Brooklyn. He was trying to focus on something in the middle distance.

"What are you staring at, Maxey?"

"The water," he said.

"And what are you thinking about?" I asked him.

"I'm not thinking about anything; I'm just trying not to puke."

I told Maxey I would be back the next day and headed out, but soon found myself lost in a maze of identical hallways, trying to find the right bank of elevators. I passed several families vibrating with excitement on their way to the maternity ward with congratulatory balloons in tow. I passed a lone figure in a hospital gown and slippers walking gingerly up and down the halls, dragging her rolling IV behind her, with encouraging family members two paces behind. I'm usually not a bad navigator, but I kept getting distracted on the way to what I thought must be the exit; maybe my seeming inability to escape the hospital was in sympathy with Maxey, who couldn't. Eventually, I asked for directions and a kind orderly helped me find my way.

When I visited the next day, Maxey was in bed and gave me a groggy hello. Pam and Tyler were both in the room, as they had been the day before; once again, I'd just missed the other kids and Maxey's sisters. Maxey described how Katie, the "glue" of the family, had helped summon everyone, and how Lizzie and her husband were putting everyone up. We talked for only a few minutes; it was still hard for him to speak. He told me that Brocq had come all the way from South Africa. I acted surprised, as though he hadn't told me the same thing the day before. When he spoke about his kids, tears started flowing from the eye on the side of his face that wasn't frozen; the other couldn't cry. Soon he nodded off to sleep.

Pam motioned me outside the room to give me a report on the operation, and Tyler followed.

"They got almost all of it, but they didn't get it all. It was just too risky—the last piece was deeply embedded. Too much chance that they might cut a nerve that would lead to permanent paralysis of his face, or something much worse." I knew from our previous discussions that the "something much worse" could include death. "It was much trickier than they expected, but they consider it a success. They don't think the tumor will grow back, and even if it does, not quickly. There will be a long road of rehab ahead. The auditory nerve on the left side was severed, and he's lost all the hearing in that ear, but he didn't have much hearing in that ear anyway, so it shouldn't be too big an adjustment. The facial paralysis should just be temporary. The biggest concern is dizziness. He may have balance problems for a long while or forever."

"That would be rough," I said.

"Nothing he can't handle," Pam responded. "We're not out of the woods yet, but I see a clearing. It looks like he was really lucky. We all were really lucky. And the surgeon was amazing. Lucky on that, too."

Lucky. That's the word my mother had used constantly during her life and even more so as it was coming to an end. As I stood there, I, too, felt lucky.

"How about you?" I asked Pam. "How are you doing?"

She laughed. She had spent most of the night in the chair next to Maxey's bed and hadn't gotten more than an hour of sleep. Still, having all of her children there was a tremendous help and comfort. And she was so relieved that she had trouble expressing it.

Tyler then jumped in with a story of Maxey's antics from just a few hours before. Maxey had declined all pain medication until that morning. He was terrified of becoming addicted and never took any medication stronger than an aspirin and rarely even that; some of his friends from the military had been prescribed opioids for injuries and were struggling mightily to get off them. But the pain had become too much for him after breakfast—blinding flashes of light and a searing headache—so he agreed to try half a Vicodin, at the doctor's urging. The result was an extreme bout of looniness, complete with trying to stand on his own and singing nonsense verse at full volume.

It was only a few minutes before I'd arrived that he'd finally exhausted himself.

After a few days more Maxey was sprung, ahead of schedule. He was recovering faster than anyone could have expected, having walked endlessly up and down the corridors of the hospital—mostly with Tyler but also on the arm of whoever happened to stop by to visit. For the next week he and Pam would stay with his sister Lizzie and her husband, who lived near the hospital; this would make it easy for him to do the rehab he needed and get back to his doctors quickly if anything went wrong.

While everyone was at work or running errands, I went to spend an hour or so keeping Maxey company. He answered the door when I rang and then grabbed my arm as he led me to the living room, which had a bank of windows facing south. It was a cold, bright day, with no snow.

"I think the smooth half of your face is getting some of its wrinkles back," I told him.

"Yeah, it's coming along. The doctor asked me if I wanted some Botox in my face so that the nonfrozen side would match the frozen side; he said he'd throw it in for no charge while he was cutting into my brain. I declined but maybe I should have said yes." Maxey was slurring his words a little, but I could understand him.

I thought it might help if I talked for a while, so he could rest after the short walk to the living room. I told Maxey about attending a dinner party where I had railed against Botox. "Can you believe that people actually inject the stuff that causes botulism into their face out of vanity?" I'd said. After the dinner the host had told me that one of the guests had been really upset by my comments. "But he didn't look at all upset," I'd said. That was the problem, the host explained: the guest who was upset had just had Botox the day before and so he was incapable of displaying any expression whatsoever. But he'd been furious.

Maxey half smiled at the story.

"Still dizzy?" I asked.

"Yes, pretty dizzy," Maxey said.

Then Maxey had a sudden burst of energy and became more talkative. It was clear that he had a lot he wanted to say and was determined to get it all out.

"You know, I've been thinking about what I really want to do with the rest of my life," he said. "Nothing like having your brain cut open to focus you on the future. And for me it's all about education. I want to help reinvent the whole thing."

I knew that Brittney was the only one of his four children who had gone to college—she had graduated from a university in Argentina three years before, with a degree in business communications. I asked Maxey whether he regretted that his other kids hadn't.

"Not for a second. I want everyone to be able to go to college who wants to, but I don't think everyone needs to go to college. I also think we put way too much emphasis on tests and grades. I've been part of this group trying to come up with a whole new kind of transcript for students, something that would allow them to show schools who they are as people and the ways that they've grown. I mean just think if a ten-year-old spent part of her school day reading for elders in a home. Shouldn't that be on a transcript, too?"

Maxey was on fire with the topic, though I had to ask him

to repeat himself a few times because he was slurring more of his words. He told me that he had books he wanted me to read: *Gaviotas: A Village to Reinvent the World* by Alan Weisman, about an eco-village founded in South America, and *Creative Schools* by Ken Robinson, who had done a TED Talk about the way that traditional public schools squeeze the life out of students. The books were somewhere in the apartment; I should find them and take them with me.

"I want to see if I can expand the school way beyond where it is now. Not bigger, not more, just share the story. We're bringing students down from Boys Hope Girls Hope in the Bronx and Promise Academy in upper Manhattan and from the Harbor School on Governors Island, and that's great. But I really want to bring what we're doing and learning to *those* schools for *all* those students. I also want to bring what we are doing to our neighbors in all the communities in the Bahamas."

I brought up the subject of charter schools, a hot topic in New York at the time. Didn't they siphon energy and funding away from the public schools?

Maxey disagreed. He saw a need and place for charter schools.

"But wouldn't we be better off if we concentrated all our efforts on the schools that are for everyone?" I asked.

"I can't believe you're arguing with me about charter schools when I've just had half of my brain cut out," Maxey said, smiling on the side of his face that could smile. But then he got serious. "That operation scared the shit out of me, Schwalbs. I mean—how much time do we have left? I want to leave the world better. I blew up a ton of shit when I was in the navy. I've got a lot of repair to do to this planet. That's what I want for the school. I want to show people what's possible."

"Maxey," I said. "I think we've all caused a lot of damage to the planet over the years. Maybe I could also try a bit harder to stop using so much plastic. And I could take shorter showers and turn off some lights."

"Now I know I must have been dying because you're the last person I thought would start talking eco. You got to come back to the school again and see it in action. And there's one thing I want you to promise. When you visit, I want you to try free diving. It will change your life. That's diving without a tank. Without scuba gear. You go down only on your breath. You totally relax, quiet your brain, minimize movements. The mammalian diving reflex kicks in. And you're just part of the ocean.

"It's the thing I've been chasing all my life, to be one with the ocean, and I've found it. Free diving." Maxey paused and took a sip of water from a cup that had been set on a table next to him; it required intense concentration. "I don't know how long it will be before they let me do it again, but the minute I can, that's where I'll be: below the waves."

"I don't know, Maxey," I said. "I think I'd freak out."

"Of course you freak out," Maxey said. "Your brain starts yelling: *Dude, you got to breathe.* But that's just noise. You can push past that. It's amazing. It's the opposite of exertion. There are moments when I'm free diving that I literally think I'm not."

"Not what?"

"Just not. Not here. Not me. Just not. Like I think I'm not ever going to the surface. I'm just going to be a fish. I rarely scuba anymore. All that equipment. When you free dive, you're free. Just fins and your mask. That way you don't just explore the ocean, you explore yourself."

The sun was starting to set behind the brownstones across the courtyard. Maxey said he wanted to close his eyes for a bit and that I could just leave him there: Pam or one of his sisters would be back soon.

I'd brought a copy of my new book for him, a book about the books that had changed my life. He told me that it would be at least a few weeks before he'd be able to read. His eyes couldn't focus on words.

I left Maxey dreaming about the ocean, and that night I dreamed about the ocean, too. For the first time in my life, I dreamed about the Bahamas.

From that day on, when I took to bed every night with my freezing feet, I would think of Eleuthera. I dreamed of being warm.

CHAPTER SIX

Middle Fifties

NERVES

On January 4, Maxey told me that even though it had only been a few weeks since his operation, he had to get back to the sea. He and Pam left New York for Eleuthera the next day.

By February 2017, Maxey was already traveling for the school, with a fundraising trip from Eleuthera to Lawrenceville. He wrote me, "You would be proud of me. . . . I was trying to do my yoga headstand and was off-balance and just quit. . . . I rang the bell!!!" Ever since he'd told me about Navy SEAL training, I'd always joked that I would have rung the bell to quit within seconds, and in the book that I'd just published there was a chapter on *Bartleby, the Scrivener* and the virtues of quitting. "Yes, ringing the bell for a while sounds very wise," I'd written him. "I am proud of you."

Over the next few months, we spoke or wrote every week or two. Maxey's operation had changed our rules of engagement.

I realized then that for the last thirty years of my friendship I had always felt I needed an excuse or reason to call Maxey—

even if that was just a funny story I recalled, or something I'd seen on television that I thought would interest him, plans for an upcoming visit, or an update on a mutual friend. That was true with almost all my friends—especially those who had entered my life in a pre-digital era, a time when even calling a romantic partner on the phone simply to express affection was such an odd thing to do that it inspired a Stevie Wonder song. There had always been a few friends with whom I spoke on the phone almost daily, but those were the people I also saw constantly in real life—it was more like one long conversation.

Now, during moments when I might have turned on the television and Maxey might have stepped outside to fiddle with his boat, we found ourselves on the phone. My conversations with Maxey inspired me to call others as well: my first boss, who was living in Southport, Connecticut, looking after his beloved wife who no longer recognized him; a friend in Kansas City I'd met on book tour; a cousin in Florida. Maxey had been on the phone calling old friends as well. When we talked, he now often had a story about a fellow wrestler from college or a SEAL he'd barely spoken to since underwater demolition training.

For me, the phone remains miraculous in a way that electronic communication just isn't. A phone brings the voice of a friend. It's live. Email is a movie—once you get it, nothing you do will change it. A call is theater—surprising and unpredictable. What's more, your presence is essential.

At some point in every conversation, I would ask Maxey how he was feeling.

"I'm still dizzy," he would always reply, "but I'm getting better at living with it every day."

Maxey was back to being the kid who was constantly in motion. His balance hadn't totally recovered. Still, he had resumed doing the four-mile swim with the students and faculty, exercise (except for anything that involved wagging his head), yoga (minus headstands), running the school, and trying to return to the literal kind of running.

In one of our calls, he told me that he was free diving again.

Curiously, Maxey said, the only place he was never dizzy was when he was holding his breath at the bottom of the ocean. There was a particular place he sought out that was sacred to him, a rock formation that jutted out from a steep ledge. He called it the Cathedral. He could sit on the ocean floor beside it and look up at the sky through a lattice of coral. Some days, he said, when he was especially lucky, there were schools of small purple fish, Creole Wrasse, filling the water between him and the surface, spinning like stars.

Maxey told me that he'd signed up for a free-diver instructor course that was scheduled for June. Of course he pushed himself too hard in every way and then would crash for a few days, worrying Pam and his kids—but he always bounced back. And the scans he had after the operation indicated that what was left of the tumor was, unlike Maxey himself, staying dormant, and there was no reason to believe it wouldn't remain so.

He would share with me the progress on his face paralysis. Much better, he said, but not back to normal. This worried him. We would also talk about how it could be discouraging to think that the dizziness might never go away or that he might be off-balance for the rest of his life.

But when Maxey asked me how I was feeling, I didn't have a reply at the ready.

I had told Maxey in one of my emails that spring that I had a weird problem with my feet, that they were always cold. He had told me to get myself down to the Bahamas for a warm-water cure. I didn't tell him anything about a blizzard of new symptoms I had been experiencing, which were so random that I was sure they were unconnected. I told myself that they would vanish as unpredictably as they had arrived.

IN THE WEEKS and months after my feet began to feel like they were blocks of ice I'd started to experience other strange and unwelcome sensations and maladies. Curiously, next came the sensation that my feet were on fire. Then shooting pains, more intense than anything I'd ever encountered—like a dentist drilling without Novocain. That was followed by the feeling that someone had just stomped on my feet with steel-toed boots.

After a while, I started to have trouble walking, with my right leg so heavy I could barely lift it.

All the symptoms were worse at night, so sleep became ever more elusive. If my sheets even touched my legs, it was like sandpaper on raw skin. Cold made the symptoms worse, but heat did, too.

Soon after, I began to have trouble getting food to stay down and would vomit up totally undigested food if I ate more than the smallest meal. I had the most intense fatigue I'd ever experienced, which would come on within minutes. When it did, I would have to lie down on the floor. It was as if my muscles just didn't hear what my brain was telling them.

I, too, was dizzy—almost all the time now, with my heart

racing whenever I changed position from sitting to standing, standing to sitting. Only lying down would bring me back to equilibrium.

In addition, I developed a strange rash on my legs and had lost all the hair on them. I also frequently found myself pouring with sweat from my forehead but unable to sweat at all on my legs and arms. And the painful symptoms were starting to spread to my face and hands.

At the time I was still frequently on the road promoting my new book; I decided that I just needed some time to rest and I would return to normal. Looking back, I don't know how I could have convinced myself that this was so, but I was so focused on completing every part of the tour that I wasn't thinking clearly. There was one day when I was driving between Tallahassee and Miami that I had to pull into a rest stop because my right leg was so numb that I worried about my ability to control the accelerator. Eventually, enough sensation returned to allow me to drive on.

When I returned home after the book tour, the symptoms started getting much worse, and several days a week I was too sick to leave my bed, so David finally told me that I had to go see my doctor. After hearing all I had to say and examining me, my doctor told me that he couldn't figure it out and suggested I see a vascular specialist, a cardiologist, and a neurologist.

The vascular specialist and cardiologist said my veins and heart were in great shape. They didn't know what was wrong with me. So I wasn't hopeful when I went to see the neurologist in May. The pain was pretty bad, I told her—but the intense fatigue, vomiting, and dizziness were far harder for me to manage.

As soon as I started rattling off all my crazy symptoms, she began to nod. It was as though she knew what I was going to say before I even said it. When I was done, she told me she thought she knew what I had: small fiber neuropathy. She explained that the small fibers are the body's temperature and pain sensors. (Large nerve fibers control muscles, feel vibration, and let you know where your limbs are in space.) Small fibers also work behind the scenes as part of what is called the autonomic (think: automatic) nervous system, influencing your circulation, breathing, digestion, and immune and glandular function. That's why small fiber neuropathy typically causes such a strange range of symptoms across every part of the body.

When you have small fiber neuropathy, the small fibers within the nerve bundles become damaged and start misfiring—causing pain and, often, systemic chaos. It's at their tips that nerve fibers usually start to malfunction and can eventually shrink back, which is why peripheral neuropathies so often begin in the feet. It's not the dead bits at the end that hurt; pain signals come from the more central ailing parts sending out an alarm.

This was a lot to take in. She would do a series of blood tests to try to find a cause, which might include diabetes, celiac, or one of a few rare genetic diseases. Sometimes small fiber neuropathy is a side effect of chemotherapy or HIV medications, but I'd never had the former and didn't need the latter. There was the possibility that the neuropathy had been caused by antibiotics I took for my sinus infections but no way to prove that. She warned me that in about half the cases, the cause remained a mystery. Would it progress? Probably not, but it might. Would it get better? Probably not, unless they could find out what was causing it. Still, there were medicines that could help lessen the pain and nausea.

Millions of people have some kind of peripheral neuropathy, I would later learn, but in only a small sliver of cases does it manifest exclusively in the small fiber pain-sensing nerves. Maybe 175,000 or so people in the U.S.; four million worldwide.

However, we shouldn't jump to any conclusions, she added. The first thing was to rule out large fiber neuropathies or mixed neuropathies; to do this they would conduct electromagnetic tests.

Eventually, they could do a simple skin biopsy if the other tests didn't reveal anything. This would confirm with more than ninety percent certainty whether I did indeed have damage to my small fiber nerves. The test had only recently become widely available and most doctors didn't know to offer it. "It's quite unusual to have a neurological condition," another doctor would explain, "that can be diagnosed with a large degree of certainty simply by counting the number of nerves that you have under your skin."

I WAS RELIEVED to have a likely diagnosis that wasn't something fatal or even something that would definitely progress. My mother had a phrase she always used: "In the grand scheme of things . . ." Whenever something happened that wasn't optimal, she would always qualify it by pointing out that "in the grand scheme of things" it could have been a lot worse. There was no doubt that "in the grand scheme of things" I was incredibly lucky. This was driven home by a comment the neurologist made after the first tests that day in the office. "It isn't ALS, Lou Gehrig's disease," she'd said. It hadn't occurred to me that ALS was a possibility.

During the months of accumulating symptoms, while trying to get appointments with the various specialists, negotiate the world of health insurance reimbursements, and manage my free-floating anxiety, I decided not to tell most of my friends that much was amiss. That was before I saw the neurologist.

I'd leaned heavily on my husband and a few friends throughout the process, including David Singer. He came from a medical family and had worked in biotech. He had proven himself over the years to be sympathetic to whatever I was going through, but never overly so, which I found helpful and comforting. His signature candor was exactly what I most needed. At several points he rightly chewed me out for using the Internet to try to help diagnose my ailment. "So I guess medical school isn't really worth the time or money, right? And all you need is Google? Why don't you wait and hear what your doctor has to say?"

At the same time, Singer encouraged me not to be overly reverent toward my doctors and to come prepared with lots of questions.

At one point he wrote me to say, "I think the core challenge in this is how to dig deeper to find out what is going on without chasing down blind alleys that are more interesting to your care team than anything with a high probability to make you better. I know that is an issue but not sure how to translate it into advice so will send love instead."

There was one other part of this ordeal. My neurologist

strongly recommended that I stop drinking alcohol. I was not happy at all about this but dutifully obeyed. Singer was, as always, mildly but not extravagantly sympathetic. He reminded me that he had stopped drinking for extended periods several times in his life—usually for overall health—and hadn't really missed it.

Singer then pointed out I could probably get down to my desired weight now that I had quit drinking. I replied that I was replacing alcohol with chocolate.

I also leaned on David Kelly, my MTV pal and Singer's roommate. He and I had kept in close touch in the early years after graduation and had become even closer after he came out as gay. David had gone to business school as part of an executive program and then law school at night—all while working as a banker in New York during the eighties and nineties—but was always game to get together, especially if it involved a meal at a new restaurant.

After he moved to California in 1999 for a finance job, we made sure to call each other regularly. He decided once there to become a caterer and chef. In 2006, David was diagnosed with HIV and found new purpose as an HIV/AIDS activist and as an emotional support group leader for people who had recently been diagnosed. He later discovered and was embraced by the gay leather community in Southern California. In 2018, he was the reigning Mr. Palm Springs Leather, which meant a year of raising funds and awareness for causes important to gay people in his new hometown. And he'd found love with Clayton Koppes, a historian and professor he met there, who had just retired from Oberlin after serving as a dean, provost, and acting president.

David Kelly's work as a counselor had made him an enormously skilled listener, with just the right blend of empathy and practical wisdom, so I called him a lot. But in all my phone calls and emails with Maxey between January and May, I didn't say anything about my medical problems, other than my one mention of mysterious foot pain. It seemed embarrassing to complain to Maxey about my bundle of symptoms and peculiar nerve disease when he had just had his skull opened up and a chunk of tumor removed. When he asked how I was, I always just said, "Fine."

Then one day in May we had a very different kind of call.

It was a Sunday, and I was watching *CBS Sunday Morning,* my favorite show. I love the languor of its segments. The show also has a superpower: the ability to make me weep. I'm superstitious about it, too. It always ends with a half minute of nature, an unnarrated segment where you just look at and listen to a river flowing, or birds gathering, or ice melting. I have to see this part or I'm convinced that the following week will go badly. It's not rational, I know that.

Just as we were about to get to the nature segment, the phone rang. I let it go to voice mail and called back as soon as the segment was finished.

Maxey got right to the point.

"I'm really pissed at you."

I thought he was joking; he so rarely got mad at me. "What did I do this time?" I asked.

"No, seriously, I'm really, really pissed."

He sounded angrier at me than he'd ever been. I remembered when he'd been angry at my inability or unwillingness to express affection. I hadn't made much progress. I wondered if it was that, or if there was something new. I figured I had better just ask. "Really? What did I do?" I asked.

"Every time we talk, I ask you how you are doing and you always say you are fine, but I just got off the phone with Singer and he says you aren't fine. He says you feel like crap. I've been asking you how you are doing, and you never say anything. So that's kind of bullshit."

"Yeah, I'm sorry. I mean, it's this weird thing with my small nerve fibers, and it's pretty painful and makes me dizzy, and they don't know what caused it, but it's not going to kill me."

There was a long silence on the phone.

"Hey, Pam's calling me," Maxey finally said. "We're heading out on *Kokomo*." *Kokomo* was their boat.

"Hope it's a beautiful day on the water."

There was another long pause.

"Later," he said. And then he hung up.

My first reaction was defensive: my illness was my business; I didn't have to tell anybody anything until I was ready. But then I thought how much Maxey had shared with me over the past few months, before, during, and after his possibly fatal operation: the nausea, the dizziness, and the fears that he would never be fully better. He had allowed himself to be completely vulnerable with me. Meanwhile, even though I was grappling with some of the same fears, I had trusted him with nothing. I had thought that I was being noble, keeping my less dramatic medical problems to myself. But in fact I was being furtive and selfish.

NOISE

The next day I wrote Maxey a long email telling him the whole story about my small fiber neuropathy. I informed him that the new medicine I was trying made me "low-level stoned" all the time—so there was, indeed, a silver lining. I wrote that I knew I was super lucky as I had fantastic doctors and they had ruled out all the fatal things it could be so that it would just involve some adjustments. How many and what kind, I wasn't yet sure. I added that walking any distance was proving difficult, so he should be ready to "include me out" on the five-mile run the next time I visited Eleuthera. I also told him that alcohol was off the table, literally and figuratively.

I heard nothing back.

That evening I realized that I'd missed a call from Maxey. I now wore hearing aids—after years of straining to follow conversations at gatherings and turning up the television far beyond loud—but had taken them out, so hadn't heard my phone ring. He'd called just a few minutes after he got my email. There was a voice mail:

"Hey. It's Maxey. Pam and I are going to come to New York in July. You're forgiven if you and David come to dinner with us. You have to let us buy dinner. And if I ask you how you are feeling, you have to tell the truth. Sending you strength. I miss you." Then there was a pause in the message before Maxey wrapped it up: "Oh, and I'm drinking too much and need to be around friends who don't drink."

After I listened to Maxey's call, I grabbed a fizzy water, put on a record (*The Low Spark of High Heeled Boys* by Traffic), and just sat for a while as night fell outside the grubby windows that we'd neglected to clean for months. David was working late so I had the apartment to myself for a while, with time to think. I was still low-level stoned from the new medication, which had the harmonious name of Lyrica, but it wasn't helping my pain or my mood.

In the song, Traffic asks: "If you had just one minute to breathe, and they granted you one final wish, would you ask for something like another chance?"

Maybe the reason I hadn't said anything to Maxey wasn't really because I believed that my medical problems were trivial compared to his brain surgery. After all, I rarely failed to mention even the slightest discomfort—a paper cut, a hangnail. Maybe I hadn't told Maxey about my neuropathy because I liked being the one who *offered* help and advice, the one whom people could lean on as they learned to regain their balance. Being that person gave me a sense of purpose, even a kind of pleasure. I did not like being the person who needed help. Not one bit. So I had never considered whether in refusing to be that person, I had denied my friends something essential. In fact, before that moment it had never occurred to me that I had denied them anything; I just thought I was being stoic. Selfless, even.

I thought back to a book I'd read as a teen, *The Best Little Boy in the World*. It's a memoir written by Andrew Tobias under the pseudonym John Reid; the author wasn't out of the closet when he wrote it. Tobias/Reid chronicles a life of obsessive overachievement all in the service of hiding his true gay identity: if he's the best little boy in the world then maybe no one will see who he really is, a kid scared of rejection for being gay in a society that places more value on straight lives.

In trying to be that best little boy myself, had I ever really been myself? When Maxey took me to task and insisted that I let him help me, he had opened up a door for me. I suspected that he was the person in my life who could best guide me through it. It was time to ask for another chance.

SINGER TOOK THE lead in scheduling our New York City get-together with Maxey and Pam in July. When Maxey emailed that Tegan would be in town and asked if he could bring her, Singer replied that not only was that fine, but that we would all much prefer to see Tegan and Pam without Maxey, but that Maxey should come if he must. (As always, Maxey had signed his email to me and Singer "Respectfully." I vowed finally to ask him what was up with that.) So, with my David, we would be seven. I volunteered to find the restaurant, suggesting we start with drinks on our building's communal roof and then head out to a place in the neighborhood.

I thought carefully about the restaurant. I wanted a place that wasn't too expensive, where we could all sit and talk without feeling rushed. I called all the quiet, cheap restaurants in my neighborhood, and none of them had a table for seven. Making things more difficult, the city was broiling hot. Because I'd lost the ability to sweat, I quickly became overheated. So we needed to be inside and with good air-conditioning.

When the day for our get-together arrived it was blessedly cool, so we started the evening on the communal roof as planned. Tegan was still working at a start-up in Brooklyn, and I gave her way too much avuncular advice on the dos and don'ts of start-ups, which she took in good humor. Mostly we talked during drinks (soda for me) about the Island School. Singer's oldest child had gone for a weeklong program there and had the experience so many other young people had: he returned home more confident and more focused, and less interested in the world of electronic devices.

Then it was time to head out to dinner at a restaurant nearby that a friend had recommended. As soon as we came through the door, though, I realized I'd made a mistake. There was wall-to-wall sound: the clanging of cutlery, shrill laughter from several tables, ear-shattering music. The restaurant had brick walls, stone floors, and metal furniture with no cushion or fabric in sight. Forced into overdrive, my hearing aids started to squeal. I looked over at Maxey, who winced. He had only the one ear that worked.

I should have suggested we bail. I should have brought everyone back to our apartment and just ordered some pizza. But we were immediately seated at a table and had ordered some appetizers to share before I fully realized that we really weren't going to be able to hear one another very well. Could the restaurant turn the music down? They couldn't, they said. Was there a quieter table? There wasn't; this was the quietest they had.

I looked around the restaurant and it seemed that everyone was having fun and enjoying the clamor. I felt sheepish and old for trying to get the restaurant to change its vibe, so I decided to make the best of the evening.

Whether it was from the noise or the neuropathy, I started to feel nauseated. Pam was telling a story about a family crisis that hadn't yet been resolved. She was telling it as a somewhat comical tale, but I could tell that she and Maxey had lost sleep over it. I heard only every few words but was able to piece it together as it went. Singer and Tegan were fully engaged in their own discussion; I couldn't hear what they were talking about.

I looked across the table at Maxey, who clearly couldn't hear a word of either conversation. Pam was drowned out by the restaurant noise and by constant loud laugher from a table nearby; Singer and Tegan were on his deaf side. His face was wrinkled more than usual, almost evenly on both sides now, as he strained to hear Pam. Occasionally, he would add an observation, a beat or two ahead or behind where she was in the story. I guessed that he was growing increasingly frustrated. Why were the people at the next table relentlessly shrieking with laughter? Nothing could be that funny.

It did occur to me that I had been at plenty of occasions with Maxey where he was the loud one and the table next to ours was probably wondering the very same thing. But New Yorkers are by nature hypocrites: we only mind the noise we don't create ourselves.

I was about to launch into a cranky rant about the cacophony when I noticed something. Singer and Tegan were enjoying themselves. David and Pam were deep into conversation, even if they could barely hear one another. And Maxey seemed totally at peace. I had been wrong; he didn't look frustrated at all. He was sitting back in his chair, cradling a beer, looking around at his family and friends; his chest was rising and falling as he took in deep lungfuls. It was almost as though he were free diving right in the middle of the restaurant.

I would need to ask him how he did that.

* * *

WHEN I GOT back to the apartment, I realized that Maxey had left his aviator sunglasses on the building's roof.

I texted him right away to let him know.

He texted back: "You keep them for now and bring them when you come to do some free diving."

QUIET

On Friday, March 16, 2018, at six a.m., the alarm went off. I was leaving for the airport to fly to Eleuthera and had an hour to shower, pack, have some breakfast, and get out of the house.

David had been encouraging me to go on the brief trip: the flights were cheap, Maxey and Pam would put me up, and I didn't have to take more than a few days of vacation. He thought that the combination of sun and warm water and old friends would do me good. Plus, he needed to go home and see his family in Hong Kong. Still, I wasn't sure; as always I had busy weeks of work ahead and more on my to-do list than I could ever hope to accomplish.

But the tipping point for the Eleuthera trip had been the February meeting of my peripheral neuropathy support group. We were ten people age twenty to eighty, meeting in a conference room in an office that belonged to none of us. It was helpful to trade information and I usually enjoyed it. At the February meeting a fellow member had asked, "Does gabapentin affect your memory?" That was the drug I now took, which didn't make me as dopey as Lyrica. "Yes, it can," the moderator helpfully answered.

A few minutes later, the same person had another question he couldn't wait to ask. He hoisted his hand high in the air until he was called upon. "Does gabapentin affect your memory?" he asked. Patiently, the moderator replied it could indeed. On it went throughout the meeting. I was sympathetic but wondered how quickly I would become that person. It was time to get out of New York and my own head.

At 6:55 a.m. on the dot, I was ready to head out the door, just as planned.

"Don't forget your passport," David groggily shouted from bed.

"I have it right here in my pocket," I said, patting my pocket. It wasn't there. It wasn't in my knapsack or my small duffel. It wasn't in my coat. It wasn't on the bedside table. Minutes were ticking by, leaving less and less margin for error. There would be traffic. There would be long check-in lines. And there was a nor'easter on the way. I was growing more and more frantic—not just because of the flight but because of my worry that I had already become the guy in my support group who couldn't remember if he'd asked the memory question.

At 7:15 David ordered me to sit down. He would look through my bags. My passport was right there in the outside pocket of my knapsack, which I could have sworn I'd checked a dozen times in the last fifteen minutes during my frantic search. What wasn't in my bag was my gabapentin. I had almost forgotten that.

I had hours of layover in Nassau. I still hadn't calmed down after the morning's panic. My feet were on fire and my forehead was dripping sweat. I found a seat in the lounge next to some teenaged girls sweetly playing the ukulele and singing "I'm Yours" by Jason Mraz, one of my favorite songs: "I fell right through the cracks / Now I'm trying to get back."

Then it was on to the small prop plane. Within minutes we were noisily flying over the calm blue waters that surround the Bahamas, with only the occasional boat visible below; the sky was almost the same color as the water, which caused the horizon to disappear. The pilot flew steadily, and I lost myself in the Mraz song that was happily stuck in my head. Fifteen minutes later, we landed at Rock Sound Airport on the island of Eleuthera.

Maxey and Tyler were there to greet me; Maxey gave me a big bear hug and then Tyler did, too, which made us all laugh. "He told me you hate that," she said.

The hour-long ride from the airport to the house gave time for me to get all the news, some of it grim. A hurricane had been through and, tragically, swept a young man off a bridge into the water. His body had not yet been found. On a happier note, I asked about Tyler's girlfriend; she was well and in Argentina but would be visiting soon. Maxey also told me with great pride that the van we were riding in was powered entirely by biodiesel, which a team of students had made from used cooking oil. About halfway through the ride, I noticed that Maxey had a vivid wound on his calf that was all the colors of the rainbow. Once I saw it, I didn't know how I'd missed it. It was oozing pus.

"How the hell did you do that?" I asked him.

"Oh, that. Basically, I tripped, fell, broke my glasses, and gashed my leg. It'll heal."

"It's hot to the touch, Dad," Tyler said. "You really should go see a doctor." Maxey didn't answer. Then Tyler turned to me. "He won't. And another thing—he's coughing his lungs out. I think he has pneumonia."

"No, I'm not," Maxey said, annoyed. Then he proceeded to cough his lungs out, forcing Tyler to throw up her hands in the universal gesture for the intersection of "See what I mean?" and "I surrender."

When we arrived at the house, Pam greeted me with another huge Maxey hug. She looked a bit frazzled and immediately explained why. While we were on our way from the airport, the Maxeys' dog, Jag, an ancient, mostly blind terrier, had gone exploring on the dock and fallen into the water—immediately drawing the attention of several bull sharks, who began circling him. "I had to cantilever myself over the dock and reach down and grab him before the sharks ate him," Pam said.

Jag seemed no worse for his adventure and was wandering cheerfully around the condo.

"Maybe Jag doesn't want to live any longer," Tyler suggested. "Maybe he's trying for suicide by shark?" Pam gave Tyler a stern look but then admitted that Tegan had suggested the exact same thing. In a few minutes, we were joined by Tegan, who had been out jogging. The house was full of life. The last time I had been there it was just Maxey, with Pam and the kids back in the United States. Now it was Pam and Maxey, with Tyler teaching at the school and Tegan visiting. Brittney and Brocq had also recently been through.

My old friend grabbed my bags and motioned me toward the guest bedroom in the back of the condo. Like the rest of the place, it was decorated in blues and greens. There was art everywhere made from seashells, more than when I'd been there last. The curated piles of seashells had also grown. The walls were covered with family pictures and bright paintings by local artists. Maxey showed me the bathroom and reminded me of the rules: Navy showers. Also, no flushing if you just took a leak. Only if you took a dump.

"Hey, Maxey, are you going to do something about that ugly gash on your leg?" I asked him. "It looks horrific."

"Nah, it'll be okay. It's healing nicely."

"Thanks for trying, Will," Pam shouted from the kitchen. "But good luck convincing him. He'll let it get gangrenous before he'll agree to see a doctor or take a pill."

THAT AFTERNOON WE headed over to the school to join the end-of-day ritual. All the students were in a circle around the flagpole, mostly boys on one side and girls on the other, but with some overlap. This was the moment the kids often gave kudos to one another. One girl said of a schoolmate, "She wasn't feeling well but still helped everyone out today."

I'd been worried we were going to have to all hold hands—another thing I don't like—but that wasn't part of the program.

Back at the house, Pam was making coffee. I grabbed a mug and settled into the rattan sofa as the Maxey family life swirled around me.

Tyler needed to get some lionfish for a science demonstration at the school. These spiny, venomous creatures weren't native to the Bahamas and were posing a threat to the local marine life. The question was how to halt the spread of this invasive fish; one popular approach sought to introduce them onto menus. Humans were capable of overfishing every kind of popular seafood to the point of extinction; why not lionfish in this particular locale? Ironically, Tyler hadn't been able to find any that day. Tegan was in between calls back to her Brooklyn start-up; she had some ideas for locating lionfish that Tyler took to be criticisms. Soon they were in a full-fledged quarrel, shouting barbs and obscenities at maximum volume. Pam tried to calm the waters, which caused both Tyler and Tegan to lash out at their mother.

During all of his, Maxey stood silently, leaning against a wall for balance. He'd told me that day he was still almost constantly dizzy—on land. But he was smiling. I wondered how long I could live in such a boisterous house, but it was a pleasant change from the winter quiet of my New York refuge.

"Any regrets about not having children, Schwalbs?" Maxey asked me. I laughed but said nothing. "I didn't think so," he added.

After a family dinner of pasta and spiny lobster, Maxey and I wound up sitting on the dock. Pam had admissions work to do for the school.

From my spot near the door I could hear the sisters in the kitchen.

Tegan: "You can't stay mad at me, can you, Tyler?"

Tyler: "No, I really can't."

Tegan: "And do you know the reason why?"

Tyler: "I don't."

Tegan: "Because I'm the best little sister ever!"

They came out, arms around each other's shoulders, and announced they were heading over to the school to hang out with some of the young faculty.

"Seriously, Maxey," I said when they were out of earshot, "don't you worry about them all the time?" One of the reasons David and I didn't regret not having children was because we couldn't imagine having to be responsible for other humans for life.

"Of course, all the time. Never not. I worry about all of my kids."

"And you're also in charge of other people's kids. And the young faculty."

"Yeah, in loco parentis. You want to treat them like your own children but go even one step further. Still, kids need a little constructive risk to help them become resilient and teach them to judge danger for themselves.

"Like the forty-eight-hour solos we have the students do during the sea kayak expeditions. One of the highlights of the school term for these students is the solo." Maxey had explained the solos in his long letter about Andy, the gay student who had initially hated him, but I let him tell me again; I didn't remember exactly how they worked. "We leave each student alone on a patch of beach all by themselves. They have to create their own shelter and entertainment, and just deal with being alone for two whole days. The amazing thing is they all learn they have resources they never thought they had. Of course, we've got a system for checking to make sure they are okay and some strong emergency procedures in place. But most of the time they truly are alone. For many of them, the solo is the first time in their entire lives they've ever been totally by themselves for more than a few hours.

"And it's not just the solos. The rule we have about phones helps make them more resilient, too. The rule is simple: We take their phones the minute they get here and they don't get them back until they leave, one hundred days later. We do let them call home once a week, from a landline in the office. Separating them from their smartphones also helps them be present with all the other students—and with themselves."

I thought of my own smartphone and how much I relied on it. I was good about putting it away when with others and being present with those around me, sure. But was I spending too much time on it when I was alone? Without a doubt.

"That's also why *querencia* is key. It's not just training for the solo. Though it is that. And it's not just a life skill. Though it's that, too. It's one of the most important things they discover. Young people come here thinking the most important thing they are going to learn will be diving, or studying marine biology, or doing research. None of those are. The whole Island School is about learning to be present where you are, and to appreciate not just this special place but *every* place—the whole planet."

I was going to tease Maxey or tune out, as I'd often done when he started to wax philosophical, but decided not to this time. Maybe that was because I was finally ready to listen. After he finished, we sat for a while in quiet. There was a huge moon that night casting shadows from the boats moored around the dock onto the water. In the distance ahead, at the mouth of the cove, was the Harbour Pointe Restaurant, whose lights seemed to dim as they were outshone from above before they were turned off for good.

"So, remind me about this *querencia* thing," I asked Maxey.

"I've explained it before," Maxey said.

"Yeah, but I wasn't listening."

"You sure you want to hear this, Schwalbs?"

"I'm sure."

"I told you that all the students, before they arrive, read *The*

Rediscovery of North America by Barry Lopez. It's a book about the way Columbus and the Spanish conquistadores slaughtered the Indigenous people and destroyed everything they touched in their hunt for gold. It was actually a talk Lopez gave. A call to arms. It's about how we're doing the same thing to our planet right now. It's a short read and great for students because it's honest and painful, but it's hopeful. It's written out of the belief that we really can turn this around. Near the end of the book, Lopez introduces the idea of *querencia,* a physical place. The word is derived from the Spanish verb *querer,* to desire. Lopez wants to instill in his readers the idea of loving a physical place—not superficially but with a deep and emotional attachment, as well as a concentrated sense of anger. I first found the word in a book by Hemingway, who defined the *querencia* the way Lopez does: as the place where a bull in a bullring goes to make a final stand. It's a place of courage and comfort and resolve.

"We begin the first morning of each new term lying on the beach in a circle, close together so that our shoulders are touching. We just lie there for a while, on the sand, looking up at the sky. We want the students to wonder about this place, the kind of wonder that was totally natural to them when they were all five years old. There's a quote I love from a marine biologist named Edie Widder; I can't remember it exactly, but she says that we're all born scientists with innate curiosity to touch, smell, and even eat the new substrate that comes into view." I made a mental note to ask Maxey what substrate was but didn't want to interrupt. "It's amazing to see teenagers who have lost contact with their five-year-old selves let down their guard and be curious again. We want to bring them back to that magic age of exploration.

"And on that first morning we tell them to pour sand over their faces, to smell and even taste this new land. That's what Lopez asks to us do. To rediscover this land, to become intimate with it, to fall in love. We then tell them that while they are at the school, we want them to spend time alone, and explore the seascape around the campus. And that's why we challenge each of them to find a place to be alone, to find their own *querencia,* a special place all their own where they can go and gain comfort, find solitude, and explore in real time the intimate beauty of this place and find their best selves.

"While they're here, they live twelve students to a dorm, sharing one big room, so *querencia* is also a chance to get away from the others for a bit. That's why every week includes three hours of *querencia* time. We give them some assignments for that time over the course of the term, but very few. Mostly it's just time for them to be there with their own thoughts."

All of the Maxeys have the same tattoo. Two numbers. The longitude and latitude of the island of Eleuthera. Their family home. Their *querencia.* I started to wonder if I had a *querencia.* I'd always found solace and strength in books. Books were a *querencia* of sorts. But books also took me *out* of the physical place I happened to be and brought me somewhere else. If that night I'd gone to bed early with a book, I wouldn't now be sitting on the dock with Maxey, and I'd never have seen this night's moon, water, boats, and lights. I wouldn't have heard what my friend had to say. It wasn't a choice: books or life. Still, I started to wonder: Had I too often retreated into the former instead of engaging with the latter?

I thought about how Maxey and I had started on such different paths. His talents were physical, and he loved to compete. His whole life had steered him toward other people: only around them could he be peak Maxey. He'd also lost a third of his family as a child, only later finding the clan he craved. I was a kid who'd lived largely inside my head, scared of spending too much time with others in case they got to know the part of me I felt I couldn't reveal. So I hid in plain sight, spending endless hours with others but only comfortable in my room, alone, or with one or two carefully chosen friends. Then, just a few years after I came out, being with people took on a whole new cast when sex began to equal death. Nothing was safer than a book.

One of the best things about books is that they are always there for you; they will forgive you endless amounts of neglect and still be ready to greet you, unchanged. I will always love books, but, in that moment, I thought that maybe, sometimes, I could keep them waiting for me a bit longer. That's the thing about a true *querencia,* I realized: the knowledge that it's always there if you need it allows you to go out bravely into the world.

Maxey had managed to control his coughing for a while but then it started up again. At that moment, a toddler from one of the nearby houses, up way past his bedtime, shot past us on the dock, with his mother laughing and running after him. I thought of the dog Jag and his close call with the sharks but the small hellion was quickly scooped up and brought laughing back to his home.

It had been a long day, and my feet were burning from the neuropathy. I was starting to think it was time for a fistful of gabapentin to literally calm my nerves.

Maxey had his eyes closed.

"Tired or dizzy?" I asked him.

"Dizzy, I guess," he said. "I've been dizzy pretty constantly since the operation. It's not getting better but I'm getting better at living with it." He'd said that before. It was almost like a mantra, I realized. The more he said it, the more it would be true.

"Do you think your dizziness might also have something to do with the enormous, festering gash on your leg?" I asked him. "Or the fact that you sound like you belong in a tubercular ward?"

"Don't you get on my case, too, Schwalbs." And then, "I wonder if it would help if I poured some rum on it?"

At that moment, Pam came out to join us. "Please don't waste the good rum," she said.

When Maxey went in to take a leak, I asked Pam if Maxey could be convinced to see a doctor for that leg. "Not a chance," she said.

"One thing I've always wondered," I asked her. "Is Maxey different with his SEAL friends? I mean, I've never met any of them. I've always kind of wondered if the Maxey I know is the same as the Maxey other people know."

Pam paused for a second before answering. "You know, I think for better or worse he's pretty much the same around everyone. He might be a little more thoughtful around you." Then she had a question for me: "Are you the same around Maxey as you are around your other friends?"

I thought about that for a moment. "I didn't used to be, but I think more and more I am. But maybe I'm a bit more butch around Maxey. Just a bit." Pam laughed.

Soon, Maxey was back.

"Hey, I left a book for you by your bed," Maxey told me.

"Some bedtime reading. But don't read too long. Tomorrow I teach you to free dive."

When I got back to my room, I saw perched on the top of my suitcase a well-worn copy of *The Rediscovery of North America* by Barry Lopez. I started reading and didn't stop.

"We cannot, with Huck Finn and Mark Twain, light out for the territory anymore, to a place where we might continue to live without parental restraint. We need to find our home. We need to find a place where we take on the responsibilities of adults to the human community. Having seen what is going on around us, we need to find, each person, his or her *querencia,* and to believe it is not a matador in a bullring we face, a rigged game, but an assailable beast, another in our history like Tamerlane or the Black Death."

This, I realized, wasn't just a book Maxey had students read before they arrived to introduce them to the school's values; it was a text that had given Maxey the language and the insight he needed to settle in this place, to find stillness here, and to face whatever demons were challenging him from outside and from within. Pages later, I came to a passage in the book that connected our *querencias:* "If we feel wisdom is lost, we need only enter a library. We will find there the records of hundreds of men and women who believed in a world larger than the one defined by each generation by human failing. We will find literature, which teaches us again and again how to imagine."

In a sense, this book didn't just help Maxey find his *querencia;* it was an essential part of it. Our paths weren't so different, after all. If he could find himself in my element, books, then maybe I could find myself in his: the water.

Before drifting off to sleep, I also wondered whether Maxey

was using the book to introduce me to his much larger quest: to not only find his place in the world but do his part to save it.

DIVING

Maybe it was the humidity, maybe the change in temperature, maybe the flying, but for no reason I could entirely decipher, my neuropathy was particularly intense and my feet felt like they were on fire that whole night. Which made it almost impossible to sleep.

I also felt an overwhelming sense of anxiety and doom, and each time I did nod off, it was only to wake up soon afterwards from nightmare after nightmare—none that I had ever had before but more garden-variety ones that involved monsters and the like. I couldn't figure out the source of my terror—unless it was that I really didn't *want* to learn how to free dive.

Maxey had suggested I watch some videos about free diving before I visited, which I had eventually done. Before that, I had thought free diving was just holding your breath, hanging out underwater for a while, and then coming up for air. But no. There was a whole complicated breathing procedure and you had to learn to clear your ears and sinuses. Then you had to try to trigger your "mammalian diving reflex," whatever that was—something about slowing your heartbeat way down. Then there was a series of complex instructions about resurfacing and what you did right after. Get any of it wrong and you could black out and die.

The last time I looked at the clock that night, it was five thirty in the morning. The next thing I remember was hearing a crash in the kitchen right outside the door to my bedroom. I looked at the clock again. Unbearably, it was only ninety minutes later. I threw on some jeans and headed out to see what had caused the commotion.

Maxey was making coffee. Nothing seemed broken. Nothing even seemed like it had been dropped. I sympathized with Pam. How could anyone make that much noise making coffee?

Maxey poured me a cup. It had a strong cinnamon flavor. Not bad. He then took a seat at the kitchen table, which looked out over the dock, the boats, the marina, and the neighbors. I started talking to him but he ignored me, which is when I remembered that I was on his deaf side. I came around and sat next to his good ear.

"Doesn't it bug you to live in a fishbowl?" I asked him.

"It's not a fishbowl," he replied. Just then, one of his neighbors walked by and waved at both of us. Maxey motioned him in and they chatted for a bit before the neighbor went on his way. Maxey laughed. "Well, maybe it is kind of a fishbowl."

"I mean, not just your home," I clarified, picking up a theme from our discussion the night before. "You're always surrounded: family, friends, students, teachers, scientists, neighbors. I couldn't do it. I need quiet time. Lots of quiet time. Otherwise, I turn feral."

"I don't believe you turn feral. I've never seen you turn feral."

"You haven't seen me when I didn't get time to myself."

As we were talking, Tyler came into the kitchen. She told us how mad she was at herself for not being able to catch a lionfish for the demonstration at the school. She wouldn't be able to get one this morning because of a misunderstanding with Pam about some errands that needed running. There was more to the story, but I quickly lost the thread. It was one of those moments when you are temporarily embedded in a friend's family and realize that battle lines have been drawn and that the best thing you can do is keep out of the line of fire. I certainly didn't want to get between Tyler and Pam on this. Nor, as it turned out, did Maxey.

"Hey, buddy, time to go free diving."

"Are you sure you feel up to it, Maxey? Don't you want to just relax today, lie down, take care of that cough?"

"When I'm sick and lie down, I get sicker. A run and a swim and a dive always make me feel better."

"Tell that to pneumonia," I said.

"I'm telling you, Schwalbs, it works for me. I know this." Maxey sounded a bit annoyed—in part because he hated me getting on his case along with his wife and kids, but also, I think, because he rightly suspected that I was trying to use his cough as an excuse to get out of free diving.

Seconds later we were in the Maxeys' electric car heading to school, with Maxey belting out one of his non-songs—a mélange of "Oh, What a Beautiful Mornin'" from *Oklahoma!*, Tom Petty's "Free Fallin'," Lynyrd Skynyrd's "Free Bird," and some genuinely unrecognizable caterwauling—but whenever it swung back around to the chorus of "Free Fallin'," Maxey replaced "fallin'" with "divin'," which resulted in the chorus "I am free . . . free divin'!"

That day, I was either going to become an underwater sea creature, flexing my instinctive mammalian breathing reflex, or I was going to drown.

I thought back to the video. If I died while free diving,

except for a brief period before I lost consciousness, I wouldn't be around after to feel like a horse's ass for doing something I knew I shouldn't be doing. Still, I wasn't keen to experience those few seconds of pain and self-recrimination. There was a distinct possibility my sinuses weren't going to be happy with my new hobby. There was also the possibility of deafness.

We pulled into the school and Maxey plugged his car into a charger.

The school's blue roofs seemed to float against the sky as though the world was upside down and I was underwater already, unsure if I was looking into the depths or toward the surface. I was dripping with sweat and keenly aware of every inch I might have missed with the sunscreen lotion I'd attempted to smear all over myself before heading out. My bald spot felt especially exposed.

At the boathouse, a few dozen students were gathered, sprouting snorkels and masks and fins. This was the first time in a decade that I'd seen Maxey among the students. They were excited to see him and he knew each one. I also noticed a change: they treated him more gingerly than they had before. They didn't swarm him the way they used to, or clamber over him. Maybe they knew he'd recently had his head cut open. Or maybe it was just that he and I were that much older, now firmly the age of their parents, or probably older still.

Maxey had everyone form a circle on the boat dock, which perched on the edge of the ocean in front of us; the water was indigo where there were reefs below and robin's-egg blue where there weren't. It was only ten or so in the morning, but the sun was already high; I kept reaching back to my tube of sunblock to slather more on my bald spot.

Before we headed off, it was yoga time. Maxey led us through a series of poses. I was delighted to see that I was not the least-limber person—one or two of the students mimed their way through the poses just as I was doing. I kept avoiding Maxey's eye. It didn't make any sense to think he cared about my yoga competency, but I didn't want to disappoint him—and if I did disappoint him, I wanted to look as though I was doing my best. As one pose resolved into another, I kept waiting for downward facing dog, hoping that that would signal we were nearing the end.

Eventually, I gave up and just crouched there awkwardly, looking around the circle at the students and faculty.

"I can never remember," Maxey said, in what looked like a perfect downward facing dog, "if this is downward dog."

One of the students confirmed that it was.

Next, Maxey led us in the breathing pattern that would slow our heartbeat and prepare us mentally and physically for the free dive. He encouraged us to keep doing it periodically while we were on the boats heading out: We were to take a big, two-second inhalation, then hold that in for two counts, and then let it out real slow, for eight counts. Then hold for two. Then inhale again. Deep. Audible. Into our diaphragm. Slowly letting it out each time to that eight count. Inhaling for two. Holding for two. Exhaling for eight. Holding for two. Again, and again.

I breathed along with the group. Soon, I did feel calmer. Was calming my mind really that simple? I would need to remember this.

Next, we all lined up and counted off—one to thirty-three. I was thirty-three. Numbers one to thirty-two paired up as buddies, charged with keeping track of the other for the rest of the morning: not just as they got on and off the boats at the start of the excursion, but above and below the surface on every dive. My buddy was, of course, Maxey.

The students were itchy to get on the boats and into the water. They looked literally itchy, scratching themselves where they'd been bitten by mosquitoes, scraped by plants, abraded by sand. Before we headed off, Maxey wanted to run us all through the basics of free diving once more. He did this every single time they headed out to dive.

First, there's the business of clearing: how to pinch our noses and reduce the pressure in our middle ears. He also told us not to go deeper in the water than felt comfortable. Not to use anything to weigh ourselves down. Not to time ourselves, ever: trying to stay below for a set amount of time might cause us to override our body's natural signals. He said we'll know when we need to surface. He also told us that if we drop something, leave it. And when we surface, we need to interact with our buddy, who will be waiting. Look your buddy in the eye, he said. Fist bump. Spend a minute. If someone is going to pass out, it will most likely happen as they are surfacing. If that happens, we should shout and use our arms to give the signal that we need help, and Maxey or one of the faculty will come find us. If you think anything is wrong, Maxey told us, take it seriously. When in doubt, always get help.

"Got it?"

Everyone got it.

We were split up among three boats. I got the *Dave and Di,* and my mind went right to Singer. I bet he could learn to free dive in his sleep. I tripped as I boarded and whacked my knee on the steering wheel. The kid who correctly identified the downward dog sweetly asked me if I was okay. As his reward, Maxey gave him the wheel. The kid turned around and flashed me a smile. He introduced himself: Arlo. "Like Guthrie?" I asked. "Hold on," Arlo said, nodding yes in answer to my question.

The students let out a big cheer, led by Arlo, who went full throttle. Even with a dozen kids plus Maxey and me aboard the boat, the bow was cresting. I recalled Ratty's famous declaration from *The Wind in the Willows:* "There is *nothing*—absolutely nothing—half so much worth doing as simply messing about in boats." But this wasn't messing about in boats—this was drug-runner, cigar-boat-style, full-on wind-blasted adrenaline-fueled propulsion. Not terrifying. Thrilling. Or at least it felt that way to me. Most of the kids seemed to feel that way as well. Maxey sat still, one eye on the ocean, one eye on Arlo.

We rounded the curve of the cove and headed into open water; it was all now the same robin's-egg blue. Then we were at a buoy, and moored to it, and all the kids plopped into the water like olives into martinis, and Maxey and I were left on the boat.

I realized I didn't even know how to get in the water.

"You can go in Jacques Cousteau–style," Maxey told me, as he mimed falling backwards off the side. "Or, you can just kind of climb out of the boat and into the water." I opted for the latter.

Right away, I started drinking the ocean. The first problem was that I couldn't get my snorkel to work. Maybe it was broken? Maxey swapped snorkels with me. I finally figured out how to use it, but by this time I'd swallowed so much salt water I was certain I was going to vomit. I started thinking that the salt was acting like an emetic. I was momentarily distracted by the pleasure of having remembered the word *emetic*. Then I got nauseated all over again.

The other two boats had arrived and disgorged their olives into the brine. The students had swum in pairs to a point about fifty yards from the boats and started to dive, one at a time from each pair. Maxey and I swam toward them, but I was having trouble with the fins, snorkel, and mask combo. I'm not a bad swimmer; I've swum all my life. Yet I was continuing to flounder, like a fish on land, and to swallow water.

"Take my hand," said Maxey.

"I'm okay," I said.

I wasn't. I was embarrassed to take his hand but more embarrassed to be flopping around so helplessly. I thought back to how awkward I felt grabbing Maxey around the waist when he gave me a ride on his motorcycle after the retreat the year we met. Had I really changed so little? Was I still worried about the dynamic between a gay man and a straight one, being misunderstood? Or was it just my usual mammalian avoidance instinct? I took his hand and he pulled me swiftly toward the dive site.

On the way there, I realized I needed to distract myself from my nausea. I thought of a book I'd just finished, a slender novel called *Mrs. Caliban* by the American writer Rachel Ingalls. It's about an achingly unhappy woman who lives in the suburbs, mourning the death of a small child and the loss of a pregnancy, and suffering in the void that stands in place of her marriage now that she's discovered her husband is cheating on her. Then into her life comes a sea monster escaped from a local lab; she hides him and rescues him. And, to reference a popular movie about a streetwalker and a billionaire, he rescues her right back.

In Ingalls's tale, the sea and its creatures are comforting and terrifying, beautiful and savage, gentle and violent. It's a more intense version of our terrestrial world, and most definitely an alien one.

Now, as Maxey pulled me through the waves, I thought of Larry, the sea creature in the novel, so ungainly and misunderstood on land, and so at peace in the water. My zodiac sign is Cancer, a water sign, and I love the ocean. But mostly to look at; I'm not made for it.

This was the first time I had ever seen Maxey in his element. What astonished me was how fluid he became in water. His movements were barely perceptible and yet full of power, nothing wasted. He propelled both of us without a splash. He seemed to breathe in tune with the swells. I almost couldn't tell where Maxey ended and the water began.

Soon, we joined the others.

"Look down," said Maxey.

I was stunned by what I saw: there was an underwater cliff, stretching down as far as I could see, maybe a football field down. Or so it appeared. One side was a wall of coral; the other side water. Then, suddenly, Maxey took the smallest of breaths and dove below the surface, with just one duck kick (as I've now learned to call it) to propel him to the bottom.

I put my masked face into the water and peered down. In seconds he seemed impossibly far away and, in a heartbeat, ever farther, sinking to the bottom of the ocean. I looked up; no one else was in the immediate vicinity; it was just me, there, above the waves, and Maxey ever farther beneath me. One member of each of the other pairs was bobbing in the distance, watching their partners below.

I looked back down and now Maxey was all the way at the

bottom of the ocean, sitting cross-legged, Buddha-like on the ocean floor. He wasn't moving. At all. Was he dead? Between him and me the water was alive with a school of purple fish, pulsing with color, electrified.

I was sure a minute had gone by; now two and three. I was thinking that Maxey was dead, never to resurface. Seconds later, I was certain I should scream for the other instructors. Or should I? Maxey did say that if someone was going to pass out it would likely be on the surface. I decided to give it a few more seconds before I screamed. I didn't have a watch, but it felt like five minutes that Maxey had been on the ocean floor. Was that even possible? I needed to get help. I needed to shout.

Then Maxey started to levitate, rising slowly, ascending, toward the light, and finally breaking the surface. And then he was next to me with his hand out for a fist bump.

I wanted to tell him that he scared the crap out of me, but I didn't. That would have been too embarrassing.

"You good?" I asked.

"I'm good," he said.

Maxey looked around, catching the eyes of each of the other instructors. All good. He scanned the water, dunked his head back in to look down through his mask, and then popped his head up and motioned for me to put my face in the water again. I was still nauseated and soon more so when I managed to swallow even more water. In my dizziness, it looked as if the little fish I saw right in front of me were spinning like whirling dervishes. I felt as though I were about to barf into the ocean, even after I realized that it wasn't my vertiginous mind making the fish seem to swim like that—they were doing it all by themselves.

I tried to look past the spinning fish to something solid, and that's when I noticed the light streaming through the reef wall below; Maxey had been at the base of it, forty feet down. This reef formation was the cathedral Maxey had talked about, his sacred space. And the fish were the young Creole Wrasse he'd mentioned. Unless I learned to dive, I would never be able to experience this place in its full beauty, from inside and below, gazing up; and unless I learned to free dive, I would never be able to know the peace that Maxey felt when he was down there.

AFTER I PULLED my head out of the water again, I realized that either we had drifted to the center of the scrum of diving students, or they had come to join us. Around us were all thirty-two students and their instructors, diving in pairs, some deep, some shallow, fist bumping, arms and legs and fins everywhere. I looked down into the water: the school of purple fish had scattered and I could no longer see the cathedral. Just a flurry of youthful limbs thrashing in the waves.

When I was a teen and would drink alcohol, I sometimes got the spins, that horrible feeling that the entire room is whipping around you, and you are helpless to make it stop. Or, at least, I was helpless until a friend taught me a foolproof trick: you had to head for a bed, any bed, but first take off a sneaker (we always wore sneakers). You then needed to take the lace out of that sneaker and tie one end of the shoelace through one eyelet and knot it tight. You would take the other end and tie it to the bedpost. So there you'd be, on the bed, holding a sneaker that was tethered to your bed by a long lace. Next, you simply had to drop the sneaker over the side of the bed: it would act as an anchor, mooring the bed to the floor and stopping it and the room from bucking and twisting.

Every time I had to employ this trick, it worked for me—largely, I think, because the amount of concentration I needed to exert to execute all those steps sobered and grounded me. I thought of this trick now, as I bobbed around in the water and continued to inhale the ocean. I caught Maxey's attention, pointed to my chest, and then to the boat, far in the distance. He got the hint, took my hand again, and swam me over to it.

After climbing aboard, I sat myself in the pilot's chair. My T-shirt, clammy and stiff with salt, clung to my chest. It was then that I realized my sneaker-over-the-side-of-the-bed trick had never made even the slightest sense. I was now on a boat that was properly tethered to a buoy and I was every bit as nauseated as if the boat had been floating totally free; it rose and fell with every swell and swiveled side to side. Anchors and tethers keep boats in one spot; they don't keep them still. Desperate not to become "Maxey's friend who barfed," I fixed my eyes on the horizon and counted to ten over and over again. Finally, after what seemed like hours but was only twenty more minutes, the kids were clambering aboard, sharing stories with one another of their free dives—with some of them describing the light pouring in through the cracks in the coral cathedral.

While they had been finding religion, I had simply been trying to find a modicum of equilibrium. I was reminded of a friend in Hong Kong who loved to go on the water every weekend in a boat he nicknamed Church. Whenever anyone asked him what he was doing on the weekend, he could say, "I'm going to Church." At the time I thought he, someone who had no time for traditional religions, simply enjoyed the joke. But maybe it *was* his church, just as the cathedral was Maxey's and was becoming the same to some of these kids.

Looking around the boat, I marveled at them: strong young women and men, confident in their bodies. Exhausted and exhilarated, they formed a tangle of kid. I could never have been that free at that age, or at any age.

Once we were ripping through the waves on the way back, my nausea subsided completely. Now I was free to focus again on the water below, which, in the late morning light, had striated into a half-dozen stripes of different-hued blues: robin's-egg, azure, teal, indigo, turquoise, sapphire. And before long, the full hive of buildings that made up the Island School came into view.

After we docked the *Dave and Di,* and the other two vessels had arrived back as well, it was time to scrub down the boats. I watched as Maxey, two of the instructors, and several students hosed everything down. The students were still a little giddy, and were sharing new thoughts they'd had about free diving, about breathing, about the cathedral, or fish they'd seen.

When everyone was done, Maxey and I sat on the dock, looking out over the water as the students and instructors scattered.

"So, what's it like?" I asked him. "Being down there on the bottom. Diving. The cathedral."

"I can't really explain it. You know I didn't learn to scuba dive until sophomore year in college. I think I told you that."

"I forgot." Or maybe he hadn't. Or maybe he had, and I hadn't listened. It was all the same now.

"I had this summer job and my boss felt bad for me because

he thought that there would be the opportunity for me to learn about the work that they were doing, but it was a slow summer, so I spent all day every day filing. It actually wasn't too bad: I wore a suit; pretended to be a businessman. But the guy felt like he'd broken his promise, so at the end of the summer he bought me a ticket so I could go to Key Largo and paid for me to take a scuba course. I don't know why he thought of that, but I'll never be able to thank this guy enough."

"Wow, that's crazy."

"I know. It's nuts how one out-of-the-blue generous thing like that can change your life. I got lucky again because I had a great instructor. This guy was a real old-school hippie. After just one dive in a swimming pool, he said to me, 'Dude, you are super comfortable in the water. Let's go blow some bubbles with Jesus.' The instructor promised that there was a statue of Jesus on the ocean floor."

Maxey told me about heading out in a boat the next day with his hippie instructor, who was talking about yoga and meditation. Maxey had little knowledge then of either; it was only decades later that he would become steeped in both.

"Then we stepped off the back of the boat," Maxey said. "Next, we slowly drifted down to the bottom. I had this urge to swim around and try to find the bronze statue of Jesus. There really was a statue of Jesus down there, but we couldn't find it. Well, we didn't really try. Instead, we just lay down on the bottom of the ocean, next to each other, rising slightly and falling with every breath. It was really cool to be weightless, magic to be breathing under the ocean. Remembering the yoga talk I'd been given on the boat, I thought about trying to slow my breath. Then I forgot about breathing at all, and started to look out at a large rock on the ocean floor only a foot in front of my mask.

"After a minute or two of staring at that underwater rock-scape, it turned into a brilliant stage dancing with life. These insanely colorful little fishes started to appear, spinning and twisting—kind of like the purple fish we saw today—but there were also feathery worms and these medusa bundles. Wild stuff. I was mesmerized, and the more I stared quietly, the more the rock came to life. I went back day after day until it was time to fly home. And you know, eventually, I did see that bronze statue of Jesus."

"What was that like?"

"No match for the reef." Maxey paused. "Scuba was every-thing to me, until I discovered free diving a few years ago. Free diving is something else entirely. It's totally quiet. It was like before I was in a noisy church in a big city. Now it's like I'm in a beautiful monastery that no human has visited for a thousand years."

"All right," I said. "I'm sold. I'm going to learn to free dive. For sure." Then I paused. "But on another visit, okay?"

It was only when Maxey started coughing again that I real-ized he hadn't coughed for hours; but if anything, the cough sounded worse now. The gash in his leg, however, did look a bit better.

"How you feeling, Schwalbs?" Maxey asked.

"Like I'm going to barf after drinking so much seawater." Maxey meant the neuropathy, and it was no better. I didn't want to say anything. I know he was really hoping that the sea would cure me.

*   *   *

BEFORE WE HEADED back to Maxey and Pam's house for dinner, there was one more thing Maxey had to do. No longer nauseated from all the seawater I'd drunk, I accompanied him.

When we got to the dining hall, he found his way to a table that had a huge conch shell on it. Before I knew what was happening, there was an epic noise as Maxey blew the conch shell to summon everyone back from *querencia* to the flagpole for the evening ceremony. Maxey's cheeks puffed out as he went for maximum volume.

"You sure love blowing that damn conch," I said after the ceremony was complete.

"You have no idea how much," Maxey replied.

As it turned out, the school day would continue. Maxey had arranged for me to speak with the community after dinner. He wanted me to talk about books, writing, and reading; in other words, about my life's passion.

There were about fifty students gathered in the open-air boathouse when we returned to it. We waited for a few stragglers to join, and then Maxey stood up to introduce me.

"Good night. It's great to have our community coming together in a circle with the ocean lapping under the dock and our friends the no-see-ums reminding us how tough we are.

"It's my honor to introduce a friend who has stayed with me on the crazy ride through life. It makes me think about all of you on this intense journey together—I'm confident that many of you will find a way to stay connected for decades after you graduate. I am proud to share that my friend Will is a writer and editor. He has always challenged me and others to think in new ways. Most of his career has been helping writers, coaching and editing and polishing their stories. You might remember when you read the book *The Perfect Storm* or saw the movie that there was a strong woman who was a great sword-fishing boat captain and who survived the storm: Linda Greenlaw. Will was her editor and helped her bring her stories and writing to the world." Maxey then named other authors I'd edited. "His career is no surprise, as he is one of those people who loves to help others. But then it was his time to be an author and tell his own stories. In his writing, he shares how powerful books can be in helping people connect and navigate life. Please join me with a bold Island School welcome to Will Schwalbe."

The last time I'd been present at a meeting, it had been at my neuropathy support group, but this time I was supposed to lead the discussion. I was both touched and embarrassed by Maxey's introduction, but I decided I wouldn't say anything funny or self-deprecating. If that's how my friend wanted to describe me, I would let it stand. So I said a simple thank-you and began by asking everyone to tell me about a book that changed their life.

One boy told about being dyslexic but discovering he could read Hemingway; *The Old Man and the Sea* had set him off on a path toward studying the ocean. A girl raised her hand next and talked about three books: *Lord of the Flies* by William Golding, *Carrie* by Stephen King, and *Into Thin Air*, Jon Krakauer's book about a disastrous Everest expedition. All variations on a theme, she said: the need to speak out when groups run amok, no matter what the cost.

The next hand that shot up belonged to one of the Bahamian students. He said that when he was a little kid his mother had read him a book about a shark, and he made her read it to him again, and again. That's what got him interested in conservation, in preserving the place where he lived. That's why he was there.

I looked over at Maxey. He had a goofy grin on his face.

BREATHING

That night I slept right through until morning. No nightmares. And not even Maxey's banging around the kitchen stirred me for long. By the time I roused myself for good, it was nine a.m. I found Pam in the kitchen with a pot of coffee.

"How'd you sleep?" I asked her.

"Terribly," she said. Maxey had kept her up all night coughing. "He won't slow down. He left hours ago to join the students and the faculty in the morning run, swim, and yoga."

My memory of that ritual still vivid, I was grateful that he hadn't knocked on my door.

"He won't see a doctor and he won't take antibiotics," Pam continued. She then launched into a series of stories: Maxey eating a fly-covered fruit he found on the ground when they were on a family vacation: he was sure it would be fine, but it almost killed him; they had rushed him to the island clinic, but he snuck out before they could pump his stomach. Or the time he was splashing around having a great time swimming with dolphins until he discovered they were alligators.

I told Pam about the conversation with the students the night before, and their favorite books. She wasn't surprised by the choices. Still involved in admissions, she knew all of the students well. I asked her what hers was. "*Crossing to Safety* by Wallace Stegner is definitely one of them," she said. I had expected she would say this. I recalled the emails and conversations we'd had over the years about *Crossing to Safety*, a novel about two marriages and a friendship between couples that lasts decades.

I also thought back to the conversations I'd had with my mother about this book, which was the favorite of so many people I know, but still nowhere near as famous as it deserved to be. Before I'd read Stegner, I thought of him as an academic writer from the West whose name was attached to a fellowship and whose works probably wouldn't speak to me. But he was the author who first gave my mother and me a language to talk about her dying, whose books I most often suggested, and who had helped Pam and me forge our own friendship—connected to mine with Maxey but also separate from it.

"And Maxey's?" I asked her. I realized in all our time together I'd never asked him that.

"Ask him," she said. "I think it will surprise you."

Not long afterwards, Maxey came home for lunch. Pam and I were startled; we had assumed he would eat at the school. Instead of fixing himself a sandwich, he went right upstairs to have a nap. Pam told me that was something he never did.

When Maxey woke up, he seemed a little better.

"Everyone is worrying about you," I told him.

"Can we change the subject?"

"Okay, sure. Last night I asked all of the students their favorite book. This morning I asked Pam hers. What's your favorite?"

Maxey paused, thinking. "Well, there are lots of books about the ocean, conservation, and marine life that I love. And I'm guided now by *Antifragile* by Nicholas Taleb and *The Obstacle Is the Way,* about the Stoics. I know I told you about *Gaviotas*—that's the story of creating a new kind of community. But my favorite? I don't think I'll ever forget reading *The Agony and the Ecstasy.*" I didn't know what book I was expecting, but it wasn't Irving Stone's novel about Michelangelo. I remembered it from my parents' bookshelves, where it had been gathering dust since just about the time when I was born.

"Why that one?"

"I loved the story about someone guided by a passion like that. Someone who goes up against everyone to follow through on his dream. I read it right after we graduated, when I wasn't sure the SEALs were going to take me and I wasn't sure what I was going to do if they didn't."

My mind returned to the time we spoke during the summer after graduation, when Maxey and I were both feeling so lost, and I smiled. Whatever our present challenges were, we had each found our place in the world.

Maxey continued: "Funny, I went to Yale for four years, and it was only after graduating that I really fell in love with reading."

"How come you never told me about the books you were reading?"

"I don't know. Maybe it's because you never asked."

AFTER LUNCH WE returned to the school. Maxey wanted to give me the full tour. We walked on a bridge over a mangrove swamp to the research facilities they'd built. He showed me a building with tilapia in tanks whose waste was channeled into planters to provide nutrients to spicy greens, which fed the school and the community. He tore off a few leaves for me to try.

He also wanted to show me a tank full of crabs, and a building they'd just built to house the scientists. We then walked back to the main campus. I asked him how many of the students' names he knew.

"Not quite all, but it's early in the term." Then as if to test himself, he addressed two students we encountered, "Hey, Taylor; hey, Tabor." They corrected him: "I'm Tabor," corrected the one. "I'm Taylor," the other.

Soon we encountered another student. This one's name Maxey got right. He was a scrawny kid. He walked up to Maxey and playfully punched him in the arm. "We've been betting—I think I could take you," the kid said. Maxey laughed. I realized then that the new students saw Maxey as I first saw him: a warrior, even if an aging one. But over the course of the term, they would learn he was someone very different. Like Andy the argonaut, these students would find out in a few months what it had taken me decades to realize—although, to be fair, it had taken Maxey a long time to realize it as well.

BEFORE DINNER MAXEY and I headed back out to the dock right behind his house. He seemed much better for his nap and was no longer coughing.

The sun and water and island breezes still weren't helping my neuropathy, but several days away from work with no set tasks or responsibilities had done wonders for my mood. I could have easily spent weeks there. Tempted as I was, I remembered the old Benjamin Franklin line: *Guests, like fish, begin to smell after three days.* I also was excited to get home and see David, who would be coming back soon from Hong Kong.

I knew it wasn't Maxey's favorite topic, but I couldn't help asking: "You feeling better?"

"Much," he said.

"And you?"

"Much," I said. Maxey fixed me with a look. "Well, I haven't thrown up undigested food since I've been here, so that's something. I do that a lot in New York."

Maxey interrupted: "I guess we should take that as a compliment."

"But," I continued, "I'm still pretty nauseated. And not just because I drank all that seawater. My feet and hands constantly feel like they are burning. And I'm still dizzy and exhausted."

"Want me to teach you my favorite breathing exercise? I don't know if it will help you, but it's done great for me. Especially with being dizzy."

"Sure, yes—thanks," I said. I was especially dizzy right at that moment and wanted the dizziness to stop.

"The breathing pattern is basically a deep, full, forced inhalation, and then a pause. And then a prolonged exhalation. Then a pause. Two seconds to inhale. A second or two to hold. And then twelve or fourteen seconds to exhale. Two more seconds to hold. Then you repeat. That simple. It's the same basic pattern we do before we free dive, but with a longer exhale. That's what slows your heart."

"And that helps you?" I asked.

"It's amazing. When I was going in for a colonoscopy—I got one when I turned fifty—they were freaking out about how low my heartbeat was. I was controlling my breathing to the point where my heartbeat was down in the thirties, and the machine kept beeping a warning, which panicked everyone. I love that.

"The best thing is the realization that you can control something most people don't realize they can control. And when you slow your heartbeat down just by breathing deeply, you fully oxygenate your body.

"One of the things I've learned while free diving—and this is tied to some of my more spiritual beliefs—is that our bodies know that we came from the ocean. That all life came from the ocean. And then there is this obvious connection between the womb and the ocean. Just the buoyancy of the womb for literally the start of our life—it's all connected to where life came from. We have a physical and spiritual connection to the ocean.

"That's what the mammalian diving reflex is. What's amazing is that if you can overcome the mental anxiety—with meditation or techniques like that—your heartbeat starts to slow down whenever you put your face in water. Naturally. Just a reflex. There are sensors in our face that trigger a slower heartbeat—and a relaxation response—when they are immersed in water. And another thing that is really cool: if you get into trouble underwater and have a blackout or something like that, your body shuts down naturally and protects your lungs.

"So that's all it is. I control my breathing on land just like I do in the water. I slow down my heartbeat. I oxygenate my body. I try that first. And if it doesn't work, then I go to the doctor. But it's not either/or. It's what got me through the brain operation and it's helped me heal after." Maxey paused. "It's ancient stuff. But you have to be open to it."

"Okay," I said. "Let me give it a try."

When Pam came out to summon us into dinner, she found both Maxey and me breathing in, holding our breaths, and then slowly breathing out.

CHAPTER SEVEN

Pushing Sixty

SCREENING

My neuropathy wasn't getting better. I was trying to remember to follow Maxey's breathing pattern, and while I was pretty sure it was helping when I had sharp, breakthrough pain, I was feeling uncomfortable and dizzy most of the time. It was often a challenge to go to the office, but I was lucky: thanks to the nature of my work and an understanding boss, I could do my job from home when necessary.

My doctor had adjusted my medicines during my twice-yearly checkups, but it seemed that I was feeling as well as I could with what current science had to offer.

In February 2019, my doctor did share a welcome bit of news: research indicated that having a glass of wine or a beer once or twice a week shouldn't affect my particular condition at all. The hospital also had something else to offer. They were recruiting for a two-year, double-blind study of a new medi-cine. Well, not a new medicine: a new use for an old medicine. Double-blind, I was told, meant that neither I nor the person running the study would know if I was on the medicine or on a placebo. Only someone at the National Institutes of Health would have that information.

My doctor referred me to a colleague, who walked me through the risks and benefits, explaining some of the possible side effects of the drug they might have me on. One was weight loss. That sounded like a good thing, as I still was a bit pudgier around the midriff than I wanted to be. But others were not so desirable: changes in the way food smelled and tasted, confusion, anxiety, depression, and, most concerning, memory problems that included loss of access to language—the inability to find the word you wanted. For an editor and writer, this last one was particularly worrying. They said that your memory and ability to articulate thoughts would return once you stopped taking the drug, which you could do at any time. But what if they didn't?

There seemed to be plenty of reasons not to give this a try. But on the plus side, the medicine might help. I would be tested more intensively, so perhaps they would find the cause. I could also help others. Medicine needs people willing to be studied. My mother's voice in my head weighed in. She would have done the study.

I decided that I would go in for the screening and see if I qualified. It was a way of delaying the decision. They were looking for people who were more or less alike. If my blood sugar was too low or too high, for example, then I wouldn't qualify. I was amused to note that they needed people who were a little bit overweight but not too overweight, a little bit unhealthy but not too much so. Was I sufficiently pudgy and unhealthy? We would see. I returned the next week for a minor battery of tests: heart, lungs, blood, skin. They would get back to me with the results.

After years of symptoms, I wasn't growing discouraged but I was growing tired. One of the hardest things was the feeling that I was somehow to blame—not for the illness but for failing to come up with a more effective way of handling it. I was always second-guessing myself. Should I have taken my anti-nausea medication earlier in the day, or later? Should I have eaten more, or less, or something different? When I was in pain, I beat myself up for walking too much or too little, for working out at the gym too hard or not hard enough.

I was also tired of the constant need to come out as someone who had a chronic illness to explain why I couldn't do things I couldn't do, but also aware how dull the subject was and how tricky: I was always worried that I was unknowingly complaining to someone with something far worse.

That week I bored all my friends with my deliberations, making a decision only to reverse it hours later. I would definitely participate in the trial. I would definitely not. I wrote to Maxey and laid it all out. He wrote right back: Come down to Eleuthera for a week to recharge. Don't make up your mind until you get here. You'll know the answer when you leave.

There was room at the research center if I wanted to stay there instead of with Pam and him, he added. He knew I liked my privacy and some quiet.

And I should bring David.

I discussed it with David, who couldn't get time off from work. I also think he needed a week away from my deliberations. He thought I shouldn't do the trial. If I wanted to keep flip-flopping, then that was on me.

A week later I was back on JetBlue to Nassau and then Pineapple Air to Eleuthera.

I would be told on the last full day of my trip whether I qualified for the trial.

THE ROOM WAS simple, almost monastic, but any decoration would have been a crime, as it full-on faced the ocean. The lines between room and balcony, balcony and beach, beach and water disappeared when I lay in bed; it was as if I were floating above the surface of the water.

I'd brought a big stack of books. I could have breakfast at the school, Maxey said, and then he'd join me most days for lunch; in the evenings we'd have dinner back at the house with Pam and Tyler, who was again teaching at the school. I would also get to meet Tyler's girlfriend, who was visiting from Argentina.

Maxey left me a bicycle and a mask, fins, and snorkel so I could explore the island and find my own *querencia*. But, looking around the room, I was pretty sure I'd already found it.

"One thing, Schwalbs," Maxey said. "We've got a lot of beautiful stingrays this year."

"Are they dangerous?" I asked.

"No," Maxey said. "Just don't step on them. And don't get between them and the surface."

IT WAS A busy week for Maxey. The Bahamian minister of education was coming to the Deep Creek Middle School to see it in action. The minister was an admirer of experiential learning and was thinking about partnering with the school to create a lab school for students from kindergarten through high school, which could then expand its programming to all the schools in the Bahamas. The students and teachers had been preparing for weeks for the minister's visit. One of the boys was particularly excited to perform a rap he'd composed about protecting local fisheries.

There was also a massive high-tech research vessel anchored off the island. It was owned by the founder of a hedge fund who was a fan of the school; Maxey had arranged for the students to tour the ship and meet with the scientists.

Finally, it was high school admissions season, so Maxey was working with one of the administrators at the school to help get local students into American boarding schools. She had been in the first class at Deep Creek Middle School, along with Brittney, and then gone to a U.S. boarding school before returning to Eleuthera. That was one of the things he was most proud of, Maxey explained: almost all of the local young people who left to go to boarding school in the U.S. returned to the Bahamas for college and stayed to contribute to the life of the islands.

The school itself wasn't in session, but it had groups of students from abroad doing temporary programs; there were also scientists in residence; and the faculty were training new teachers for the start of the next term.

The first few days I got sunburned, avoided stingrays, and took my breakfast and lunch at the school. I met several of the teachers and administrators there, all of whom wanted to know stories about Maxey back in the day. I gave them nothing. They told me what had brought them to the school. There were writers, scientists, mathematicians. One had been a student at the school and had always dreamed of returning to teach. Another had worked with at-risk kids in Chicago and had family ties to the Bahamas; he would be directing a leadership program for young men in the community.

This program had been founded by a former student at the school named Stan Burnside, who had gone to the U.S. and Ithaca College before returning to Eleuthera. His father, Stan Burnside, is an iconic cultural figure in the Bahamas: a world-renowned painter and sculptor. The younger Stan had wanted to do something to help give the young men of South Eleuthera a better shot at a future; jobs were scarce and it was easy for them to lose their way. He and a friend of his had devised a week-long course to be sponsored by the school and held on campus between terms. The idea was to have Stan and his friend, Will, lead younger Bahamian men through a course that would challenge them physically, emotionally, and spiritually.

Stan and Will designed the course and had started it with a dozen participants, thirteen and fourteen years old; many of them had been in trouble. The idea was to help these young men find purpose. On the first night they were shown a clip from a global track meet: a British runner had pulled his hamstring and collapsed on the track; his father came down from the stands, put his arm around his son, and helped him across the finish line. The students in the program wept openly while watching it. Many of them didn't have strong men in their lives and had no one cheering for them. Stan and Will would try to help them find that in one another.

Evenings at the Maxeys' were spent with teachers, neighbors, friends. This visit it was Pam who had an angry gash. She'd been tiling the kitchen and sliced her arm open. Unlike her husband, however, she'd gone to get stitches. On the first night she served me homemade seafood spring rolls so we could photograph them and make David jealous: he was. Over Face-Time, he promised he would accompany me on the next visit.

At the end of each evening, I was exhausted. Attempts to help with the dishwashing were always rebuffed (I think they were partly scared I would use too much water). So after dinner, I would hop on my bicycle and wobble back to my room at the school.

A few days in, I realized that I had given no thought whatsoever to the decision I had to make, and it was a huge relief to know that I'd gone days without thinking about it. I still didn't know the answer, but I was delighted to have had a break from the question.

TWO NIGHTS BEFORE I was scheduled to leave, Maxey and I found ourselves at the end of dinner with energy to spare. We grabbed some Kaliks and headed outside.

"You know, the craziest thing, Schwalbs. I was looking through some old papers, and I found my journal. I didn't even remember I kept one. It goes all the way from junior year of Yale right up until I was accepted by the SEALs, a few months after graduation. Mostly it's just me writing about wrestling matches and drinking at the Rude Bar and about how much my mom and dad do for me and kind of beating myself up for not letting them know how much I appreciated it. There's a lot of stuff about my girlfriend and our ups and downs. And about me wondering what I'm going to do with my life."

"You didn't strike me as the diary type," I said. I later

recalled that when we'd talked soon after graduation, he'd mentioned to me that he kept a journal—and how much that had surprised me.

"I know. But whatever: I wanted to see if you remembered this one thing. The entry was from 2:50 in the morning on March sixth, 1984, a few months before we graduated. I must not have been able to sleep. In the journal, I wrote that I'd slipped up in the hall and had been calling everyone homos. I was furious with myself. I wrote that wrestling achievements don't matter and that failures don't matter either. What matters is being a good person."

Sitting out on the dock, drinking a beer, in one of the most beautiful places on earth, that incident seemed more than a lifetime ago. It seemed like it belonged to someone else's life. At the same time, I did remember that night, and the hurt I'd felt afterwards. I hadn't felt it for decades, just recalled it. Yet I was glad to learn that Maxey had regretted his words the very night he said them. The guy who said he would beat up anyone who hurt me had, in fact, beat up himself.

For a moment I considered telling Maxey that I didn't remember any of it. Instead, I decided to do the opposite and tell the truth. I told him that what he had said that night had bothered me for years. Not a lot. But enough. I also said that I wished I'd told him right away that he'd upset me, because I would have discovered that he'd upset himself, too.

"Karma sure is funny," I added. "I mean, you were kind of homophobic when I met you and now you've got a gay daughter, gay and trans kids in your school, and you are sitting drinking beers with your gay friend."

We sat and drank for a while longer and then I decided to

ask Maxey something I'd always wondered: "Hey, Maxey, when I rode back to Yale with you, that first weekend, and had to wrap my arms around you to keep from falling off the bike, I was worried you would think I was coming on to you. Did you worry about that?"

"That you would come on to me or that you would think I thought you were coming on to me?"

"Either. Both."

"Dude, I honestly just thought I'd give you a lift. You didn't seem to like me much. I wanted you to like me."

"Why did you care?"

"I wanted everyone to like me back then."

"Well, that hasn't changed much, Maxey. You still want everyone to like you."

"I know. And you do, too."

"Maybe that's why we're friends," I said.

"And maybe that's why we don't know each other better after all these years."

We sat quietly, watching the stars. Drinking crisp Kaliks. My burned skin was also ravaged by itchy bug bites, and I knew I would have trouble sleeping, but I was past caring. I had a few Ambiens at the ready.

I thought back to some of the other things I'd worried about over the years: the way I'd behaved the night I met the other members of our group; which bedroom I would sleep in on the retreat; why I'd neglected for so long to send even a small check to help with Maxey's school in its early years; whether Maxey and Pam minded that I couldn't remember the names and ages of his kids; who had last called whom, and whose responsibility it was to get in touch; if I'd said the right thing when Maxey confided in me and if I'd confided sufficiently in him; why Maxey hadn't called me some of the times he came to town; whether I should have brought up my feelings about charter schools so soon after his operation; if I was too needy as a friend or not needy enough; whether I had listened as much as I should have and asked the questions Maxey wanted me to ask; if I had shared too much or too little, been too honest or not honest enough. Ultimately, I worried whether I had been giving enough of the one thing that we have to give our friends: our true selves.

That night, on that dock, I realized that most of the things I had worried about for the last four decades lived only in my head, and that while it was almost certain that I am the bigger nutcase, Maxey was a nut, too. He had his own list of things he'd worried about. I also knew that all my friends carried similar lists in their heads. Maybe that's part of the reason my friends are my friends. We care enough to spend time worrying about the ways that our actions, including the times we neglect to act, affect one another. And, of course, we enjoy one another's company. We like the people our friends are, and the person we are when we're around them. After decades of worry, maybe it wasn't more complicated than that.

"You know, I think you know me as well as anyone knows me, Maxey. The truth is, and I mean this, there's not much to know."

"You, know, that's another thing we have in common, Schwalbs. I'm pretty shallow, too. I guess we are just two middle-aged shallow guys who are pretty frickin' lucky to be here."

"I'll drink to that," I said.

"But let's make a deal for the last years, decades, whatever is left: If I'm mad, I'll tell you. And if you're mad, you tell me. Then we don't have to worry about it."

"It's a deal," I said, thinking that we could have agreed on that decades before, but that back then it never would have occurred to either of us to propose it.

When we got to the end of our beers, we walked into the kitchen to stick them in the recycling bin.

"I was such an asshole when we met," said Maxey.

"I think I was a pretty big asshole," I said.

"Dude, I was a way bigger asshole," Maxey said.

"Yeah, you kind of were," I agreed. But I wasn't so sure.

THE NEXT MORNING, I woke up to rain in Eleuthera and a message on my cell phone from the medical administrator in charge of the trial. They'd run my blood. To be eligible you needed a blood sugar of over 5.6 and "good" cholesterol of under 40. My blood sugar was exactly 5.6 and my "good" cholesterol exactly 40. I didn't qualify; I missed by a tenth of a point. I didn't have to make a choice; it had been made for me.

I realized right after the call that I had decided to participate if my numbers were where they needed to be. My mind had made itself up at some point over the last few days; I wasn't even sure when. I also realized that I wasn't disappointed that I'd been excluded. An enormous decision had revealed itself to be a very minor one. What I'd really needed, more than anything else, was a breather. Maxey and Eleuthera had given me that. Now the trick would be whether I could do the same for myself in the future without leaving the island of Manhattan.

There was still, however, one day and night left for me on *this* island.

TESTS

I spent that last day in Eleuthera bicycling around the island. After many hours, when I was even more sunburned (reminder to self: you need suntan lotion even when it's overcast) and mosquito-bitten, I returned to my room to read and nap.

There was time for a swim in the ocean before the small send-off party Pam and Maxey had arranged for my final evening. The water was clear in the cove and magnified my feet. I waded in up to my knees and stood in the still air, feeling the sun on my now-lotioned chest and back. I decided to try Maxey's breathing technique. I tried to clear my mind. It all seemed to be working. I felt a kind of peace I hadn't felt in ages.

I would need to wade in deeper to swim. I closed my eyes to stay in the moment and started to walk forward, feeling the softness of the sand on my feet.

Then I had a thought: stingrays. I looked down and there one was. Sure, it probably would have lighted away if my foot got near it. Though maybe not. I delicately retraced my steps. All my worries, all my neuroses, were there for a purpose. Some I needed to let go, but many had served me well. The challenge was to distinguish which was which—while at the same time accepting that it wasn't always possible to know for sure.

I rode my bicycle over to the Maxeys' house and immediately related my momentous encounter with the natural world. Maxey didn't think that either I or the stingray had been in any danger. When I shared the tale with another guest, her response was "And that's it?"

After the party I realized I was too burned and bitten to pedal back to my room at the school, so Maxey drove me. Even with the burns and bites, there was nothing I would change about the day.

Because I was leaving the next morning, Maxey and I decided it was a matter of thrift to finish off the two last Kaliks that he and Pam had left for me in the communal fridge, so we grabbed them and headed to the breezeway and a patio with a bench that overlooked the ocean.

The wind had picked up; for the first time all day, I was outside without being surrounded by a mosquito cloud. Still, I felt welts rising all over my body from the bites.

"How come they don't bite you, Maxey?" I asked.

"I think my skin is like leather at this point. I've been curing it in salt water and sun all my life."

We sat quietly for a while and then I asked: "What's next? For you? For the school?"

"I don't really know, but it's time for some transitions. It's been twenty years. Time to put the school in some new hands."

"How do you know it's time?"

"I don't, really. Part of me dreams about not waking up worried about six different management and educational challenges; the other part worries about waking up with nothing to worry about. That's when the real worry starts. I also have to earn a living. But it's important for the school that we support the new leaders that are emerging and allow them to take it in new directions. And we are in the Bahamas and need to become more Bahamian."

"I've always wondered something, Maxey. I know why you left the computer company for teaching. And why you founded this school. But I never understood why you left the military."

"How come you didn't ask me?" Maxey said.

"I don't know. I guess I figured it was something you didn't want to talk about."

"What gave you that idea?" Maxey looked genuinely puzzled.

"I don't know. I really don't," I replied. "But I guess, like many people, I've been sort of in awe of the military. I don't worship it. But I respect it. A lot. My dad enlisted during World War II, as did all his friends. And I know that people from all over the country serve for all sorts of reasons—but it never even crossed my mind to enlist. In fact, you are the only friend I had who did. I mean, every time you talked about SEAL training, as I've told you before, all I could think of is that I would have rung that bell so fast it would have made everyone's head spin.

"And I think about that Jack Nicholson speech from *A Few Good Men.* About how people want the truth but can't handle the truth. How I *do* want someone on that wall, protecting us. I just don't want to be on that wall myself. Maybe I didn't ever really want to know what goes on and know the reality of how we as a country use our power. Plus, there's the way we treat vets when they return from deployment. I've never known what to say when someone tells me they were in the military: 'Thank you for your service'? It doesn't seem enough. But I guess it's better than nothing. Also, there's the unfairness of it all. I realize that if I grew up in a different part of the country or grew up differently, then many or even most of my friends would be serving. And I might be, too."

"I never knew you thought about this stuff so much," Maxey said.

"You never asked," I answered right away, and we both laughed. Then I added, "You know, Maxey, I just realized something this second. The whole subject makes me feel so awkward that I've avoided it all these years—and I put that on you."

"It's really complicated," Maxey admitted. "I love my SEAL brothers, and it was an honor to serve with them. They're amazing guys and there's nothing I wouldn't do for them or them for me. There's a reason it's called a SEAL *team*. But I went into the navy largely because I wanted to push myself physically and be close to the water. I would love to say it was because of my father's service or some awesome blast of patriotism, but it just wasn't that deep. Or I don't think it was.

"I mean, of course I'm patriotic. I also really did want to be useful. To be of service. That's always been important to me. But when I joined the SEALs, most people hadn't really heard of them. It's not like today, after all these books and movies and television shows. We were this bunch of people in the navy who did underwater demolition. We were proud as hell to be SEALs, but part of the culture was not to talk about it. It was never supposed to be about me as an individual, not something to brag about."

"Except when picking up girls," I reminded him, recalling his story about the night he met Pam.

"Yes, well, except then. But today it's the only thing about me anyone wants to talk about. And then you have these guys like Gallagher. That makes me crazy." Six months before, a SEAL officer named Eddie Gallagher had been charged with stabbing a teenage captive to death and posing for a picture with his severed head, and with other war crimes, including shooting civilians; the men under his command had turned him in. "That guy is an insane criminal who did horrific things and deserves to be in jail. Good warriors fight for respect and decency and freedom. The guys on Gallagher's team are like my SEAL friends. That he lost the respect of his team tells you everything you need to know."

Maxey paused for a bit, lost in thought. I said nothing. "Everyone assumes I'm pro-military—I *am* pro the people who serve—but I'm really more of a pacifist in most situations. We need a military, but I don't always approve of the way we use it. And that, Schwalbs, is a big reason why I resigned my commission after six years. Even though I loved the guys I served with. Maybe *because* I loved the people I served with. I'd become disillusioned, I guess. I'd had enough."

"What made you actually decide to leave? Why after Panama?"

"Well, the Pacific tour had been frickin' awesome. The captain of the ship was a total hard-ass but I respected the hell out of that guy and he taught me more than just about anyone in my life about leadership and responsibility. It was while I was on his ship in Subic Bay that Pam flew out and she and I got married the first time.

"And then you know came language school and that was awesome. And then we deployed to Panama. Early on, I was sent to Cartagena to work with the Colombian navy. Our job was to help train Colombian marines to intercept coca leaves coming by river from the countryside. The idea was to stop drugs while they were being transported from their source instead of when they came across our border. It was part of Operation Snow Cap. It seemed like a good idea—honestly, I didn't give it too much thought.

"Two weeks into our work, I'd formed a trusting relationship with the Colombian sergeant responsible for coordinating the training. We were sharing a beer and some personal stories when he turned and asked if he could tell me something that might piss me off. He said that he'd been on a boat patrol up on the Magdalena River early one morning. They'd come alongside an old man guiding his canoe downriver. The canoe was full of coca leaves heading for a processing plant. The sergeant had ordered the old man to dump the coca leaves in the river—that was the protocol—and the old man smiled through his fear and said, *'Lo siento, sargento, no puedo tirar la coca en el rio. Mi familia necesita la plata que me darán por ellas para sobrevivir.* I'm sorry, sergeant. I can't dump the coca plants in the river. My family needs the money I'll get for them to survive.' And then the sergeant, my colleague, said to me, *'Es su problema. La gente en su pais usa las drogas, y estamos luchando con nuestros campesinos.* It's your problem. The people in your country use drugs, and so we have to fight our own peasants.'"

Maxey told me that he knew the sergeant was right and was relieved when he learned that the patrol had let the old man take his coca leaves and go. In the months after that, Maxey thought more and more about the people he'd met in Colombia and during other parts of his journey. He started feeling that serving in the military was a chapter in his life, but not his whole life. And then came our invasion of Panama: Operation Just Cause.

In 1989, Maxey was based in Panama helping to coordinate cross-training between SEAL teams and in-country police and military to combat drug trafficking. "I was essentially a desk monkey with some heavy travel," he said.

"There was very little warning or preparation for the invasion. Those of us with families had just enough time to get them on the last plane out. Pam was woken up early in the morning on December eighteenth—greeted by me in full fatigues, which was far from the norm—with the call to pack quickly, as we were heading to the airport. Our residence on Fort Amador shared space with the Panamanian defense force. I told Pam that she and Brittney, who was only six months old, would be flying out of the country in an hour, and that I would be working from a desk at the base to support the operational platoons coming in from the U.S. That's what I'd been told I would be doing.

"I remember my commanding officer being shocked that we were sending in three platoons—that's about sixty men—to secure Patilla Airfield, right outside Panama City. Even one platoon of fourteen men out on an op is unusual. More often than not, a group of four or maybe eight SEALs would be deployed on a mission. The airfield was a key target because they were trying to prevent Noriega from escaping and that's where the guy's Lear jet was hangared."

"Wait," I interrupted. "Remind me again what the story was on Noriega?"

"He was a military guy who was head of the government," Maxey explained. "And a massive drug lord at the same time. So he was a foreign leader flooding the U.S. with drugs. The idea was to capture him, topple his government, and bring him to the U.S. to stand trial. But first we had to keep him from escaping."

"Oh, yeah, that's right," I said, embarrassed that I hadn't paid more attention at the time. "Sorry, go on."

"Well, the large SEAL Team Four contingent, sixty men

strong, landed that evening at Patilla. They'd arrived by water and reached the shore in Zodiacs: inflatable boats. At twenty-three hundred hours—eleven p.m.—I was at headquarters at my desk and was told that several SEALs had been injured and at least two had been killed in the operation to seize the airfield. It had turned into a battle. They were requesting a helicopter and reinforcements. My buddy Julio Gomez—the senior officer among the SEALs in the office—volunteered to help our fellow SEALs who were pinned down. Without a thought, I volunteered along with a few others to jump on that helicopter with him.

"Julio was my neighbor and close friend. He's this crazy Cuban-American, built like a pit bull. Our daughters were born a few months apart, and we owned a boat together and got into all kinds of adventures. We gathered out on this dark field, waiting for the helicopter. While we waited, Julio reviewed important protocols, like how to switch off the safety on our guns and how to set perimeter. He helped us focus our minds and ready ourselves for combat. This was the first time I'd had a rifle in my hand in maybe six months, and it was good to have Julio walking us through everything like we were new guys in training. Our ad hoc team included a few veteran enlisted SEALs with lots of experience in a shitstorm. For me, this was the first real call to arms.

"In the darkness, we could hear the dual blade helo whipping in to land. Lights were deployed on the field and the master chief cranked off a smoke so the pilot could see wind direction. The back ramp released, and we climbed on board. We practiced how after landing we would take up positions around the helo so that the wounded and dead could be loaded up. There were lots of rumors running around the headquarters when the call came through. Everyone thought there might be a Panamanian armed vehicle deployed by Noriega that would have heavy firepower. That's why some of us were armed with forty-millimeter grenade launchers and even larger handheld missile launchers.

"I leaned into Julio, who was sitting next to me and who would be the first to head out when the ramp opened. *'Hey Gomez,'* I shouted above the rotors, *'Tengo miedo.* I'm scared.' Julio yelled back into my ear, *'Yo tambien.* I am, too.' It was equal parts comforting and unnerving to know that Julio was just as frightened as I was."

Maxey explained to me that the flight from the base to Patilla was less than ten minutes but seemed like forever, like some kind of journey down into one of Dante's circles of hell. "Panama City was blacked out and it felt like we were falling the whole flight. Then, without warning, the wheels hit the runway and the ramp was down. I could hear Julio shout, *'Let's go, set perimeter.'* I was up and awkwardly running with gear and ammunition, med-kit, water, and rations: all gear I hadn't carried for almost a year. I veered slightly to the right of Julio—maybe ten meters out—and hit the ground like I was sliding into second base with the base attached to my chest. I couldn't hear and see much, but as I was concentrating on protecting the perimeter, I saw through the periphery that people were loading bodies onto the helo behind me. I knew these were my wounded and fallen comrades. I hoped to hell that they wouldn't be loading my ass in the back of the helo the next time it landed.

"I stayed in that prone position for hours, moving slightly

to awaken sleeping limbs and muscles. I watched the sunrise revealing the dirt-poor barrios surrounding the airfield. As the sun rose fully, I looked around: There we all were in full combat gear, holding the perimeter, and a hundred feet away local women were starting small fires, boiling water, and making food for their families. I was fine and Julio was fine, but we'd lost four men the night before.

"Operation Just Cause was this fucked-up operation right from the start. And the more I learned about it, the angrier I got. All the brass knew it would be a very short-lived conflict and everyone was hungry for medals. The way to get medals was to get your guys into the action—maybe that's the reason the SEAL teams were given the job of securing Patilla Airfield. That's why my commanding officer was so disturbed: SEALs aren't trained in command-and-control covering multiple platoons, and we aren't trained to secure airfields. That's a job normally reserved for Army Rangers or Marines. One of the four guys who was killed was a good friend, Don McFaul, and he left behind a pregnant wife. I'd served for six years by then, and I decided I wasn't going to re-up. I was going to do something else with my life.

"But it wasn't just Operation Just Cause. My two years in Colombia and Panama changed me. The military is all about power and control, but the four men who died that night were killed because they did the right thing: they followed the rules of engagement that were put in place to protect civilian life. They could have blasted their way out of that situation, but they were absolutely committed to following the rules. It crushed me that we lost them. But then I woke up that morning and found myself looking over my rifle at a Panamanian mother bathing her child. The guys who died were real heroes because they protected civilian lives at the cost of their own. That's who we were supposed to be fighting for, after all—civilians, the Panamanian people. But the whole situation was fucked."

We sat quietly for a while, looking out at the ocean. Then I said the same thing I'd said to him several times before over the years when bad things happened: "I'm sorry."

"And that's why I hate those books by SEALs bragging about their exploits and killing and all of that. And you know another thing that's frickin' messed up? Some of these assholes running around talking about being SEALs weren't even in the service. They just make it up. A few of us have the energy to expose them—there's a whole website that tracks fake SEALs—but most of us just get on with our lives."

All those years I'd wondered what happened. Now I understood that Maxey's reasons for leaving the military were both simpler and more complex than I could ever have imagined. I realized that in the years after college I had built a mythology around both Maxey and his service. When I introduced him to others, it wasn't just as my friend Chris Maxey. It was usually my friend Chris Maxey the Navy SEAL. And while I was making such a big deal out of that, while we all were, that was only a part of who Maxey was. A proud part, sure. But just a part.

I thought of the need so many of us have to lionize the people in our lives, introducing them to others by what they do and not who they are. If our friends do amazing things with their lives, it's as if that makes us amazing, too. Reflected glory. Why isn't it enough that our friends are just our friends? Why couldn't Maxey just be Maxey? Why couldn't I just be me? Maybe that was what was behind Maxey's passion about the new kind of school transcript. A transcript that captured not only what young people had done but who they were.

"You know, Schwalbs, I wrote about my experience in Panama in a letter to the Yale alumni magazine while I was still a SEAL, right after it happened." I had missed the letter when it was published. It was during the years when we weren't in close touch.

"A professor had written an article about how anti-military Yale had become while we were there, and I wanted to say that that wasn't the case—that my friends had mostly supported my decision. I also wanted to say that while I had some real problems with the military, I had seen my teammates make the ultimate sacrifice to protect civilians. That nothing was clear cut, that it's complicated."

"Maxey, there's another thing I always wanted to ask, but it's about me, not you. I've always wanted to know how you felt about the AIDS stuff—when I talked about it at audit or in the hall. What did you think?"

Maxey paused. "I hate to say it, but it just seemed really far away. I mean, I was worried for you, of course, but it seemed like this thing that gay people needed to worry about, not me. Then in the late 1990s there was a guy I knew a bit from high school. His cousin and I were really close. And this guy was diagnosed with AIDS. I wish I'd talked to you about it then. I wished I'd asked you more about it after we graduated. But I did worry about you during those years, when AIDS was in the news so much, and there were no treatments—whether you would be okay. I think I never brought it up because I just thought it was something you wouldn't want to talk about—that maybe you thought I couldn't understand what it was like."

"I understand," I said, meaning that I understood why he thought that but would have liked it if he'd asked. I hadn't known he'd worried about me.

Then, in that moment, I couldn't resist parroting Maxey. "I never knew you thought about this stuff so much," I told him.

"You never asked," Maxey said, unable to resist copying me.

It was getting late at night and our beers were almost finished. We moved on to end-of-night conversation, about plans for the next day. When I would eat breakfast; whether Tyler would join us on the drive to Rock Sound Airport; the time of year to return with David (ideally, the season with the fewest mosquitoes).

"Good night. Love you, man," Maxey said over his shoulder as he headed back to his truck to drive back to his house.

"Love you, too, Maxey." It was the first time, after nearly forty years of knowing Maxey, that I'd ever said that.

Coda

Back at the Hall

IN MARCH OF 2019, I had a long phone call with David Kelly. After an hour of reminiscing, we decided to plan a get-together for our group at our upcoming thirty-fifth reunion. It was not one of the big ones, but worth celebrating. I immediately texted Maxey; he was in. As it happened, Maxey's father had a Yale reunion that weekend, too. Pam would be with him. David Kelly was particularly pleased about that as he would be bringing Clayton.

Brooke, our group's president, was coming. She was married with two children, living in Massachusetts, and working on her governor's presidential campaign. Singer needed to visit New York on business a few weeks before the reunion and couldn't manage another visit east so soon; he was crushed to miss it but had to send regrets. Molly, who had outrun Maxey up the rock, was writing an oral history of a Benedictine monk, living with her husband in Baltimore, and hoping to be able to join us back at the hall.

Renata was heading a college dance program in Massachusetts, and none of us could find her email soon enough. She was now married with a son. Morris, the wiry-haired journalist, had launched a start-up, and had a deal looming, so couldn't make it. He and his wife had four children. A few others from the group said yes, there were a couple more regrets, and there were some of us who had fallen out of touch, either on purpose or by accident. There was no way to know.

We arranged to meet up at the hall on the second day of reunion weekend, Saturday, May 25, at 4:30 p.m. We'd have the place to ourselves for two hours.

MAXEY, PAM, AND I met up after a lecture; we'd arranged to walk over to the hall together.

I spied them before they me. When I approached them, I put out my arm for a handshake. Maxey gave me a bear hug. Then Pam did the same.

"I'm never going to get used to that," I told him.

"I don't give a shit," Maxey said.

"Where's David?" was the first question Pam asked me.

"He decided to take a pass. It was between this and a weekend at the beach, and he chose the beach."

"I don't blame him," said Pam. "I would so much rather be at the beach. If it wasn't for Chris's dad, I'd have stayed home." For a second, I thought: *Who is Chris?* And then I remembered: Maxey.

By the time we got to the hall, several members of our crew were already there. Soon, everyone who was expected had arrived, including David Kelly and Clayton. There were others there, too, from different years. When we had found out how few of us could make it, we'd abandoned the idea of having the place to ourselves; it seemed selfish.

Of course, we needed to go up to the roof. So we headed toward the ladder up. But there was a padlock on the door between us and the ladder.

We found the hall's caretaker and asked her for the key. "Oh, it's been years since anyone was allowed up on the roof," she said.

"Got any Special Forces tricks for locks?" I asked Maxey. He didn't.

We hovered over the cold cuts in the main hall until the platter was empty. We all talked in pairs and in triplets, but not as a group. There were so many of us missing that the day felt incomplete. It was easier to re-create some of what we'd had together when we were outside the hall, outside New Haven even. That day we felt keenly how much separated the adults in that room from the kids who had been given it for a year. And it was at reunions like this that we all felt most intensely the absence of Huei-Zu and her full-throated laugh.

THERE WAS A moment in the hall when Maxey and I found ourselves together, separate from the others.

"How are you doing?" Maxey asked me.

"My feet are kind of burning and I'm nauseated and exhausted as usual, but good. Really good," I said. I meant it. I'd been doing Maxey's breathing exercises when I experienced moments of acute pain. They calmed me. What's more, my dreams had become blissfully boring. In one recurrent one, I had trouble opening a pickle jar but eventually succeeded. It had been decades since I'd had the nightmare about my friend Ben being killed by a mob, and several years since the angel of death with his rusty knife had visited me. I was now convinced that, for whatever reason, the angel of death wasn't coming for me. Not yet.

"And how are you doing?" I asked Maxey.

"Dizzy, of course. But good. Really good."

"You know, there's something else I've wanted to ask you for years, Maxey. That 'Respectfully' thing you do at the end of emails. What's that all about?"

"I always sign letters and emails that way. I respect you, you psycho." Then, "Is that strange?"

"With friends, yes."

"Well, we're just going to have to disagree on that one."

I decided then to tell Maxey about an article I'd read years before in the *New York Times*. It mentioned a study done at the University of Virginia that sought insight into the way that friendship might help people cope with some of the less pleasant aspects of daily life. Researchers had accosted students near a hill on the college's campus and asked if they minded helping out with an experiment. The researchers had given heavy backpacks to the students—some of whom happened to be alone, others who happened to be walking along with friends. In all cases, the backpacks weighed twenty percent of the students' body weight. (I guess they weighed the students and adjusted accordingly.)

The students thought they were going to be asked to climb the hill. But instead, the researchers just told them to guess how steep the slope was. The students who were alone when they were approached thought the hill was very steep, while, surprisingly, those who had been walking with a friend thought it far less so and guessed it wouldn't be arduous to climb, even with the backpacks.

The study revealed something even more surprising, I told Maxey: "The longer the friendship, the gentler the slope of the hill seemed to both of the friends."

"That makes total sense to me," Maxey said. Then after a minute: "So, you going to try free diving again?"

"You bet," I said.

"When?"

"Sometime." I instantly recalled the classic *New Yorker* cartoon of a man talking into a phone, so I almost quoted that: "How about never—is never good for you?" But then I thought that maybe I *might* learn to free dive at some point. After all, I had done a lot of things over the years I hadn't anticipated doing—like share a motorcycle with a jock who I was certain didn't even like me. Without Maxey guiding me—not a chance in the world. But, with my friend, maybe it wasn't impossible. Maybe I wouldn't ring the bell on that particular challenge just yet.

Maxey laughed. "I'll get you free diving before too long. Are you practicing, like I told you?"

"What?" I asked.

"Breathing. I can't take you free diving until you learn how to breathe."

So I did the breathing exercise for him right there: the two-count breaths in, the eight-count breaths out, holding for two seconds between inhaling and exhaling. Maxey had a soda water at hand. I had an iced tea nearby. My gut spilled a bit over my belt. The top of my head felt a little cold—not much hair left for cover. I had also just heard the little automated voice whisper in my ear telling me that my hearing aids were almost out of batteries; they talk to me when they are low on power. As for Maxey, his face was still a bit lopsided, especially when he smiled. His hands were mottled and swollen. He kept kicking one leg out—I guessed in order to uncramp the muscles that had frozen around one of his two fake hips, which tended to bother him.

Soon I became aware that Maxey wasn't speaking and that I wasn't feeling the need to speak either—to fill the airtime with a question, a story, a quip, or an observation. After almost four decades, we had finally reached the point where we could talk to each other about almost everything. Perhaps the greatest reward for that was that we no longer felt compelled to say anything at all.

We were two guys pushing sixty, with maybe a few decades ahead of us. The angel of death had taken so many people from us, but it hadn't come for either of us yet. If our luck held, there were plenty of conversations still to come.

After a while my hearing aids did stop working, and the sounds of the room became more blurred and indistinct. I looked over at Maxey. He, too, was breathing. And for the two of us, in that moment, it felt great simply to be breathing and in the company of an old friend.

Acknowledgments

I had the gift of Sonny Mehta's wisdom, support, and steadfast friendship from when I met him in 1998 until his death in 2019. He was the publisher of my books and the reader whose opinion mattered to me the most. It's hard to believe that there will be no more lunches or drinks with him. He was a great man and I miss him greatly.

Dan Frank was the editor of my previous book and this one. He guided it and me in the years I spent writing the manuscript. In January 2021, just as I was about to deliver my first draft, I got an email from Dan telling me he had metastatic cancer of unknown origin. He said he would still like to edit my book and would then find the right colleague to take it over. Dan gave the book his signature rigorous and brilliant edit just eight weeks before he died on May 24, 2021. Mine was not the last book Dan edited; he worked right up until his final days. Dan was truly the editor's editor, and one of the smartest and kindest people I will ever know.

I need to make clear that any passages that should have been cut or improved are ones I added after Dan's edit.

Dan placed my book in the hands of Jordan Pavlin, Knopf's editor in chief. Jordan has always been one of the editors I most admire. I now see firsthand why her authors and colleagues treasure her so much and am grateful to her for taking such superb care of this book and me.

My immense thanks to everyone at Knopf, especially Reagan Arthur, Kristen Bearse, Penelope Belnap, Gabrielle Brooks, Madeleine Denman, Sara Eagle, John Gall, Chris Gillespie, Chip Kidd, Kim Thornton Ingenito, Nicholas Latimer, Maya Mavjee, Beth Meister, Jo Anne Metsch, Lisa Montebello, and Sean Yule. To Isabel Meyers, for her thoughtful assistance and attention to every detail. And to Victoria Pearson, kindred spirit and production editor extraordinaire. I also want to give special thanks to Erinn Hartman, Kate Runde, and Angie Venezia. Publicists are among the unsung heroes of publishing; these three are phenomenal, and it's been a joy spending time with each of them over the years. My appreciation as well to Karen Thompson for her careful copyediting and to Kate Kinast.

I'm equally fortunate to have Louise Moore, Ariel Pakier, and their colleagues at Michael Joseph publishing the book in the UK and honored to be on their wonderful list. And, as always, thanks to the remarkable team at Brockman, Inc., for their guidance and wise counsel.

Right from the start, I've been blessed to have Alice Truax in my corner. Alice is a genius at puzzling out language, paragraphs, books, and people. Her range of knowledge is astonishing, and she asks the best questions: she has an eagle eye and a huge heart. I've come to rely on her to help me decide what stories I want to tell and how to tell them. I can't thank her enough for her years of inspired advice and friendship.

David Shipley supplied constant encouragement and extremely helpful comments, macro and micro. Marty Asher gave me the benefit of his great wisdom. Elisabeth Dyssegaard and Bob Miller were, as ever, crucial early readers.

Other friends who helped me enormously on this book include Josef Astor, Kedron Barrett, Rich Benjamin, Rick Brenders, Derek Brown, Mike Bryant, Robin Desser, Will DeYoung, Nick Even, Molly and Linc Frank, David Kelly, David Kissinger, Peter Lynn, Georganne Nixon, Morris Panner, Marco Pasanella, Rebecca Robertson, Alex Rockwell, Brooke White Sandford, David Singer, Kelly Sullivan, David Webster, Will Winkelstein, and Hanya Yanagihara. I'm also tremendously grateful to the members of my writer's group for their joyful and unwavering camaraderie.

Endless thanks to Bill Reichblum, who has literally been a partner in crime since we were in our teens. To Bob and Sally Edgar, for decades of sublime conversations. And to Louise Penny, whose marvelously warm, funny, and caring messages always arrive when I need them most.

I also want to thank Joyce, Nora, Miriam, Ryan, Toby, and Troy at Three Lives Bookstore. And Pooh Shapiro of the Washington Post. Both Maxey and I want to thank our doctors: Dr. Stephen Dillon, Dr. Sam Selesnick, Dr. Tina Shetty, and Dr. Louis Weimer. My thanks as well to Craig Sloane, LCSW.

I am, as I hope is evident, immensely grateful to everyone in the secret society. While I've checked details wherever I could, I know that each of the people with whom Maxey and I shared the hall would have a different story to tell about that year. I want to thank all of them for sharing part of their life with me; they all changed my life.

Maxey asked me to add a special acknowledgement to Dr. John M. Daly, who was one of the people most important to Maxey and his parents, and who was always there to guide Maxey and help him find the best road.

Lisa Queen has always been my very first reader. She is willing to spend hours with me obsessing over every little thing in my books and my life. Lisa is one of the smartest, most caring, most intuitive people on the planet, and one of the funniest. I don't know what I would do without her.

I was lucky enough to get the coveted Andrew Brimmer and Tom Molner fellowship while I was still at college. I'm not required ever to produce anything—but I get the pleasure of their company over meals several times a week, daily phone calls checking how I am, and two of the best friends anyone could ever have.

My deep gratitude also to Tom and Ann Maxey and to the entire Maxey family. To my siblings. And to my father and Larry Kramer. Dad and Larry didn't live to see this book finished, but they, along with my mother, are present on every page.

There are no words sufficient to thank my husband, David Cheng. I'm forever and completely indebted to him. I know Maxey feels the same way about Pam. The real miracle of our lives is that they've stuck with us. Why, we don't exactly know.

Finally, I want to thank Chris Maxey—for giving me a ride on the back of his motorcycle and for joining me on this crazy journey.

A NOTE ABOUT THE AUTHOR

Will Schwalbe has worked in book publishing (currently as an editor at Macmillan); in digital media; and as a journalist, writing for various publications, including *The New York Times* and the *South China Morning Post.* He is the author of *Books for Living* and *The End of Your Life Book Club,* and coauthor, with David Shipley, of *Send.* He lives in New York City.

A NOTE ON THE TYPE

This book was set in Garamond, a typeface originally designed by the Parisian type cutter Claude Garamond (c. 1500–1561). This version of Garamond was modeled on a 1592 specimen sheet from the Egenolff-Berner foundry, which was produced from types assumed to have been brought to Frankfurt by the punch cutter Jacques Sabon (c. 1520–1580).

Typeset by Scribe, Philadelphia, Pennsylvania

Printed and bound by Berryville Graphics,
Berryville, Virginia

Designed by Jo Anne Metsch